FILM STUDIES

The History & Art of Cinema

Frank Beaver, *General Editor*

Vol. 3

PETER LANG
New York • Washington, D.C./Baltimore • Bern
Frankfurt am Main • Berlin • Brussels • Vienna • Oxford

FILM STUDIES

Women in Contemporary World Cinema

EDITED BY

Alexandra Heidi Karriker

PETER LANG
New York • Washington, D.C./Baltimore • Bern
Frankfurt am Main • Berlin • Brussels • Vienna • Oxford

Library of Congress Cataloging-in-Publication Data

Film studies: women in contemporary world cinema /
edited by Alexandra Heidi Karriker.
p. cm. — (Framing film; vol. 3)
Includes bibliographical references.
1. Women in motion pictures. I. Karriker, Alexandra Heidi. II. Series.
PN1995.9.W6 F52   791.43'652042—dc21   2001050657
2002   ISBN 0-8204-5235-1
                     ISSN 1524-7821

Die Deutsche Bibliothek-CIP-Einheitsaufnahme

Film studies: women in contemporary world cinema /
ed. by: Alexandra Heidi Karriker.
—New York; Washington, D.C./Baltimore; Bern;
Frankfurt am Main; Berlin; Brussels; Vienna; Oxford: Lang.
(Framing film; Vol. 3)
ISBN 0-8204-5235-1

Cover design by Joni Holst

The paper in this book meets the guidelines for permanence and durability
of the Committee on Production Guidelines for Book Longevity
of the Council of Library Resources.

Printed in the United States of America

For Katy, Sonia, Lexie, and Monica
for sharing laughter and providing
wise counsel beyond their years

Table of Contents

Chapter 5

Chapter 6

Chapter 7

Chapter 8

Chapter 9

Chapter 10

List of Contributors

Acknowledgments

I would like to thank the Arts Council of Oklahoma, the Oklahoma Foundation for the Humanities, the University of Oklahoma, and the Jeanne Hoffman Smith Fund for their support of the Women in Film Conferences that gave impetus to this volume; Dr. Heidi Burns for her superb professionalism; Susan Houck for her technical skills; and Bob Karriker for his infinite patience and good humor.

Preface

Alexandra Heidi Karriker

In the late 1990s, several Women in Film conferences were held at the University of Oklahoma to explore how the roles, representations, and productivity of women have been reflected in contemporary world cinema. This book represents a refereed selection of essays from the conferences, which grew from regional to international in scope within a few years. Featuring colloquia, keynote addresses, and workshops, the conferences focused on the texts and theories of contemporary sexual paradigms; women and violence; new interpretations of traditional stereotypes; and women of color in film. Documentary and independent filmmakers Carroll Parrott Blue, Su Friedrich, Barbara Hammer, Jan Krawitz, and Gaylene Preston joined film historians and critics such as Lucy Fischer, Judith Mayne, Patricia Mellencamp, and Janet Staiger in an investigation of gender issues in film.[1]

This volume provides a variety of narrative stances, including theoretical, descriptive, aesthetic, and production orientations.[2] The authors look at various constituencies of the texts and audiences, where age, class, politics, and socioeconomic status play significant roles. Many areas from around the world are the foci of the essays: France (the essays by Sutton, Patterson, and Boyle); Great Britain (Allison); Ivory Coast (Martin); Paraguay (Nash); Russia and the former Soviet Union (Knox-Voina); New Zealand (Hardy, Thornley, and Boyle); and the United States (Maxfield). The visual texts under discussion include mainstream and independent films, television programs and series, and advertising. The subject matter encompasses a wide variety of topics: film theories (feminist, psychoanalytical) and their practical applications (Martin, Patterson, Knox-Voina); religion (Hardy); women and violence (Boyle, Allison, Sutton, Thornley); postcolonial studies (Martin); history and geography (Thornley); adolescence (Maxfield); politics (Nash); and myths (Knox-Voina, Maxfield, Thornley).

Susan Smith Nash is the author of chapter 1, "Female Desire in Paraguayan Filmmakers Maneglia and Schembori's *Artefacto de la Primera Necesidad*: Revenge Fantasy, Camp, or Post-Dictatorship Self-Loathing?" Framing her essay with a discussion of writers critical of Paraguay's repressive dictatorship, Nash mentions the works of Augusto Roa Bastos, who lived in exile in Buenos Aires and wrote moralistic novels critical of the regime. Nash comments that irony and ambiguity are often lost as writers turn to morality plays, but the same is not true for the filmmakers Juan Carlos Maneglia and Tana Schembori, whose work is replete with ironic manifestations of angst, making it akin to that of Almodovar in the unorthodox and irreverent treatment of political and religious constraints. Nash dissects *Artefacto de la Primera Necesidad*, an eight-minute short, from the stance of aesthetics, musical soundtrack, and technical dimensions. The narrative is interspersed with campy visual references to Hitchcock's *Psycho*, DePalma's *Dressed to Kill*, and Cooper and Schoedsack's *King Kong*. Comic elements of the film lead to a discussion of a particular kind of Paraguayan humor based on certain linguistic peculiarities of the Guaraní language. In fact, Guaraní, along with Spanish, is the official language of Paraguay. Suffixation and prefixation enable Guaraní speakers to create words with many possible meanings, allowing for ironic or humorous effects. Differentiating among humor, camp, and kitsch, Nash maintains that Maneglia and Schembori undermine the authority of the visual citation of other films in the narrative, a process that leads to multiple interpretations. Nash follows female desire, the erotic gaze, and pornography within the context of the film, thus offering both a political and an allegorical reading of the film. This approach subverts the expected cultural situation of the macho philandering male and the ideal, submissive woman. Discussing the issue of censorship during the thirty-five-year dictatorship of General Stroessner, Nash ends her chapter with a look at Maneglia and Schembori's next project.

"Deflecting Desire: Destabilizing Narrative Univocality and the Regime of Looking in Agnes Varda's French Film *Vagabond*," by Katherine Patterson is the subject of chapter 2. Agnes Varda uses nonlinear, nonchronological narration and female voice-overs to deny scopophilia. Using a pseudo-documentary style, the director deflects the gaze through structural elements, such as flashbacks and "interviews" with the characters who had seen the murder victim. Basing her analysis on Varda's techniques, Patterson analyzes both cinematic and contextual elements as vehicles that refocus the attention of film viewers away from the expected point of passive looking, and toward an interactive viewing experience. She sees Varda's utilization of narrative nonlinearity and documentary-style "interviews" as effectively reformulating both the cinematic gaze and the orientation of its traditional object—the female body. Specifically, Patterson cites Varda's use of contextualized nudity in the film as a backdrop, rather than as sexual focal point; thus, the nudity does not eroticize the body. A close analysis of several scenes substantiates the contention that Varda consciously and conscientiously denies viewers the traditional fetishistic opportunity for gazing at the solitary female in distress, thereby making the viewer find a new point of reference for assessing the narrative events.

Karen Boyle, in chapter 3, "'Not All Angels Are Innocent'— Violence, Sexuality, and the Teen Psychodyke," considers the linkage between sexual transgression and crime in the films *Heavenly Creatures* and *Sister My Sister*. Looking first at the historical incidents on which the films are based, she discusses the similarities of the two cases, specifically that the girls "acted in pairs" and murdered women. Although the crimes were committed twenty years apart, both films appeared within months of each other in 1995. Considering the events which led up to the murders, Boyle discusses the verdicts and the fact that homosexuality was linked with insanity in the Parker-Hulme case. She also notes the ambiguous usage of the word *gay* twice in the commentary accompanying the travelogue at the beginning of *Heavenly Creatures*. Boyle provides detailed analyses of key sequences in the film, showing the blurring of fantasy and reality, and the suggestion of a reversal of attackers and victim. The girls' homosexual love is manifested in the kiss on the boat, which functions as a "coming out." Boyle pays close attention to recurrent motifs and to the details that cement the girls' relationship; the murder was in fact planned and called "the happy event." Boyle considers the pace of narration, the chief elements of the soundtrack, such as the foreboding contained in the ticking of the clock on the day of the murder and the strains of "The Humming Chorus" from Puccini's

Madame Butterfly, which occurs in the opera before the suicide. These details position the girls as victims, as did the opening sequence, thus featuring characteristics of a slasher film. Boyle takes into account viewers' possible responses to and sympathy for both the victim and the perpetrators of the murder. The murder, in fact, is shown on the screen but in truncated form. Boyle differentiates between the fantasy of the middle class and the fantasy of desire. The filmmaker shifts the focus from the horror of the murder to the tragedy of the girls' separation.

Boyle then turns to a discussion of *Sister My Sister*, exploring the theme of separation and considering the lyrics of the recurring song in the film's soundtrack. She examines instances of containment and its effect on the film's narrative structure. The tragedy of Christine's never again voicing her sister's name between her incarceration and her death is revealed as a primary example of containment. The final act of containment in the film occurs in the postscript when a male voice-over asks whether it was "simply sisterly love." Again, lesbianism is adjudged as "illness."

Chapter 4, "Executing the Commoners: Examining Class in *Heavenly Creatures*," by Davinia Thornley, reviews the critical literature on Peter Jackson's film. Thornley, though, shifts the focus from the girls' sexual relationship to a discussion of New Zealand national identity and notions of class. She explores Jackson's cinematic vision in the context of New Zealand society of the 1950s. Reconsidering the myths surrounding New Zealand's egalitarianism, Thornley gives a historical overview of the settlement of New Zealand and delves into discussions of class divisions and cultural identities by looking at diverse reference materials, including travel guides. She analyzes the social situations of the two families portrayed in the film and the fissure that exists between the working-class Riepers and the well-educated Hulmes, who are expatriates from Britain.

The beginning of *Heavenly Creatures* functions like a travelogue of New Zealand, with views of prominent buildings and monuments of the city Christchurch. Thornley demonstrates that the choice of scenery plays up the inherited traditions from England, with a lack of depiction of the native environment and indigenous groups. She traces how New Zealand culture is shown to be inferior to that of Britain through several key scenes in the film. Although the main characters, Pauline Rieper and Juliet Hulme, are both rebellious, Juliet insists that she is from England and

and has the audacity to correct the French teacher, thereby emphasizing class and cultural differences. Pauline's mother, Mrs. Parker, reminds her of "her proper place." Feeling trapped, the girls invent a fantasy world that enables them to transcend the limitations of their allotted gender and class roles. However, their final violent act cuts short these possibilities.

Ann Hardy, in "The Heroine's Journey? Women and Spiritual Questing in New Zealand Film and Television—A Production Study," addresses spiritual and gender concerns in chapter 5. She calls the traditional male hero an "endangered species" in New Zealand film because for the past fifteen to twenty years male characters have been portrayed as brutally domineering or pathetically stressed. At first, looking at several films, Hardy examines the historical manifestations of the process that has made the adult white male in New Zealand society uncertain of his position. Then concentrating on the film *Saving Grace* and the television miniseries, *The Chosen*, Hardy describes a series of interviews she held with the cast and production crew before filming, when filming was almost finished, and during postproduction. Hardy does not limit herself to the visual texts, but she also considers production factors and audience response. The main female protagonists, Grace from *Saving Grace*, and Sarah from *The Chosen,* are portrayed as undergoing spiritual searches in which they question patriarchal power and the position of men as the harbingers of the word of God. Hardy discusses the effect the making of *The Chosen* had on Radha Mitchell, who played the role of Sarah, and on Jeremy Sims as Peter MacAllister, the cult leader. The actors of *Saving Grace* attested to the changing interpretations of the narrative as the film production progressed because the script was constantly being reworked. Hardy analyzes the actors' opinions and draws conclusions; Grace, for example, moves from a "psychological discourse of spirituality" with self-reliance at its core, into a "discourse of dependency" with memories of the security that the figure of Jesus can provide. The shift from acceptance to dependence is surprising and somewhat disturbing.

Chapter 6, "*La Femme Nikita*: Violent Woman or Amenable Spectacle?" by Paul Sutton, eschews the comfortable interpretation of *La Femme Nikita* and most of Luc Besson's work as *cinéma du look*. The *cinéma du look* is characterized as youth-oriented, emphasizing style over content in favor of a more analytical evaluation of the apparent contrast between the unfettered punk character presented in the opening scenes and the refined *femme fatale* assassin developed to do dirty work

for the state. Sutton argues, following Susan Hayward, that the film deals
with the nature of containment at various levels. The punk junky of the
initial scenes is defined or contained by the very elements that identify
"punk" to the western audience, namely the stylized clothing and hair,
the nihilistic attitudes, the androgynous look of the character. The "way
out," which is offered by the police after Nikita's capture, is also seen as
containment because in this situation she is deprived of free will to
choose her response. Even after her training, Nikita remains constrained
to do only the bidding of her male "handler."

Paul Sutton argues that in John Badham's *Point of No Return*, the
American version of *La Femme Nikita*, the happy Hollywood ending
serves to contain the ambiguity of the original. It is interesting that the
name "Nikita" in Russian is a given name for males; its usage in the film
for a female reaffirms the androgynous aspects of the character, making
her akin to prototypes of masculine action heroes. Her other name,
Maggie, is a hypocoristic diminutive, distinctly nonambiguous, even en-
dearing, and thus accentuating the femininity and perhaps the youth of
the character.

Chapter 7, authored by Jane Knox-Voina, is "The Myth of Beauty
and Eroticism: Female Icons in Recent Russian Film, Advertising, and
Popular Journals." Knox-Voina examines images of women in Russian
popular culture by presenting a historical overview of their portrayal in
classical Russian cinema and in the media since the fall of the Soviet Union, with the beauty myth superceded by the "flesh movement." Examining Soviet and Russian attitudes toward beauty, Knox-Voina emphasizes
the need to consider the concepts within the context of Russian cultural
traditions. Perspectives rooted in the history of the Soviet State's prohibition of overt female sexuality and stylish dressing—it showed obeisance
to "decadent" western influences—in recent times has led to vociferous
condemnation of American feminists' attitudes toward beauty. After the
Bolshevik Revolution lauded woman as worker, as an equal to the male
in the labor force, screen images of women showed them dressed in
ubiquitous overalls and with their hair worn short or covered. The female
body was not allowed to intrude upon or detract from the great task of
building the new Soviet State. Knox-Voina refers to Alexandra Kollontai's *The Autobiography of a Sexually Emancipated Communist Woman*
and discusses views of gender differences as a "bourgeois construct."
The monumental, desexed worker bodies, both male and female, rechan-

neled sexual energy to the service of the State. Analyzing specific sequences from a large group of films, Knox-Voina shows that not only was kissing missing, but sex was tantamount to pornography under the proscriptions of Soviet Socialist Realism. During the war, depictions of women demonstrate the "sublimation of actual physical passion into patriotism."

All this changed dramatically after the dissolution of the Soviet Union, and a rehabilitation of the flesh was characteristic of the aftermath of *glasnost* and *perestroika*. In the 1980s a Leningrad woman appearing on the satellite link-up of Russian and American cities exclaimed, "We don't have sex in the Soviet Union!" In the nineties, conversely, it seems that there is nothing but sex in print journalism and feature films. Knox-Voina discusses the objectification of women by focusing on iconographic images in advertising, the proliferation of beauty pageants, and the appearance of new glossy women's magazines that show the transformation of the Russian worker into a beauty queen and goddess of seduction. Women's roles in the workplace and the family have been dramatically affected by the rise of the "New Russians," wealthy, powerful men who prefer their women young, beautiful, and unemployed. The concept of a career woman is demeaned in the media, and publications devoted to the business woman fold, while many other magazines advocating home, hearth, and beauty are thriving. Knox-Voina discusses film images of Amazonian career women dressed in black with a black eye patch. Such icons suggest an imperfectability in women who choose a career over family.

Knox-Voina also looks at the depiction of women in many Russian films of the 1990s, which often objectify and marginalize women. She discusses the theme of prostitution in films such as *International Girl* (1989) and *Land of the Deaf* (1998), and she analyzes several films from the viewpoint of violence, most notably evidenced in the frequent rape scenes in films such as Balayan's *Lady Macbeth of Mtsensk* (1989) and Todorovsky's *Moscow Nights* (1995). Both films are based on Nikolai Leskov's nineteenth-century novel, *Lady Macbeth of the Mtsensk District*.[3] Although heroines who break out of loveless marriages are not new to either Russian literature or film, the portrayal of male dominance in sexual encounters is a recurrent motif. This one-sidedness raises questions about the displacement of love and affection by forceful sex that only provides gratification for the male. Other themes Knox-Voina considers are sex as a commodity, the Cinderella myth, and the search for a new hero. Ending on a hopeful note for more honest depictions of women in the Russian media, Knox-Voina cautions readers and viewers to consider historical and cultural factors when deciphering icons and images of post-Soviet film.

Margaret Allison, in chapter 8, "Women Behind the Grave," examines three case studies of women who kill. She takes examples from real life and fiction: The case of Fred and Rosemary West, accused of killing twelve people, all of them female; *Shallow Grave*, a 1994 film directed by Danny Boyle; and episodes from the British soap opera, *Brookside*, involving the murder of an abusive man by his wife and younger daughter. Allison examines the chronologies of the three narratives, showing points of similarity between actual events and the fictional stories. Furthermore, Allison discusses the concept of women's space, women who conspire to kill, the consequences of domestic abuse, and the rights of the abused. More specifically, the analysis highlights the frequent failure of social services to intervene in abusive domestic situations and the "net-curtain syndrome," the protection of the privacy of the home, even in the case of violent actions because they are hidden from those on the outside. A subtheme of "Women Behind the Grave" is perceived female deviance and its manifestations.

Amanda L. Maxfield discusses the portrayal of adolescent girls in American mainstream and independent film in chapter 9, "The Quest for External Validation in Female Coming-of-Age Films." Their paths to maturation are distinctly different from those of boys, who are most often portrayed in films as encountering and overcoming obstacles through journeys of self-discovery. For girls the process of maturation involves desire, approval, recognition, and love, whereas in boys, it is linked with separation.

Maxfield sees film as not just a reflection of society, but the creation of "a society with unique values, stereotypes, and expectations that can be made to seem as authentic as or even more authentic than reality." The work of psychologists, anthropologists, and social psychologists provides a theoretical basis for her interpretations of films that serve as guidebooks for the behavioral patterns of adolescent girls. Teens struggling with their self-image also seek role models in the media. Maxfield presents a reprise of the maturation of boys in films such as Rob Reiner's *Stand By Me* (1986), Jeff Bleckner's *White Water Summer* (1987), and

Gus Van Sant's *Good Will Hunting* (1997). The boys overcome fear and feelings of physical inadequacy to emerge more confident and strong. Demonstrating that this pattern is unsuitable for girls, who seek approval from peers, parents, teachers, and boys, Maxfield focuses on the themes of sex and romance, peer acceptance, and performances. In discussing Bernardo Bertolucci's *Stealing Beauty* (1996), Maxfield provides a perceptive analysis of the protagonist's road to the loss of her virginity. Her reading of the narrative shows blatant, repetitive cliches of sex, such as the images of cherries and bee stings. I would add that the beauty of the lush photography beguiles the viewer by romanticizing a process that is fraught with anxiety and is not an end-all in itself: The sexual act does not define women.

Maxfield looks at the way films shape girls' self-image. Using examples from John Hughes's *Sixteen Candles* (1984), *The Breakfast Club* (1985), *Weird Science* (1985), *Pretty in Pink* (1986), and *Ferris Bueller's Day Off* (1986), she traces the themes of sex and romance, peer acceptance, performance, and their variations. Her reading of Walt Disney's *Cinderella,* with the story hinging on the King's desire to have grandchildren, emphasizes the feudal concept of marriage as romance is subverted to elements of procreation. Maxfield's meticulous analysis of *The Little Mermaid* (1989) uncovers some quite explicit libidinal imagery that dispels the innocence of the story line for little girls and imbeds the narrative firmly within traditional systems with a patriarchal solution: The Little Mermaid has to choose between her family (and her identity) and her man. The film *Heathers* (1989) demonstrates that maturation for girls comes through conformity to members of a clique, not through individuality. In *Mermaids* (1990), the status of adulthood is reached when one is sexually active.

Maxfield examines the teen films of John Hughes in which bonding is achieved through crime, drugs, and sex (although not explicitly pictured). In *Foxfire* (1996), wild acts lead to painful consequences, whereas in *Clueless* (1995), validation by peers and society is rejected. Maxfield next looks at films in which adolescent girls realize a dream of performance by overcoming obstacles, as in *National Velvet* (1944), *Wild Hearts Can't Be Broken* (1991), and *Little Women* (1994). Finally, Maxfield considers two independent films, *Gas Food Lodging* (1991) and *Welcome to the Dollhouse* (1995). These two films offer alternative routes, never easy or straightforward, to self-awareness and discovery.

The final chapter of the book is entitled "Sound and Visual Mispreci-sion in *Faces of Women*: Visual Difference Redefined in Thought" and is authored by Binnie Brook Martin. She addresses the challenges of view-ing postcolonial African cinema and speaks about gaps in the correlation of the visual and aural fields. Considering the writings of E. Ann Kaplan, Trinh T. Minh-Ha, Gilles Deleuze, Mary Ann Doane, and others, Martin discusses ways of seeing that contrast western expectations in synchro-nicity of sound and image and postcolonial African heautonomy, the separateness of visual and audio elements, as exemplified in the film of the postcolonial Ivory Coast filmmaker, Désiré Ecaré. Martin provides a theoretical framework for her study of Ecaré's film, *Faces of Women* (*Visages de femmes,* 1985), which follows the lives of three African women struggling for independence in economic and sexual spheres. Martin focuses her attention on the analysis of a ten-minute love scene between Affoue, a young village woman, and Kouassi, a young man who at first takes the lead in lovemaking but then responds to Affoue's needs as the scene proceeds in more coequal fulfillment of desires. Addressing the spatial discrepancy with distancing of the woman and bringing the voice nearer, Martin shows that the sound takes on a life of its own, no longer subordinate to the visual elements. Martin demonstrates that the director's techniques remove the female character from the fixed point/gaze of the viewer. Specifically, she shows that by breaking "stan-dard" lines between the audio and visual aspects of an on-screen image, the viewer may reacquire the ability to dwell on the "cracks, chinks, and hiccups" of what the spectator perceives to be continuity of the au-dio/video event as an "inventor of connections and syntheses at the level of image construction."

The essays in this book should be of interest to scholars and students in areas as diverse as cultural studies, cinema and television studies, women's studies, communication and media studies, journalism, interna-tional and area studies, languages and literature, African studies, and postcolonial studies. They provide a rich field for analysis and discus-sion.

Notes

1. The secondary literature on gender issues in cinema has been growing rapidly since Laura Mulvey's groundbreaking article, "Visual Pleasure and Narrative Cinema," appeared in *Screen* 16.3 (1975): 6–18, and a representative sampling might include the following important works: Teresa de Lauretis, *Alice Doesn't: Feminism, Semiotics, Cinema* (Bloomington: Indiana UP, 1984); Lucy Fischer, *Cinematernity: Film, Motherhood, Genre* (Princeton: Princeton UP, 1996) and *Shot/Countershot: Film Tradition and Women's Cinema* (Princeton: Princeton UP, 1989); bell hooks, *Talking Back: Thinking Feminist, Thinking Black* (Boston: South End Press, 1989); E. Ann Kaplan, *Women and Film: Both Sides of the Camera* (New York: Methuen, 1983), *Psychoanalysis and Cinema* (New York: Routledge, 1990), and E. Ann Kaplan, ed., *Women in Film Noir* (1978; London: BFI, 1998); Judith Mayne, *Cinema and Spectatorship* (London: Routledge, 1993) and *The Woman at the Keyhole: Feminism and Women's Cinema* (Bloomington: Indiana UP, 1990); Patricia Mellencamp, *A Fine Romance: Five Ages of Film Feminism* (Philadelphia: Temple UP, 1995), *High Anxiety: Catastrophe, Scandal, Age, and Comedy* (Bloomington: Indiana UP, 1990), and Patricia Mellencamp, ed., *Logics of Television: Essays in Cultural Criticism* (Bloomington: Indiana UP and London: BFI, 1990); Laura Mulvey, *Visual and Other Pleasures* (Bloomington: Indiana UP, 1989); Linda Seger, *When Women Call the Shots: The Developing Power and Influence of Women in Television and Film* (New York: Henry Holt and Co., 1996); Kaja Silverman, *The Acoustic Mirror: The Female Voice in Psychoanalysis and Cinema* (Bloomington: Indiana UP, 1988) and *Male Subjectivity at the Margins* (New York: Routledge, 1992).

2. For perspectives on issues of race in regional cinemas, see Gloria Anzaldúa, ed., *Making Face, Making Soul: Haciendo Caras: Creative and Critical Perspectives by Women of Color* (San Francisco: Aunt Lute Foundation, 1990); bell hooks, *Black Looks: Race and Representation* (Boston: South End Press, 1992) and *Reel to Real: Race, Sex and Class at the Movies* (New York: Routledge, 1996); E. Ann Kaplan, *Looking for the Other: Feminism, Film, and the Imperial Gaze* (New York: Routledge, 1997; Judith Mayne, *Kino and the Woman Question: Feminism and Soviet Silent Film* (Columbus: Ohio State UP, 1989); Robert Stam and Louise Spence, "Colonialism, Racism and Representation," *Screen* 24.2 (1983): 2–20; Ann Marie Stock, ed., *Framing Latin American Cinema: Contemporary Critical Perspectives* (Minneapolis: U of Minnesota P, 1997).

3. See, for example Molly Haskell, *From Reverence to Rape: The Treatment of Women in the Movies* (New York: Holt, Rinehart and Winston, 1974). For a discussion of violence in Russian film, see Alexandra Heidi Karriker, "Examining the Evidence: Gendered Violence in Post-Communist Cinema," in *Memory, History and Critique: European Identity at the Millennium* (N.p.: International Society for the Study of European Ideas, 1998), 1–4.

Bibliography

Anzaldúa, Gloria, ed. *Making Face, Making Soul: Haciendo Caras: Creative and Criti-cal Perspectives by Women of Color.* San Francisco: Aunt Lute, 1990.

Fischer, Lucy. *Cinematernity: Film, Motherhood, Genre.* Princeton: Princeton UP, 1996.

————. *Shot/Countershopt: Film Tradition and Women's Cinema.* Princeton: Princeton UP, 1989.

Haskell, Molly. *From Reverence to Rape: The Treatment of Women in the Movies.* New York: Holt, Rinehart and Winston, 1974.

hooks, bell. *Black Looks: Race and Representation.* Boston: South End Press, 1992.

————.*Reel to Real: Race, Sex, and Class at the Movies.* New York: Routledge, 1996.

————.*Talking Back: Thinking Feminist, Thinking Black.* Boston: South End Press, 1989.

Kaplan, Ann E. *Looking for the Other: Feminism, Film, and the Imperial Gaze.* New York: Routledge, 1997.

————. *Psychoanalysis and Cinema.* New York: Routledge, 1990.

————. *Women and Film: Both Sides of the Camera.* New York: Methuen, 1983.

————, ed. *Women in Film Noir.* 1978. Reprint, London: BFI, 1998.

Karriker, Alexandra Heidi. "Examining the Evidence: Gendered Violence in Post-Communist Cinema." In *Memory, History and Critique: European Identity at the Millennium.* N. p.: International Society for the Study of European Ideas, 1998.

Lauretis, Teresa de. *Alice Doesn't: Feminism, Semiotics, Cinema.* Bloomington: Indiana UP, 1984.

Mayne, Judith. *Cinema and Spectatorship.* London: Routledge, 1993.

————. *Kino and the Woman Question: Feminism and Soviet Silent Film.* Columbus: Ohio State UP, 1989.

————. *The Woman at the Keyhole: Feminism and Women's Cinema.* Bloomington: Indiana UP, 1990.

Mellencamp, Patricia. *A Fine Romance: Five Ages of Film Femnism.* Philadelphia: Tem-ple UP, 1995.

————. *High Anxiety: Catastrophe, Scandal, Age, and Comedy.* Bloomington: Indiana UP, 1990.

————, ed. *Logics of Television: Essays in Cultural Criticism.* Bloomington: Indiana UP, 1990. London: BFI, 1990.

Mulvey, Laura. *Visual and Other Pleasures.* Bloomington: Indiana UP, 1989.

————. "Visual Pleasure and Narrative Cinema." *Screen* 16. 3(1975): 6–18.

Seger, Linda. *When Women Call the Shots: The Developing Power and Influence of Women in Television and Film.* New York: Henry Holt, 1996.

Silverman, Kaja. *The Acoustic Mirror: The Female Voice in Psychoanalysis and Cinema.* Bloomington: Indiana UP, 1988.

————. *Male Subjectivity at the Margins.* New York: Routledge, 1992.

Stam, Robert, and Louise Spence. "Colonialism, Racism and Representation." *Screen* 24.2 (1983): 2–20.

Stock, Marie, ed. *Framing Latin American Cinema: Contemporary Critical Perspectives.* Minneapolis: U of Minnesota P, 1997.

Chapter 1

Female Desire in Paraguayan Filmmakers Maneglia and Schembori's *Artefacto de la Primera Necesidad:* Revenge Fantasy, Camp, or Postdictatorship Self-Loathing?

Susan Smith Nash

Given its long history of repressive dictatorships, Paraguay is not a country usually associated with innovative or subversive art production. Although it is true enough that Paraguay's best-known author, Augosto Roa Bastos, wrote novels that criticized not only the historical dictatorships of Dr. Francia and Mariscal López but also the contemporary regime of General Stroessner, Roa Bastos wrote with a decidedly moralistic hand, always positioning himself and his work in opposition to the dominant "Colorado" party and affiliating himself with both leftist-leaning political parties and procommunist artists living in exile. Until recently, Roa Bastos wrote from his home in Buenos Aires, in self-imposed exile, a condition which, arguably, tends to imbue the works with an aura of nostalgia and/or tragedy, as in the work of Chile's Isabel Allende, Ariel Dorfmann, and Uruguay's Mario Benedetti.

However, the existence of repressive dictatorships also can lead to a rather didactic stance wherein the political scene is viewed as revolving around a clear dichotomy between good and evil, right and wrong. In this sort of artistic economy, there is very little room for irony, ambiguity, or postmodern play, except in the sense that patriarchy and patriarchal structures are problematized if not completely delegitimized as they are held culpable for a long list of human rights violations, corruption, and atrocities. Sadly enough, in seeking to oppose what is inarguably an anti-art stance, such writers as Roa Bastos and Allende can be accused of making facile reductions to effect a twentieth-century morality play. The potential for sheer, perverse joy in the paradoxes and contradictions of such societies is often completely lost.

In contrast, Paraguayan filmmakers Juan Carlos Maneglia and Tana Schembori are not living in exile, nor have they received a great deal of acclaim (or shocked protest) for their work. Decidedly apolitical, or, better yet, anti-political, their work ironizes the idea of absolutes—absolute right or wrong, absolute male or female, absolute power. It also undermines the notion that a country that is undergoing radical political change in the form of a new democracy should necessarily play to a nationalistic theme or promote prescriptive solutions to bring about sweeping social reform. Instead, Maneglia and Schembori create a visual and auditory space in which the anxieties, self-doubts, and perversities of a culture in transition can be played out. They do not rely on allegory, although their work can most definitely be said to reflect a certain ironic commentary on the culture of authority and privilege that so characterized Stroessner's Paraguay.

Although his own work is not considered to be particularly avant-garde, Roa Bastos admired the avant-garde writers and their desire to open possibilities of freedom of expression, with the notion that such self-expression is capable of eradicating prejudices and taboos. This idea applies even more to film than to literature, according to Roa Bastos, where the attack upon convention can be taken to new levels:

> La vanguardia, a su vez, procuró investigar en todos sus alcances y posibilidades los medios técnicos y expresivos del cine en función estética. Al margen y a pesar de sus propias contradicciones, los logros alcanzados en este terreno fueron muy valiosos, especialmente en su lucha por una más amplia libertad de expresión, conviertiendo al cine en un instrumento removedor de prejuicios y tabúes con su ataque mordaz a las convenciones más reaccionarias.[1]

> [The avant-garde, in its time, tried to investigate in all its potentials and possibilities, the technical and expressive means of the cinema via aesthetic function. On the edge of and in spite of its own contradictions, the accomplishments achieved in this area were very valuable, especially in the battle for wider freedom of expression, converting the cinema into an instrument capable of removing prejudices and taboos with its biting attack on the most reactionary conventions.]

A campy, ironic cinematic response to repression and didacticism tends to be uncommon in South American cinema and found more in television and radio. However, the form does have its antecedents, particularly in the work of Pedro Almodóvar, which has some affinity with the films of Baltimore native John Waters. As Almodóvar's work has been said to have been a response to the fall of the right-wing military dictatorship of Generalisimo Franco, one can also characterize Maneglia and Schembori's work as a flamboyant statement against a harshly punitive set of "traditional" values that have historically relied upon the weight of the church and cultural heritage to repress individual thought and freedom. Working from a vantage point from within the Paraguayan culture, Asunción residents Maneglia and Schembori are involved in the production of television commercials, advertising, and print ads. Their eight-minute short, "Artefacto de la Primera Necesidad" (Must-Have Appliance), displays many of the techniques found in commercials and music videos, including jump cuts, numerous point of view shots, quick cuts, and scenes that reference well-known shots from well-known "classic" films.

Artefacto de la Primera Necesidad opens with an establishing shot, which quickly cuts to Paraguayan actress Alejandra Siquot lounging in bed during the hour(s) of siesta. In black and white, the film has the atmosphere of a 1940s film, particularly in the set, which is a colonial Spanish-style mansion, á la *Gilda* or *Notorious*. Siquot is talking on the telephone in conspiratorial tones to a friend. She is complaining about her philandering husband, saying she can tell when her husband is lying and when he has been with someone else. Angry but not defeated, Siquot expresses that she would like a change—a new lover, one who is exciting, dangerous, "atrevido."

In the meantime, Siquot is interrupted by a humorously "cachafaz" (scraggly) maid attired in traditional French maid dress, but with a cigarette hanging from the corner of her mouth, and men's striped crew socks sagging around her ankles. She is sweeping the elegantly tiled floor with a canister vacuum, and when she enters the bedroom to ask the "señora" something, Siquot looks at her impatiently and says, quite cuttingly, "¡Estoy hablando!" (I'm talking!). It is at this point the audience sees that the social gap between Siquot and the rest of the world is enormous. Siquot is clearly part of the elite, privileged class, while the maid, a

Guaraní-speaking subaltern, is immediately relegated to the marginalized.

As Siquot speaks, the camera makes quick cuts to scenes from a
graphic novel, pages that illustrate the kind of exciting lover she would
like to have. She hangs up after telling her friend, "you'll be the first to
know." Clearly titillated by the idea of an "amor atrevido," she retreats to
the shower where she refreshes herself in a scene echoing Hitchcock's
Psycho and Brian DePalma's *Dressed to Kill*, but with a campy edge,
thanks to the musical score by Tony Apuril. Although generic expectations would lead the viewer to expect the arrival of the dangerous love
(the "amor atrevido") in the shower (perhaps armed with a knife or other
similarly lethal phallic symbol), it does not happen. Instead, Siquot retreats to her bed, where she clicks on the television with her remote control and dries her hair. Although the furniture is antique, the bedspread
made of handmade lace, the scene is modern because she owns an elec-
tric hairdryer and a modern television with remote control. There is another unusual juxtaposition of 1930s and 1990s modalities, as we see the
original *King Kong* on the television, precisely at the point that the beast
picks up Fay Wray. It is a movie trailer for *King Kong*, and the large caption across the screen reads "Man or Beast?" foreshadowing what will
soon happen.

Siquot drifts off into the heart of the siesta, and it is not clear whether
or not she is sleeping or relaxing. What is clear is that strange things are
about to happen. The maid who is sweeping the floor has problems, in-
vestigates the sweeper and is promptly sucked up into it. The sweeper
then moves toward the bed, frightening Siquot, who is naked. The nozzle
enters the bed, converts itself into quite the phallic beast, raking the bed
under the sheets like a crazed Loch Ness monster, menacing Siquot, who
cowers in fear until the "beast" appears to ravish her and her fear turns
into pleasure. In a moment that invariably reduces audiences to guffaws,
she begins to moan in sexual ecstasy as the "beast" becomes the "amor
atrevido" she has been longing for.

Satisfied, Siquot falls into a deep sleep, interrupted only by the sound
of her husband returning from work. It is late, already quite dark. It is
clear he has been cheating again and he is not a bit remorseful. As he
hangs up his clothes in the closet, a noise can be heard in the background. Appearing like a large, mechanical serpent, the vacuum emerges
and, not too surprisingly, sucks him up in precisely the same way it dis-

posed of the maid. Instead of being horrified, Siquot (who has conveniently awakened and can savor the revenge fantasy) turns to the camera with a conspiratorial smile. Then she rings her friend on the telephone. "I told you I'd call you the minute I found a new lover," she says. "I did, and [she turns and looks to the camera] it's marvelous," she says in a conspiratorial whisper.

The film closes with Apuril's original music and the credits, which are whisked away as if aspirated by the vacuum sweeper. After the credits have run, we see a final scene, this time in color, where Siquot, wearing a Roy Lichtensteinish polka dot dress, her nails brightly polished, her body legs shaved and smooth, slips into high-heeled pumps and leaves the house. It is bright outside, and a Guaraní native from the countryside is selling brooms on the other side of the wrought-iron fence. "¿Escobas? ¿Escobas para la señora?" she asks. Siquot, an elegant contrast to the poor street vendor, gestures for her to wait, as she rushes toward the vendor to buy a broom. She looks knowingly at the camera, and then enamouredly at the highly phallic broom. In this moment, the male phallus has been utterly stripped of its autonomy and power, the mechanical substitute prevails. This is quintessential camp. "An alternative interpretation would be that the female has not so much assimilated the male as eliminated it."[2]

Camp and the Undermined Erotic Gaze

Artefacto de la Primera Necesidad is subversively comic on a number of levels. First, it is humorous and comic: humorous in the sense that it toys with the viewers' expectations, alluding to well-known standard films, and then deviating from the referent in a way that evokes laughter for its daring and sense of the absurd. The humor in the film is also very sly, very much about subversions of authority, which is precisely the cornerstone of picaresque Paraguayan humor, "la picardía"—the humor that simultaneously titillates, outrages, and demonstrates the buffoonery in power games. This type of humor, while not the exclusive domain of Paraguayans, very much typifies the mindset of the people. In fact, the very structure of the Guaraní language (Paraguay is a bilingual nation, with Spanish and Guaraní being the official languages) incorporates what could be categorized as picaresque mental cognitive structures that feature self-contained double entendres. Comprised of "building block" words, the language enables Guaraní speakers to construct their own vocabularies as they add suffixes and prefixes to roots and stems.[3] As they invent words to suit the occasion, Guaraní speakers seek to create the image that has the most possible interpretive possibilities—double-entendres, ironies, and self-deprecating humor.[4] The result is often outrageously funny.

In *Artefacto de la Primera Necesidad*, the comic element functions as a mechanism much along the lines described by Aristotle in *Poetics*. Thus, human fallibility and ludicrous existential states, with which the audience can identify, are played out upon a stage. In fact, the audience is the omniscient spectator, where the absurd differences between the generic norm and the scene being played out on the screen reinforce the audience's awareness of how sexual power games tend to privilege the authority of the male, and only in rather tragicomic enactments does the female gain authority, and hence self-actuating power. Further, in *Artefacto de la Primera Necesidad* it is clear that the authority of original referents (*King Kong, Psycho*, 1940s "B" films) is undermined when Siquot reacts to *King Kong* as mildly titillating and amusing, instead of sharing in the overwhelming horror of female powerlessness that the film communicates in its melodramatic way. As Siquot reclines in bed after her shower, appropriating for her own enjoyment the grotesque eroticizing of bestialized male rape that underlies *King Kong*, the authority of the genre—whether it be terror or horror—is utterly undermined. To function well, terror requires an interplay between the possessor and the possessed, and the thrill of watching is in observing the negotiations (or lack thereof) between the empowered and the powerless.

In order to become powerless, an object is made a screen on which the audience's collective desire is projected, and the meaning (that is to say, the signification) of the image is made captive to the moment. Further, the impassivity of the reflecting screen creates a false sense of unity between the viewers' projected desires and the reality. Gilles Deleuze describes the process as the transformation of a face into an inscribable surface in which the "face is a receptive immobile surface, a receptive plate of inscription, impassive suspense: it is a *reflecting and reflected unity.* "[5]

The "reflecting and reflected unity" is an aspect unique to film, and the relationship is created by the act of the "gaze." The director guides the viewer in the options open for the act of interpretation; he/she is orchestrator of the gaze. From this, meaning can be created:

Everything is meaningful, even nonsense (which has at least the secondary meaning of being nonsense). Man is so fatally bound to meaning that freedom in art might seem to consist, especially now, not so much in *creating* meaning as in *suspending* it; in constructing meanings without, however, making them rounded and complete.[6]

Therefore, by guiding the viewer to consider various interpretive options, the director opens up the possibility of multiple meanings. In this case, the meanings involve a state of suspended vulnerability and powerlessness (terror or horror), or a liberating state of anti-authority, which is actually the epitome of camp.

In *Artefacto de la Primera Necesidad*, the great "camp" moments occur when the camera deconstructs traditional roles; for example, when it dwells on the exquisitely and self-consciously female presence of Siquot. At the same time the camera is encouraging the viewer to see her as the victim, the object of an invasive gaze, Siquot herself is viewing *King Kong* and subordinating the raw power represented there for her own pleasure. When, under the power of her gaze, the vacuum sweeper is transformed from an uncontrollable, all-consuming monster to a creature domesticated into her own "amor atrevido," camp demonstrates itself to be, above all, involved in the demystification of authority and the empowerment of potential victims of the gaze. Camp is closely allied with *kitsch:*

El *kitsch* está ligado íntimamente al desarrollo de las técnicas de la reproducción, llamado por Walter Benjamin como proceso de democratización de los bienes culturales. La redundancia, característica esencial en las formas de producción masiva, es fundamental en el camino de la comprensión del kitsch y no es otra cosa que la acentuación de un significado a través de su repetición conceptual.[7]

[Kitsch is intimately connected to the development of techniques of reproduction, called by Walter Benjamin the process of the democratization of cultural goods. Redundancy, an essential characteristic of the forms of mass production, is fundamental in the road to understanding "kitsch" and it is no other thing than the act of accentuating a certain meaning by means of its conceptual repetition.]

The photographed female is ideal for the purposes of camp, because it puts into flux the definitions and delimitations that enabled the terror and horror (the gaze) to attain so much influence: "The photographed female model is visually the full revelation of the feminine at first glance; how-

ever, it also possesses qualities which undo that first glance. It transgresses femininity. . . and it challenges all levels of definition and delimi-
tation of the body, whether medical, political, or cultural."[8] Authority
and power, particularly the patriarchal as represented by the philandering
husband, are undermined by the "amor atrevido"—which has been created completely by Siquot. In another interesting power reversal, the
viewer's authority in considering Siquot a sexual object and in being seduced into viewing her through an objectifying erotic gaze is completely
undermined as Siquot takes control of the invasive "amor atrevido" and
subsumes it with her own powerful desire.

In this moment, female desire, personified by Siquot, is more powerful than the gaze of the patriarch or the audience:

> There are Lulu, the lamp, the bread-knife, Jack the Ripper: people who are as-
> sumed to be real with individual characters and social roles, objects with uses,
> real connections between these objects and these people—in short, a whole ac-
> tual state of things. But there are also the brightness of the light on the knife,
> the blade of the knife under the light, Jack's terror and resignation, Lulu's
> compassionate look. These are pure singular qualities or potentialities—as it
> were, pure "possibles." Of course, power-qualities do relate to people and to
> objects, to the state of things, which are, as it were, their causes. But these are
> very special effects: taken all together they only refer back to themselves in
> constituting the state of things ... and of course, power-qualities have an antici-
> patory role, since they prepare for the event which will be actualized in the
> state of things and will modify it (the slash of the knife, the fall over the preci-
> pice). But in themselves, or as expressed, they are already the event in its eter-
> nal aspect, in what Blanchot calls the "aspect of the event that its accomplish-
> ment cannot realize."[9]

Again, in demonstrating herself quite willing to replace her husband with
King Kong, then King Kong with a vacuum sweeper; and finally the
sweeper with an ordinary broom, Siquot demystifies the male mythos,
and reduces phallic power to a simple "artefacto"—an appliance which is
ultimately controlled by the female. From one point of view, what is being undermined is the conventional definition of pornography, because
what is occurring is essentially pornographic: "Pornography is about textual, transgressive bodies set into discourse of seduction and difference,
although the boundaries of difference are continually transgressed."[10]
Pornography occurs in the moment we witness what begins as a rape of
Siquot by the vacuum sweeper, but it clearly is no rape as we realize that
she has willed the "amor atrevido" to her side, and she is merely playing

games with it; the rape fantasy is a power reversal; the nozzle is being made to simulate rape simply to titillate her.

"Hoovering" the Oppressor:
Revenge Fantasy as Displaced Sexual Power

Despite the fact that revenge motifs tend to locate themselves squarely in the realm of the tragic (*Hamlet* is one well-known example), it is certainly conceivable to incorporate revenge as an element in gallows humor, or as British director Mike Leigh has suggested, the "tragicomic."

The idea of revenge as the place where justice is finally served is considered the ultimate form of law enforcement, although it must be pointed out that revenge almost always functions in a vigilante manner outside the law. The irony is that vigilante justice is viewed as a kind of "natural law," whereas the legal system tends to be viewed in a patriarchal society as aiding and abetting, if not in fact *creating* the entire notion that "revenge" is an aberrant form of justice. Nevertheless, patriarchy loves a good revenge tragedy, particularly if national pride, family honor, and macho sensibilities have been abrogated.

Revenge is often a theme in works that directly or indirectly promote nationalism. This element has little to do with *Artefacto* except in the most tangential way: if one were to look at the vacuum sweeper as some sort of metonymic extension of the Paraguayan psyche, the inner angst of a "sufrido" people who have been brave and long-suffering after a series of devastating wars—the Triple Alliance (against Argentina and Brazil) and the Chaco War (against Bolivia)—that left the Paraguayans feeling nationally coherent but subjected to a profound lack of respect by their more prosperous neighbors. Therefore, the sight of the vacuum sweeper sucking up the cheating husband is quite satisfying if one draws a parallel between the arrogant, insensitive, and psychologically oppressive husband and the people of Argentina and Brazil.

In *Artefacto*, sexual indiscretion is the trigger for the revenge fantasy, which is also a critique of Paraguayan machismo in what is viewed as the typical Paraguayan marriage. It is often expressed that the man possessed the privileged position as patriarch simply because he was born male. The privilege of being male has become even more pronounced by the above-mentioned wars, when the extermination of as much as 75 percent of the adult male population made repopulation a difficult task, and hence, philandering became an acceptable, even heroic act. In this situation, the woman could do very little but sit back and fantasize about ways to either legitimize the consequences of a man's philandering (pregnancy) or eliminate the competition. Options were further limited in a society that feared female sexuality and considered it to be an uncontrollable, destructive force. In attempts to control or discount female libido, the typical Paraguayan male traditionally has assumed an exaggeratedly macho stance and has tended to joke about his "favorite" wife or the existence of a long line of women awaiting their turn to have a moment with the man. Female aggression is shaped into a male fantasy as men describe, only half-jokingly, the supposed fights that break out among women competing for a rendezvous. In such a society, the ideal woman is a mother who has put her sexuality behind her in order to solidify the family unit, has committed herself to raising the children, and has learned to ignore her own needs. The ideal woman is submissive, self-sacrificing, and modest. She can no longer transform herself into the "brujita" (little witch) who can cast a spell over a Paraguayan man.

Although Paraguayan men claim they would like women to be self-sacrificing mothers, Paraguayan women are in no way passive, having long been accustomed to a de facto matriarchal society, as a result of the not-so-distant male-exterminating wars. Paraguayan women are likely to take matters into their own hands; hence the existence of revenge, whether it be a fantasy or an actual event. Is what happens in *Artefacto* a dream or reality? It matters in the sense that the dream is the often suppressed battle in the psyche:

> Dreams and nightmares are now believed by many investigators to constitute the enactment, the dramas of our waking lives, but in warped forms, with the unconscious desires and fears of loss mightily exaggerated. . . . instead of a protagonist and an antagonist who are distinct characters, we find an antagonist who plays a part of the hero that he most fears, a conjuration from his unconscious.[11]

In *Artefacto* the vacuum sweeper is the perfect appliance because it both satisfies and punishes. It is part of the equipment of the privileged (due to the high cost), which gets rid of the annoying "empleada," a Guaraní-speaking country dweller. The vacuum sweeper becomes the "amor atrevido" and thus provides extreme pleasure, not only sexual, but psychological as it devours the cheating spouse.

The revenge fantasy functions as displaced sexual power because as long as power differentials exist, there will be injustices. The desire to right what is wrong, even though the means are outside the law, is part of what makes vigilantism so antinomian, with all the attendant thrills of an anti-authoritarian work of art. Liberation of mind and spirit are held out as promises.

The *Mano Dura*, Strong-Arm Dictatorship: Hating and Loving Being Fay Wray in King Kong's Paw

An interesting phenomenon takes place in *Artefacto* that is definitely worth examining from a socio-psychological point of view. In 1989, the southern part of South America was hit by a wave of new democracies as many of the old dictatorships crumbled. Dictatorships disintegrated not only in Paraguay but also in Chile, Brazil, and, to a lesser extent, in Uruguay and Argentina. Paraguay had the questionable distinction of having had the world's longest-running dictatorship, headed by General Stroessner, a stern figure who maintained peace, order, stability (through contraband trafficking and human rights violations) for more than 35 years.

At the time of the filming of *Artefacto*, nine years after the end of the dictatorship and the second successful round of democratically held free elections, there was a groundswell of support in Paraguay for a return to a leader with a *mano dura* (strong hand). This nostalgia could be explained as a response to increased crime, economic instability, bank failures, accusations of corruption, and the fact that membership in the South American common market, the Mercosur, brought Paraguay none of the benefits and all the costs of competing against the behemoths. The first disadvantage to Paraguay was the loss of its function as an informal free trade zone—and its attendant status as a smugglers' paradise.

Economic and security issues aside, the populace of Paraguay has tended to look at dictatorship as a way to keep liberty from sliding into libertinism. However, what is often overlooked is that dictatorship is utterly toxic to the arts and that censorship occurs not only on an official level (all books must be approved by an official government committee), but also on a psychological level as writers and artists censor themselves.

Under Stroessner's regime, political commentary, critiques of the existing regime and the ruling families, and so-called "immoral" art were censored. It is hard to imagine that Paraguayans could really wish to return to that type of repressive regime. Furthermore, despite all their talk about how they like to be dominated and ruled and how a strong, dictator-type ruler is necessary, Paraguayans are the first to evade laws that do not suit their fancy. Paraguay is a nation characterized by freewheeling, anarchistic, extremely street-smart (hábil) individuals who have enormous capacity for survival in a landlocked country of scant natural resources. *Artefacto* contains a perfectly rendered snapshot of the Paraguayan psyche in a *doppelgänger* motif illustrated by Siquot contemplating her double (Fay Wray), simultaneously loving and hating being held in King Kong's *mano dura*.

At the end of *Artefacto*, Siquot walks confidently yet coquettishly out her door, the very picture of *picardía,* with the viewer knowing the vacuum sweeper monster has been conquered, domesticated, and subjected to her desires. Now that the challenge is gone, she is free to discard it and go on to the next. Siquot is not only emblematic of the freedom-loving nature of the Paraguayan psyche, she is also a reflection of self-reflexive postmodern art. More specifically, she personifies the notion that art, once defined and delimited, must undergo a metamorphosis that foregrounds the creative process itself.

Future Tense—What's Next for Maneglia and Schembori: Love in the Municipal Dump

The latest project of Maneglia and Schembori has to do with a woman who falls in love with a garbage collector, or at least that was the way it was described in a planning meeting in Asunción. The concept is a fascinating one—again, there are opportunities to build a multilayered work that comments on women's sense of self and their role in society.

Of course, under a dictatorship, such a work would be banned or censored. Disconcerting and uncompromising views of women's self-images and roles are not easy to assimilate, particularly when women are assumed to have the power to destabilize an entire society. Perhaps the most biting satires and pungent gallows humor come from the places where the issues are the most palpable. This can partially explain the genius of Lina Wertmuller's early feminist work in Italy, particularly in *Swept Away* and *The Seven Beauties*. In Paraguay, the satire of Schembori and Maneglia is refreshing, and their campiness is exhilarating. One could only hope that, if dictatorship does in fact return, the artists will not self-censor but will rise to new levels of gallows humor, satire, and camp—dangerous as all great art must be.

Notes

1. Augusto Roa Bastos, *Mis reflexiones sobre el guión cinematográfico y el guión de "Hijo de Hombre"* (Asunción, Paraguay: Fundacion Cinemateca y Archivo Visual del Paraguay, 1993), 17.

2. Susan Rubin Suleiman, *Subversive Intent: Gender, Politics, and the Avant-Garde* (Cambridge, MA: Harvard UP, 1990), 133.

3. Antonio Guasch y Diego Ortiz. *Diccionario Castellano—Guaraní / Guaraní—Castellano,* 13th ed. (Asunción, Paraguay: Centro de Estudios, 1996), 807.

4. Domingo Adolfo Aguilera, *Ne'Enga: Dichos populares paraguayos* (Asunción, Paraguay: Centro de Estudios Paraguayos Antonio Guasch, 1996), 21.

5. Gilles Deleuze, *Cinema I: The Movement-Image*. 1983, trans. Hugh Tomlinson and Barbara Habberjam (Minneapolis: U of Minnesota P, 1987), 87.

6. Roland Barthes, "Toward a Semiotics of Cinema," in *Cahiers du Cinéma: The 1960s: New Wave, New Cinema, Reevaluating Hollywood*, ed. Jim Hillier (Cambridge, MA: Harvard UP), 281.

7. Silvia Oroz, *Melodrama: El cine de lágrimas de América Latina* (México, D.F.: Universidad Nacional Autónoma de México, 1995), 45–46.

8. Brian K. Aurand, "Pedro Almodovar: On the Verge of a Pornographic Space," *CineAction* 47 (1998): 36–44.

9. Deleuze, 102

10. Berkeley Kaite, *Pornography and Difference* (Bloomington: Indiana UP, 1995), 33.

11. Albert Bermel, *Contradictory Characters: An Interpretation of the Modern Theatre* (1973; reprint, Evanston, IL: Northwestern UP, 1996), 8.

Bibliography

Aguilera, Domingo Adolfo. *Ne'Enga: Dichos populares paraguyos.* Asunción, Paraguay: Centro de Estudios Paraguayos Antonio Guasch, 1996.

Artefacto de la Primera Necesidad. Dir. Juan Carlos Maneglia and Tana Schembori. Perf. Alejandra Siquot, Edith Errecarte. Rockhold Entertainment, 1996.

Aurand, Brian K. "Pedro Almodovar: On the Verge of a Pornographic Space." *CineAction* 47 (1998): 36–44.

Barthes, Roland. "Toward a Semiotics of Cinema." In *Cahiers du Cinéma: The 1960s: New Wave, New Cinema, Reevaluating Hollywood*, edited by Jim Hillier. Cambridge, MA: Harvard UP, 1992.

Bermel, Albert. *Contradictory Characters: An Interpretation of the Modern Theatre.* 1973. Reprint, Evanston, IL: Northwestern UP, 1996.

Deleuze, Gilles. *Cinema 1: The Movement-Image*. 1983. Trans. Hugh Tomlinson and
Barbara Habberjam. Minneapolis: U of Minnesota P, 1987.

Guasch, Antonio, y Diego Ortiz. *Diccionario Castellano—Guaraní / Guaraní—
Castellano*. 13th ed. Asunción, Paraguay: Centro de Estudios, 1996.

Kaite, Berkeley. *Pornography and Difference*. Bloomington: Indiana UP, 1995.

King Kong. Dir. Ernest B. Schoedsack. Perf. Fay Wray, Bruce Cabot, Robert Armstrong.
Universal, 1933.

Oroz, Silvia. *Melodrama: El cine de lágrimas de América Latina*. México, D.F.: Universidad Nacional Autónoma de México, 1995.

Roa Bastos, Augosto. *Mis reflexiones sobre el guión cinematográfico y el guión de "Hijo
de Hombre"* Asunción, Paraguay: Fundacion Cinemateca y Archivo Visual del
Paraguay, 1993.

The Seven Beauties. Dir. Lina Wertmuller. Perf. Giancarlo Giannini, Shirley Stoler, Fer-
nando Rey, Elena Fiore. WinStar Home Entertainment, 1975.

Suleiman, Susan Rubin. *Subversive Intent: Gender, Politics, and the Avant-Garde*. Cambridge, MA: Harvard UP, 1990.

Swept Away by an Unusual Destiny in the Blue Sea of August. Dir. Lina Wertmuller.
Perf. Giancarlo Giannini, Mariangela Melato. WinStar Home Entertainment, 1975.

Chapter 2

Deflecting Desire: Destabilizing Narrative Univocality and the Regime of Looking in Agnes Varda's French Film *Vagabond*

Katherine J. Patterson

Laura Mulvey's 1975 article "Visual Pleasure and Narrative Cinema" began the flood of a form of feminist, psychoanalytic discourses of film viewing that broadened the discussion of film beyond thematics. In fact, subsequent essays have gone so far as to recognize that film techniques reemphasize the patriarchal system of gazing.[1] Consequently, the regime of looking[2] has reified male power and undermined the representation of women as empowered subjects. Mulvey's 1978 British film *Riddles of the Sphinx* attempts to destabilize the fetishization of the female body through camera techniques. Agnes Varda's (1985) French film *Vagabond* goes even further in that it employs many mechanisms that undermine scopophilia. One of these is a mobile camera technique that represents a direct inheritance from Mulvey, but Varda has combined a fluid camera with a nonlinear, nonchronological structure, a multiplicity of "voices" that deny univocality, and the power of an extradiegetic female voice-over (Varda's own voice) that enunciates power as the narrative begins. Whereas *Riddles of the Sphinx* emerged as a largely "underground" cinematic effort, Varda's *Vagabond*—it won the Golden Lion at the 1985 Venice Film Festival—is viewed by and is available for a more "mainstream" audience through the resuscitating life given films in videotape release. Although Varda's *Vagabond* lacks the egalitarianism between female and male nudity available in Claudia Weill's (1978) film

Girlfriends and Jane Campion's *The Piano* (1993), Varda accomplishes a movement in film techniques that challenges paradigms of intelligibility by forming an interactive viewing experience. Specifically, Varda's film denies passive viewing, just as its protagonist, Mona Bergeron kinetically denies the desires of a voyeuristic gaze.

Agnes Varda's French film *Vagabond* (1985) evades the classical narrative cinematic tropes of linearity and scopophilia through the subject positioning of its narration as nontemporal, picaresque, and structurally deflective of the gaze. The narrative structure defines a clear subjectivity: Bergeron's "last weeks of her last winter" as her life is investigated through an interlacing of flashback sequences and "interviews" with those who witnessed her last days "living outdoors." As Sandy Flitterman-Lewis states in the text *To Desire Differently: Feminism and the French Cinema*, "Varda lists seven main actors and thirty non-professionals who surround them."[3] Thus, these documentary style "characters," their verbal portraits, and flashback sequences create a "reformulating [of] both the cinematic gaze and its object—the body of the woman—it restructures relations of desire both in the text and for the text."[4] Mona, as all women, exists in a panopticon of intersecting glances, and many of the characters in the film are "caught looking"— committing what Laura Mulvey terms "fetishistic scopophilia."[5] Even so, the camera's look is not complicitous in the fetishization of Mona, just as the partial nudity of two other women characters is contextualized within a logical scheme. In the same way as artist Susan Valadon's nudes are painted within a sociological context (in contrast to Edgar Degas's nudes, such as 1883 "Morning Bath," which idealize and eroticize the female body), so Varda's use of nudity functions as a backdrop rather than as sexualized phenomenon.

Laura Mulvey asserts in "Visual Pleasure and Narrative Cinema" that "The first blow against…traditional film conventions is to free the look of the camera into its materiality in time and space and the look of the audience into dialectics, passionate detachment."[6] Varda's subjective intercession in the narration, a resistance to linear temporality and structural and auditory aspects of shot sequences, deny what Rosemary Betterton terms the "regime of looking which is oppressive to women"[7] in order to insist on an interactive cinematic trope in which "units of episodic demonstration" provide the access for interpretation rather than a predetermined/overdetermined "truth."[8] This narrative resistance to a univocal signifier of meaning and the spiraling of temporal sequences transcend and magnify a statement by Godard that "a film should have a beginning, middle and end but not necessarily in that order."[9]

Two film sequences structure the understanding of Varda's cinematic technique in *Vagabond* in terms of narration: the spiraling of time and space through nontemporal sequences sutured by a fade to black and characterized by thematic consistency but temporal disunity and the disruption of scopophilic desires through a fluidity of camera movement and the use of diegetic, nondiegetic, and extradiegetic sound. The first sequence occurs at the beginning of the film, and I will term it the "bathing scene." Mona, who lives outdoors, bathes in the sea and is visually "caught" by two male bikers who view her and subtly discuss the possibilities of rape. The second scene, which I will term the "forest scene" shares both thematic consistency (this time representing a rape realized) and structural techniques when juxtaposed with the bathing scene. Both the bathing scene and the forest scene depend upon narrative interlacing with ruptures of temporality and visual and auditory deflections from traditional cinematic desires.

As Flitterman-Lewis suggests, *Vagabond* "is a film about looking" in which "the film wanders between Mona and the others" with seemingly random encounters that follow no strict temporal or spatial logic or sequence.[10] What precedes the bathing scene is the discovery of Mona's corpse, found frozen in a ditch amidst the golden-shimmering, agrarian landscape of Languedoc. An extradiegetic voice-over narration connects the initiating two sequences—the establishing shot of the corpse amidst the fields and the flashback bath sequence that constructs the subjective address of this film. A linguistic hinge connects the corpse scene and the bathing scene through the use of the word *mark* articulated first by the police officers who discover Mona's body and next by Varda herself in the voice-over narration.

Linguistically this term functions like an audible form-cut, linking two segments of film and yet signifying very differently in each enunciation. The police utilize the term *mark* to suggest that Mona's body suffered no mark of violence, thereby suggesting that hers was a "natural death." The deployment of the term mark refers to the impression upon the individual left by Mona's intercession in their lives—how their memory is *marked* by her presence, the *mark* of her difference as a woman vagabond. The police, who represent the establishment, enforcement, and the law embody what Judith Butler's *Gender Trouble* defines in Foucauldian terms as that "subjugating law itself" that "ought to be reconceived as a discursive practice which. . . produces the linguistic fiction of repressed desire in order to maintain its own position as a teleological instrument."[11] Therefore, the deployment of this empowered (male) choice of word that views Mona's body "unmarked" functions ironically not merely in light of the violence and psychological suffering of Mona throughout the segments of her life that the film affords, but also philosophically, as Mona is marked by her gender. Varda's reappropriation of the term *mark* interrogates this valorization of the physical mark (as police and courts misogynistically demand cuts, bruises, and torn flesh to signify abuse) to display that a "mark" functions invisibly, denoting psychological/emotional markings as well as the value of imagination and memory as a trace of human lives.

Varda skillfully uses cross-cutting that symbolically moves from the image of Mona's corpse under multiple surveillance during its "disposal" into the plastic body bag to close-up shots of the village being "scrubbed" free of its debris of wine dregs. This clean-up thus rids the village of the traces of its complicity in the violence that brought about Mona's death. Varda's deployment of her own voice as initial voice-over narration constitutes resistance toward the patriarchal regime of storytelling that, as Kaja Silverman asserts, traditionally manifests power as gender specific—as male:

> ...the male subject is granted access to what Foucault calls "discursive fellow-ships," is permitted to participate in the unfolding of discourse. In other words he is allowed to occupy the position as speaking subject—in fiction and even to some degree in fact. Within dominant narrative cinema the male subject enjoys not only specular but linguistic authority.[12]

Varda's verbal intercession enunciates, as Silverman defines, "extra-diagetically, from the privileged place of the Other,"[13] a position Silverman astutely asserts as "nonexistent." More specifically, woman occupies the position of an "object" that "functions as an organizing spectacle, as the lack which structures the symbolic order and sustains the relay of male glances."[14] Defining woman as "lack" recognizes the phallocentric roots of these systems of iconographic representation. It correlates explicitly with the theories of Jacques Lacan's and Freud's concepts of the "uncanny" and the Medusa complex.

In traditional narrative cinema women occupy the specular landscape as silenced object functioning as the organizing spectacle for male narcissism—women become the catalyst amidst the parlance of homosocial desire devised by a controlling system of looks and language.[15] As Flitterman-Lewis suggests:

> Varda redefines cinematic visual pleasure just as certainly as she interrogates "femininity" and its cultural representations. And one of the ways she does this is by evolving a new discursive form that blends fictional constructs with documentary research in a unique articulation which defies traditional categorization.[16]

The discursive marks of enunciation reverberate with Varda's own voice, as well as affirming through word choice, her affinity with and authorship of the film text. The camera functions as a kind of surveillance, first as it scans the wind-blown ripples in the sand that accompany Varda's voice-over, and as the camera fluidly pans first left and then right until Varda's voice articulates the appearance of Mona by the pronoun "she" in the last line of her address that (in translation) states:

> I wonder, do those who knew her as a child still wonder about her?... Those witnesses helped me tell the last weeks of her last winter. She left her mark on them. They spoke of her, not knowing she had died. I didn't tell them. Nor that her name was Mona Bergeron. I know little about her myself, but it seems to me she came from the sea.

The questions Varda asks contextualize Mona as an identity—as a biographically rooted existence rather than merely "a body" viewed in the establishing sequences. As the line about the sea and Mona's origins is read, the camera's slow pan to the right ends, and the camera scans vertically through the sand until a beachfront appears in the upper third of the frame. The camera zooms into a tighter long shot upon the beach, as the image of the sand, blue water, and a diagonally traversing figure fill the screen, beginning the sequence of the bathing scene.

Mona's nude figure appears, rising from the waters in an unfocused long shot. Glowing with refracted light and bathed in shadows, Mona's figure is barely discernible as nude because Varda resists the traditional method of using a deep focus in the shot. Character movement also denies scopophilic desires as Mona walks screen right in a diagonal emergence out of the water. In fact, this continual long shot cannot contain Mona's kineticism within a centralizing framing focus, thereby fetishizing her as an "it." Varda's refusal to cut to a tighter shot enables a more

casual surveillance of the landscape as a contextualizing entity for
Mona's life—such patterns of inclusion are oppositional to the Hitch-
cockian drive for screen voyeurism that classical narrative cinema affords—creating a "repressed desire" by its "law."[17] This shot of Mona
rising from the sea functions as a "delayed preface—and indicates from
the outset the kind of temporal dislocations that will structure the film—
Varda inserts herself emphatically as enunciative source and establishes
a presence of authorship that will be felt throughout the film."[18] Despite
this stamp of authorship, Varda's voice appears only at the beginning of
the film, and the narrative structure of multiple voices and polyinterpre-
tations of Mona dissipate the "univocality" implicit in auteurist techniques.

The refusal to create a linear "closure" wrought by parallel voice-
overs like bookends to the narrative defines not only Varda's resistance
to classical paradigms but also embodies the thoughts of Randy Shiltz
(writer of *And the Band Played On*),[19] who states in his last interview
with *Sixty Minutes* shortly before his death from AIDS: "I will die before
my life is complete."[20] Similarly, Mona Bergeron's life cannot be contained within a few "parting words." The narrative remains cyclical because the first view the audience glimpses is of Mona Bergeron's body
(under the surveillance of so many eyes, a photographer, the camera's
lens, and the resulting photographs and film that sustain the panopticon
through time). To complete the circle, the last glimpse before the screen
goes black is of Mona's corpse, after her identity has been partially un-
covered, and the full ironic measure of her so-called "natural death" has
been exhaustively revealed. Furthermore, the interlacing of multiple narratives of Mona disrupt not only temporal unity but reflect multiple perspectives as these characters, who populate Mona's world, project various interpretations and memories of Mona.

Despite the "authority" of Varda's initial narrative position in the
film, the questioning and questing for the unraveling of incidents in
Mona's life displace the omniscience of this classical narrative position
and articulate an investigative desire to explore the weave of interconnectedness between Mona and others and the underlying alienation in the
tapestry of Mona's life. The unseen interviewer—except for rare, fragmented glimpses—locates the primacy of the narrative with the speaking
subject, the individual who bears a memory of Mona. Many patterns of
sequences appear in the film, and they juxtapose two incidents without

reference to the temporal lag between an incident and its interpretation in the interview format.

In this paired sequencing, Mona appears in a scene as a participant in some action (or inaction), and then the shot fades to black. The next shot opens upon a figure, who was present in the scene with Mona, relating her or his impressions of Mona. Exemplary of this sequencing is a scene when Mona wanders disconsolately onto a site of construction work, and one construction worker emerges in the background and observes Mona as she sits amidst the activity of the workers. The scene ends with the camera poised upon this worker in a medium shot as the camera fades to black. The next sequence opens upon that worker discussing his memories of Mona as he comments regretfully, "I should have spoken to her." Although none of those interviewed are informed of Mona's death, all of the figures presented bear a memory of the lone girl isolated more by the sociological context of her existence and exploitation than by the fact that she travels by herself. Specifically, a garage worker enters her tent and her body as the exchange for her tent residing on his terrain; she is nearly raped, actually raped, sexually extorted by a truck driver, and accosted at a wine festival. All these incidents highlight Mona's isolation and the fact that she is an easy target for abuse.

For Varda, filmmaking constitutes "a way of narrating," in which she solicits discursive interaction with the audience. Flitterman-Lewis explains that "The interweaving of interpretations, the critical engagement with meaning, the experience of a diverse social tapestry are all of much more consequence to our participation in the text."[21] Thus, Varda "rework[s] the function of narration"[22] into a nonchronological temporal flux which spirals into a "complex intersection of narration, vision, and sexuality."[23] Flitterman-Lewis explains further, "Each 'witness' who encounters [Mona] narrates the account, as the camera renders [either simultaneously, before, or after] a vision of the events, sometimes offering a view unanchored in the narration as well."[24] The "authority" of narrative subjectivity is cast out among a wide variety of characters who (as nonprofessional actors convey more than an aesthetic ideal) locate their own subjective interpretation as a narrative voice.

Louise Heck-Rabi's *Women Filmmakers* compares Varda's film *L'Opéra Mouffe* (1958) to the experimentalism of Dali-Buñuel,· and *Vagabond* parallels in several sequences Luis Buñuel's *Le Fantôme de la Liberté* through its use of female voice-over narration, the use of post-

cards to render a cultural critique, and the tactile contact expressed between a character and a statue.[25] Linda Williams notes in the text *Figures
of Desire* that in Buñuel's *Le Fantôme* the postcards function as an ironic
sexual metaphor because the postcards evince neither the sexuality nor
the nude images suggested by the character's discourse. More precisely,
the postcards represent a resistance to adequate audience expectations
and more puritanically function as a humorous indictment of the viewer's
salacious imagination.[26] Contrary to this use of postcards, Varda's deployment of postcards confirms the omnipresence of the objectified female body by functioning as a form-cut starting with Mona's observed
nudity at the beach to the nude bodies that populate the postcard the
biker purchases. Unlike Buñuel, Varda's voice is extradiegetic, inter-
rogative, and allied with so many other narrative voices that what
emerges is a "portrait" of Mona constructed not by any single narrator (in
a claim of "univocality") but, rather, by the intersection between screen
action, vision, and voices culminating with the viewer's subjective interaction with screen action.

In the bathing scene Mona's body refracts light, is shadowed, and is
fluidly in motion so that her body does not affect the static, passive substrate "ripe" for fetishization. As Rosemary Betterton suggests, in patriarchal regimes the nude functions as a signifier of male desire, through
which

> [m]ale artists and critics justify their enjoyment of the nude by appealing to ab-
> stract conceptions of ideal form.... Such a view renders invisible the relations
> of power and subordination involved when a male artist depicts the female
> body. It ignores or denies the difference between looking at the body of a
> woman and looking at a pile of fruit.[27]

Varda acknowledges the difference by illustrating a female subject with
"rebelliousness" to social constraints, by animating her female subject
with motion and subjectivity—thus rendering her a fluid, colorful, and
active context.

The shot sequence in the bathing scene involves a cut from Varda's
narrative perspective upon the body of Mona emerging from water to a
form-cut of static voyeurism by one of the bikers in a card shop, staring
at the postcard images of nude women at the beach. These depicted
women share a metonymic and metaphoric relationship with Mona, as
the character who reaches for these postcards "reaches" into his memory
and articulates the iconographic connection between these images and

Mona with the other biker. As the postcard "becomes" Mona icono-
graphically, the collapsing of all female identities into a nude substrate is
sociologically realized by habitual objectification of the female body.
These postcard images, similarly to Buñuel's *Le Fantôme,* spur a conversation between the bikers about Mona's nudity at the beach. This conversation cuts to a flashback sequence that enacts the kinetic voyeurism of
the two male bikers who, viewing Mona getting dressed after her bath,
discuss the possibility of assaulting her in language that eroticizes her.
The taller biker suggests: "A girl alone is easy." This statement rhetori-
cally connects Mona as the unnamed "girl"—diminutive, objectified,
replaceable, disposable—with "easy." In English and French slang the
connection to available, permeable, "microwave" female heterosexuality
typically depicted on-screen appears—as opposed to male sexuality
which is always "ready," in fact, "uncontrollable" but is never considered
promiscuous.

Varda does not deflect the sting of the patriarchal double-standard in
relation to human sexuality. Throughout the film, Mona's hypervisibility
and vulnerability within a system of exploitation are implicit. The omission of the term *rape* from the speech of the two men dislocates and denies their culpability in a conspired, if unacted, crime. This linguistic
omission of the rape signifier also reflects the latent socialized aggression of the two men who merely seek the opportunity for their violence
to become kinetic as they identify a woman's separation from the social
order—her independence—as an opportunity for parasitic gang torture of
perceived vulnerability. The presence of the signifier *rape* is to assume
responsibility for a transgressive act, yet the pervasiveness of violence
against women dissolves the stigma of such activities, and thus the two
bikers' speech is confidently overt (spoken in the broad light of day just
as the near-rape might have been enacted) and not repressed in conspiratorial whispers.

As the bathing sequence begins, Varda's narrative voice ends, as
cross-cutting displaces the viewer spatially and temporally from a frontal
view of Mona striding diagonally across the beach to an interior shot
with a close-up of postcards of nude women at the beach, thematically
linking the objectified "women" with Mona in a form-cut. The visual
analogy created by the form-cut connects auditorally with the discourse
of the two bikers who first purchase the postcard and then discuss Mona
outside the card shop. The close-up of the postcards is framed in a point-

of-view shot from the perspective of the shorter biker. The camera tracks backward to widen the frame onto a medium shot of the shorter biker's back as he purchases the card. As in Buñuel's *Le Fantôme de la Liberté*, the postcards in *Vagabond* function both as a stimulant of discourse within the diegesis of each film as each film constitutes a "revolutionary" cultural critique within the film and beyond it.

The camera maintains its position inside the shop as the shorter biker walks past the shop window and hands the card to the taller biker, dressed in black. The camera maintains its distanced position behind the dual glasses of the window and under the surveillance of the camera's lens as an act of detachment from the two bikers as the men exist in what Foucault terms the "Panopticon"[28] of multiple viewings—they are viewed simultaneously through the framing lens of the camera, through the framing window pane of the card shop (mise-en-abyme), viewed by the passers-by (through the exchange of characters' looks), as well as by the viewing audience, enacting all three looks of the cinema Mulvey defines. The linguistic privilege of the two men is expressed by the overt discussion of the missed rape opportunity verbalized amidst a swarm of onlookers—white male freedom is clearly expressed metonymically and metaphorically. "Boys will be boys"; gender excuses all transgressions and permits the unspeakable to be spoken with abandon. Varda's selection of shot sequences places these men within the very paradigm of hypervisibility within which women exist.

The taller biker glances at the card and gasps at the shorter biker: "For once we find a real naked girl . . . he chickens out! . . . That day on the beach . . . I was ready! . . . A girl all alone is easy!" After the word *easy* is articulated, the scene cuts to a flashback sequence that dislocates time and space, revealing an unknown surveillance of Mona that contrasts with the viewer's previous understanding of Mona at the beach as an isolated bather. Time is disjointed back to moments after Mona's emergence out of the water, and what is glimpsed is not Mona in isolation, in sole possession of her experience, but rather Mona exposed to the visual assessment of a voyeuristic gaze by the two bikers. This voyeurism is connected explicitly with the two bikers foregrounded in the frame through over-the-shoulder shots and *not* subjective point-of-view shots that would invite audience complicity with the bikers' perspective. Varda's selection of a chronological "moment" at which the dressing is viewed denies the audience participation in the scopophilia the two men practice. Varda's film technique "kills" the visual privilege the two bikers enjoy by not replicating the "performance" of Mona's nudity on screen. Varda denies the scopophilic pleasure of the heterosexual male gaze by cutting past Mona's nudity to a moment in which she is nearly fully clothed. Mona's positioning is viewed in deep focus, standing amidst sea grasses, in a shot that foregrounds the two bikers.

The cut back to the beach dislocates measured time into psychological time as the memory of the two bikers conjures the image of Mona and recalls the potential for rape. The narrative perspective of this voyeuristic sequence is visually revealed by the frame composition that manifests an over-the-shoulder shot of two bikers who exist in the foreground of the frame. One biker wears a blue and red helmet (the shorter biker) and sits on his motorcycle in the frame center while a biker dressed in a black leather jacket and a black helmet is positioned only marginally in the film frame, as the perspective, in terms of looking and frame composition, clearly resides with the black-garbed biker. The bikers are foregrounded in the shot sequence, as Mona's body is cloaked both in terms of camera position and perspectival narration and in terms of the timing of the shot sequence.

Temporally, the shot dislocates the audience's complicity with the on-screen voyeurism because Mona's body is already clothed at the moment the camera's surveillance begins. Mona is viewed in deep focused long shot, in contrast with the previous lack of deep focus when Mona strode nude across the beach; Mona stands fringed by two clumps of sea oats, her lower body obscured by sand mounds. The shot captures Mona adding additional garments to her clothed form as the males discuss how cold it is for anyone to bathe outdoors. The taller biker dressed in black removes his helmet, walks to the other side of the motorcycle and remarks of Mona's body "She's not bad eh? Let's go see...." The shorter biker discourages the attempt, and the taller biker reluctantly accedes to the demands of the bike owner who threatens to leave. A shot of the asphalt of the highway is split by horizontal shadows just as powerful string music splits the silence and reaches a crescendo, and the camera pans up to Mona, dressed and backpacked as she resumes her roadside journey. Mona walks toward the highway in a medium shot as the sputtering of the motorcycle permeates the scene and passes by her as she walks, just as Mona and the two bikers will "pass" each other several times during Mona's journey.

The spiraling of time backward and forward disrupts the sense of temporal continuity and insists upon a structure dependent upon the interconnectedness between Mona and those whose memory compiles the portrait of Mona; the screen affords defining the polyvocality of Varda's film technique. The fluidity of Mona's movements in the bathing scene mirrors the fluidity of the camera itself when, later in the film, Mona is raped by a man in the woods. The continuous spewing rattle of the motorcycle's engine, which passes Mona as she emerges onto the highway, begins diegetically (on-screen) and continues nondiegetically (off-screen) to define a prevailing phonic motif of power. The rattle of the motorcycle dominates the audible expanse of the scene paralleling the continual infiltration of Mona's life by the violating "engine" of male sexuality analogous to Constance Penley's phrase *bachelor machine* that systematizes the ultimate annihilation of women (Mona) as independent agents and as a life force. The implicit social commentary of the social will and its desire to punish the female vagabond, to exploit her, and ultimately to kill her resonates in the uncanny spectacle that Mona's journey represents for those who witness and abuse her.

The collision of opposites emerges as Mona is marked by her gender as a "different" vagabond from most—a difference remarked upon in the interviews by those who witness her. The construction worker says: "A young girl walking alone—it is rare . . . ," and Ms. Landier's concern for Mona is a product of this difference. The familiarity of Mona's position as vagabond reflects upon a broader social climate of exploitation through which Mona, like most victims of rape, is brutalized, randomly and systematically. However, because institutionalized oppression cannot glimpse its own mechanism, those who suffer bear an indiscernible mark of affliction, unrecognized and disdained by the larger community—the police who term Mona's death as "natural." Immediately preceding the forest scene, Mona is viewed emerging from a car whose driver, Ms. Landier, will provide the narrative voice that worries for Mona's safety in the woods when she is dropped off. Ms. Landier nondiegetically states: "I am worried for her, she's so alone."

The scene preceding the forest sequence is discontinuous temporally because many intervening narrators speak between our first introduction to Ms. Landier, who picks up the hitchhiking Mona, until the time when Ms. Landier drops her off at the wooded area. The discontinuity of the film is highlighted because Ms. Landier's interaction with Mona ends abruptly and inexplicably, and the parting sequence between the two women appears later in the film, after Ms. Landier is nearly electrocuted in her bathroom. In the attendant pain and shock of the experience, Ms. Landier recalls the image of Mona who reappeared to her "like a reproach."

Ms. Landier's words construct a segue and a linguistic form cut as danger is first feared and then realized in the next sequence. Location and time are disjointed from the inside of Ms. Landier's apartment to the roadside; time displacement is obvious as Ms. Landier appears in both scenes. The viewer experiences the moment at which Ms. Landier drops Mona off with two bags of food, money, "'bread for some bread'" Mona quips, and a kiss goodbye. This shot cuts to the forest sequence, which opens upon a thick plane-tree, viewed in medium shot, as the tree trunk is viewed at its apex, where diagonal branches cross and intersect. The tree casts a "dark" image, ominously symbolic both of the shadow of corrupt humanity, to which Mona falls prey, and as an icon of the disease that afflicted the plane-trees when the U.S. troops brought along contaminated crates and spread the contagion of violence in their wake—so Mona is afflicted by violence. The late afternoon sun casts highlighting ribbons upon the thin, intersecting branches of the trees, which are revealed in greater detail as the camera pans to the left. Both the fluidity of the camera movement and the sound in this sequence are key to interpreting both the on-screen and off-screen action.

The jarring sound dominating the rape sequence is comprised by frenetic piano and string music, composed especially for the film by Joanna Bruzdowicz.[29] It contrasts with the ribbons of diegetic music, as well as Muzak in the plasma donor scene, which presents a counterpoint to the narrative. The music of the rape sequence reflects a faster jagged tempo and aurally alerts the viewer of impending danger as the camera pans and "scans" the forest and pauses upon the crouching figure of a man clothed in shades of brown that match the forest den. The camera pauses only momentarily in its panning left, and the subtlety of this pause highlights its importance as a visual register. The camera's pan does not "follow" the male who voyeuristically—and autonomously hidden—tracks Mona's movements attentively. Just as in the bathing sequence the camera pans to deny focusing upon the nude bather. Constant camera movement denies any identification with the assailant or, arguably, the protagonist/survivor. Instead, the man moves into and out of the film frame but never is its central focus as the camera continues its panning of the trees and underbrush that surround Mona's passage. The continuous panning allows the foliage of the forest to occupy as prominent a position as the human forms that move through it, simultaneously resisting the urge to fetishize and freeing up the viewer's look to a life force that exceeds that of a troubled human realm.

The brief pause upon the crouching male reveals a figure poised behind and amidst brown, fallen branches and greener grasses. Varda's visual artistry as a film director is implicit in the constant juxtapositioning of contrasting hues that illuminate the film frame with vibrance and texture. As the camera movement resumes its panning left, the frame barely captures the human form rising out of his crouched position before the figure steps over a branch and disappears within the dense foliage as the camera passes the assailant. Varda's kinetic camera denies the viewer the option of sharing the subjective perspective of the stalker, and the viewer gains an empathetic relationship with Mona as the camera itself "flees" from the man's pursuit. As the camera continues to pan the forest, the music strains higher, and the stalker steps around rocks and moves in and out of the frame while the camera captures the stalker's continual, voyeuristic gaze upon his prey, Mona, who resides beyond the framed images. The auditory impact of the increasing crescendo of the music grips the listener with pathos for the victim, who walks through the trees calmly, not knowing that she is being stalked, in opposition to the frenetic pace of the racing musical score. This Eisensteinian collision of opposites (auditory and visual) heightens the pathos of this paradigmatic stalking and intensifies the drama of the opposition between male/female, foe/protagonist, predator/prey. The man's gaze is constant and will be acknowledged by his dialogue before he attacks Mona.

The camera pauses once more as the man, hiding behind a tree, suddenly springs out at Mona, who is bathed in shadow throughout the sequence. The camera continues its panning left as Varda resists the scopophilic urge to centralize the focus upon Mona and thereby highlight Mona's victimization, thus multiplying her exploitation. Instead, the director reveals through dialogue, music, and shadowy struggling Mona's resistance to the attack. As the man seizes Mona from behind, the camera resumes its slow pan as the man asks, "So, camping alone?" A tree foregrounds the shot, blocking the images of the shadowy struggling figures as Mona tries to flee.

"I've been watching you a while" the man asserts, as technically the constantly panning camera denies the viewer the continuity of "watching" what the stalker enunciates. During a pan to the right, Mona is glimpsed in the semi-darkness breaking away from her assailant for an instant as she flees toward the "light" of the campfire. The camera is positioned behind vines, overgrowth, and Mona, barely discernible in the firelight, as she dodges to avoid the stalker's encroachment. As the camera continues its panning to the right, mirroring the character's movement, the man collapses on top of Mona; the pan of the camera continues past the two struggling figures, decentering the violation of Mona, disallowing identification with her assailant and a view of her rape. The figures occupy the dark foreground of the shot as they struggle and are now indiscernible as the music screams at a higher pitch, and the camera continues to pan left, leaving the human figures behind as it races across foliage, panning first low to the earth and then arching higher, until it traces to the end of a tree limb and ends its movement upon the blue-veined tree-limb poised in semi-darkness. The close-up shot of the spines of the tree limb parallels the fragility of Mona's plight, as the image is viewed in isolation, cloaked by semi-darkness, appearing acutely vulnerable.

The verbal discourses of the rape in the forest scene are manifest representations of the verbal and physical gagging of a woman's will in the act of rape. "Want company?" he asks. "No!" Mona shouts. At the instant of her articulation, the man pushes Mona to the earth and states, "Sure you do!" as the two forms tumble out of the film frame and the panning movement more rapidly scans left ("running" as Mona cannot) and finally fixing upon a blue-veined evergreen limb with thin spines poised in the afternoon light issuing from the upper left of the film frame as the music thunders to a powerful crescendo of strings. The rapist unwrites Mona's answer: "NO!" and silences her linguistically by asserting "Yes, you do!" just as his body physically vanquishes her will by pushing her to the ground.[30]

Varda's active camera pans into the trees, and the utilization of dramatic musical intercession resists the desire to locate identification with the stalker, just as the camera movement denies the scopophilic urge to view graphically or hear Mona as she is being raped. Auditory cues of dialogue construct clear "rape signs" (Timothy Beneke) as Mona's voice is symbolically overpowered, just as sound (through music and dialogue) defines the constructed pathos of impending danger.[31] This denied "centrality" to the body of Mona within the film frame appears repetitiously throughout the film, as the camera movement itself comes to embody the paradigmatic "movement" of the life of a vagabond. Thus, film technique and film thematics form a dialectical interlacing motif of movement. Movement as a discourse is connected to shattering the desires of voyeurism, and despite Mona's existence within the panopticon of continual gazing (and the reconjuring of that gazing in the memory of those who observed her), the kineticism of Mona as a figure transgresses the harnessed existence of most women within patriarchal society. This elusive visibility is displayed in many sequences of the film in which the camera pans past Mona as she is absorbed in some activity, such as the brief tracking shot of Mona sitting on a concrete slab outside a kind Tunisian vinyard worker's place of lodging. The gaze afforded the viewer is brief, and Mona's body is contextualized within her concerns, as her gaze and body form itself are downward and turned in upon themselves, rather than "open" and inviting the voyeuristic gaze. The death of Mona, which might have appeared politically problematic as yet another "fallen woman" martyrdom, becomes in fact an indictment of a patriarchal regime through which women move but cannot be free. Thus, Mona, prey to the exploitation of a paternalistic system, experiences repeated symbolic violence through truck drivers who require sex for a ride and through fellow vagabonds who wish to use her in "porno flicks." Mona's demise is anything but a "natural death," as her body, will, and independence are repetitiously invaded by a parasitic gang of male figures.

Varda's direction denies the traditional narrative cinematic tropes of linearity and scopophilia not only by disordering temporal linearity, but by interlacing scenes with no linear chronological pattern except the one the viewer may provide in the act of viewing/interpretation. Varda's arrangement of shot sequences denies the traditional motif that fetishizes the female body through constructing a deflective gaze from the body of Mona and onto the complex interactions between Mona and others, who offer a subjective portrait of her for the audience. In the poem "North American Time," Adrienne Rich states, "the context is never given."[32] However, in this film by Agnes Varda, contexts are supplied and intermingled while the ultimate interpretive power resides with the viewer.

Many film directors, such as Federico Fellini and Jean-Luc Godard, among others, have attempted interactive cinema. Agnes Varda makes

interactive and polyvocal films that bear the stamp of authorship structurally, narratively, and technically, without falling within the traditional
auteur pattern that diminishes the collaborative efforts required in film
production. Nevertheless she simultaneously allows the ultimate intelligibility (or lack thereof) of a fragmented and indeterminable plot to reside wholly with the viewer.

Rosemary Betterton best determined that "fetishizing the female
body"[33] marginalizes women to object status (as in Stanley Kubrick's *A
Clockwork Orange*) and diminishes women's capacity to live free from
the damage this kind of socialization creates. To be pro-woman and anti-
censorship is to believe that "some forms of representation are better
than others on the basis that they offer women images of themselves
which are not humiliating or oppressive."[34] Perhaps through enhanced
examination of work by feminist directors, the evolution of what Betterton terms "new strategies of intervention which have a critical function
towards dominant stereotypes and also try to find...new kinds of representation for women" will result.[35] As Annette Kuhn suggests in the text
Women's Pictures: Feminism and Cinema, "a transformation in the area
of representation might in some measure be brought about if there were
greater numbers of women artists, advertising executives, film directors
and so on."[36] To be optimistic is to believe that Agnes Varda's "amaze-
ment"[37] at the success of *Vagabond* that was executed "with no compro-
mising at all"[38] might one day exist as the rule rather than the exception—such uncompromising creativity might manifest a worker-friendly
environment for feminist directors in which women in the field will no
longer be "extraordinary" or "marked" by their gender as was the vagabond of Varda's film. Only through writing about such strategic differences offered to cinema audiences by "alternative" directors will such
multiple codes of representation become better understood for their political, auditory, and visual codes of communication.

Notes

1.   Laura Mulvey, "Visual Pleasure and Narrative Cinema," *Feminism and Film The-
      ory,* ed. Constance Penley (New York: Routledge, 1988).

2.   Kaja Silverman's *Male Subjectivity at the Margins* creates an enhanced understand-
      ing of the differences between the look and the gaze—the gaze manifesting a total-
      izing force that is irreducible to the look, which (in terms of power) may be cast out
      among a range of provisional/temporary possessors. I argue that because Varda's

film technique displaces the traditional male gaze (and in fact undermines the look itself), the gaze manifest in *Vagabond* is provisional, under critique, and constantly thwarted if not altogether invisible in Varda's (1985) film.

3. Sandy Flitterman-Lewis. *To Desire Differently: Feminism and the French Cinema* (Urbana: U of Illinois P, 1990), 286.

4. Flitterman-Lewis, 285.

5. Mulvey, 64.

6. Mulvey, 68.

7. Rosemary Betterton, *Looking On: Images of Femininity in the Visual Arts and Media* (London: Pandora, 1987), 251.

8. Flitterman-Lewis, 298.

9. James Monaco, *The New Wave: Truffaut. Godard. Chabrol. Rohmer. Rivette* (New York; Oxford UP, 1976)

10. Flitterman-Lewis, 285–86.

11. Judith Butler, *Gender Trouble: Feminism and the Subversion of Identity* (New York: Routledge, 1990), 65.

12. Kaja Silverman, "Dis-embodying the Female Voice," in *Revision: Essays in Feminist Film Criticism,* ed. Mary Ann Doane, Patricia Mellencamp, and Linda Williams (Frederick, MD: The American Institute Monograph Series, 1984), 131.

13. Silverman, "Dis-embodying," 132.

14. Silverman, "Dis-embodying," 131.

15. See Eve Kosofsky Sedgwick, *Between Men: English Literature and Male Homosocial Desire* (New York: Columbia UP, 1985).

16. Flitterman-Lewis, 286.

17. Butler, 65.

18. Flitterman-Lewis, 288.

19. Randy Shiltz, *And the Band Played On* (New York: St. Martin's Press, 1987).

20. *Sixty Minutes,* CBS Television Network, 20 February 1994.

21. Flitterman-Lewis, 287.

22. Flitterman-Lewis, 286.

23. Flitterman-Lewis, 287.

24. Flitterman-Lewis, 287.

25. Louise Heck-Rabi, *Women Filmmakers: A Critical Reception* (Metuchen, NJ: The Scarecrow Press, 1984).

26. Linda Williams, *Figures of Desire: A Theory and Analysis of Surrealist Film* (Urbana: U of Illinois P, 1981).

27. Betterton, 252.

28. Michel Foucault, *Discipline and Punish: The Birth of the Prison,* trans. Alan Sheridan (New York: Pantheon Books, 1977), 171.

29. Flitterman-Lewis, 288.

30. Claudia Weill's (1978) film *Girlfriends* explores a similar undermining of the female voice as the protagonist Susan Wineblatt's voice, desires, and vision are blocked by a hairdresser who interrupts Susan, refuses to give her the haircut she desires, removes her glasses and piles hair over her eyes despite her protest "I'm blind without my glasses." While a bad haircut cannot compare with a rape in terms of violation, the parallel resides in the male behavior in the enactment of oppressive power that linguistically and symbolically violates a woman's will. Weill's largely static film techniques and character blocking discourage scopophilia while displaying an egalitarian presentation of female and male nudity.

31. Timothy Beneke, "Rape Signs," in *Women's Studies in the South,* ed. Rhoda E. Barge Johnson (Dubuque: Kendall/Hunt Publishing Company, 1991).

32. Adrienne Rich, "North American Time," in *Your Native Land. Your Life: Poems* (New York: W. W. Norton, 1986), 83.

33. Betterton, 251.

34. Betterton, 251.

35. Betterton, 251.

36. Annette Kuhn, *Women's Pictures: Feminism and Cinema* (London: Routledge, 1982), 7.

37. As noted by Barbara Koenig Quart, who interviewed Varda after the success of *Vagabond.* Her observations appear in *Women Directors: The Emergence of a New Cinema* (New York: Praeger, 1988).

38. Barbara Koenig Quart, 139.

Bibliography

Beneke, Timothy. "Rape Signs." In *Women's Studies in the South,* edited by Rhoda E. Barge Johnson. Dubuque: Kendall/Hunt, 1991.

Betterton, Rosemary. *Looking On: Images of Feminity in the Visua Arts and Media.* London: Pandora, 1987.

Butler, Judith. *Gender Trouble: Feminism and the Subversion of Identity.* New York: Routledge, 1990.

A Clockwork Orange. Dir. Stanley Kubrick. Perf. Malcolm McDowell, Patrick McGee. Warner Bros., 1971.

Flitterman-Lewis, Sandy. *To Desire Differently: Feminism and the French Cinema.* Urbana: U of Illinois P, 1990.

Foucault, Michel. *Discipline and Punish: The Birth of the Prison,* trans. by Alan Sheridan. New York: Pantheon Books, 1977.

Girlfriends. Dir. Claudia Weill. Perf. Melanie Mayron, Eli Wallach, Bob Ballaban, Anita Skinner. Warner Bros., 1978.

Heck-Rabi, Louise. *Women Filmmakers: A Critical Reception.* Metuchen, NJ: Scarecrow, 1984.

Kuhn, Annette. *Women's Pictures: Feminism and Cinema.* London: Routledge, 1982.

Monaco, James. *The New Wave: Truffaut. Godard. Chabrol. Rohmer. Rivette.* New York: Oxford UP, 1976.

Mulvey, Laura. "Visual Pleasure and Narrative Cinema." In *Feminism and Film Theory,* edited by Constance Penley. New York: Routledge, 1988.

Le Fantôme de la Liberté. Dir. Luis Buñuel. Perf. Jean-Claude Briay. 1974.

L'Opéra Mouffe. Dir. Agnes Varda. 1958.

Penley, Constance. "Feminism, Film Theory, and the Bachelor Machines." In *Close Encounters: Film, Feminism, and Science Fiction.* Minneapolis: U of Minnesota P, 1990.

The Piano. Dir. Jane Campion. Perf. Holly Hunter. 1993.

Quart, Barbara Koenig. *Women Directors: The Emergence of a New Cinema.* New York: Praeger, 1988.

Rich, Adrienne. "North American Time." In *Your Native Land. Your Life: Poems.* New York: W. W. Norton, 1986.

Riddles of the Sphinx. Dir. Laura Mulvey. BFI, 1978.

Sedgwick, Eve Kosofsky. *Between Men: English Literature and Male Homosocial Desire.* New York: Columbia UP, 1985.

Shiltz, Randy. *And the Band Played On: Politics, People and the AIDS Epidemic.* New York: St. Martin's, 1987.

Silverman, Kaja. "Dis-embodying the Female Voice." In *Revision: Essays in Feminist Film Criticism.* Frederick, MD: The American Institute Monograph Series, 1984.

Sixty Minutes. CBS, 20 February 1994.

Vagabond. Dir. Agnes Varda. Perf. Sandrine Bonnaire. France, 1985.

Williams, Linda. *Figures of Desire: A Theory and Analysis of Surrealist Film.* Urbana: U of Illinois P, 1981.

Chapter 3

"Not All Angels Are Innocent"— Violence, Sexuality, and the Teen Psychodyke

Karen Boyle

I want to begin with a quotation from Graham Fuller's review of *Heavenly Creatures,* one of the films I will be focusing on in this chapter. Fuller writes:

> When a little girl kills, it seems like the whole world's going mad (unless, of course, she's played by Drew Barrymore). When a little girl kills her mother, it's as if natural law has been overturned; or it could be the most natural impulse there is. Perhaps every female adolescent at some time harbours a Lizzie Borden in her breast, thinking thoughts that turn Maurice Chevalier's lewd homily "Fank 'eavens for leddle girls" on its head, that add some strychnine to "sugar and spice and everything nice," and that would make even Humbert Humbert bat an eyelid.[1]

Fuller sets up the equation between violence and sexuality and innocence and guilt. This relationship is the focus of this chapter. On the one hand, "little girls" are innocent. Indeed, they are *so* innocent that "when a little girl kills," such a crime threatens the entire social fabric. On the other hand, however, little girls are sexual, and their sexuality makes them dangerous—both sugar *and* spice. Put differently, as the advertising for *Heavenly Creatures* reminds us: "Not all angels are innocent." *Innocence* is first and foremost sexual innocence. However, once the little girl, played by Drew Barrymore, has fallen (or been pushed), criminal guilt is not so hard to imagine. Thus, it is easier to envisage little girls—or more appropriately, young women—as guilty of murder because they are already "guilty" of sexual transgression. The sexual and criminal transgressions of girls and women are closely linked, for both desire and aggression require an activity and subjectivity which women are denied. Lynda Hart argues: "If desire inevitably confirms masculinity, so does crime . . . the desiring subject as confirmation of masculinity to some extent depends on the presupposition that women cannot perform acts of transgression."[2] This linking of female desire and criminality has clear implications for the lesbian in representation: lesbian desire, by definition, positioning women as desiring subjects, female desire, by its very existence, being marked as aggressive.

As desiring women, then, the protagonists in *Heavenly Creatures* and *Sister My Sister* are positioned as "deviant." This deviance provides the means through which the story of their violence can be told—and arguably enjoyed—while potentially contained. The search for "why" becomes less a search for the reasons why the women killed than an interrogation of why—and how—they became desiring subjects.

Both films portray historical cases in which young women have killed. As the girls come of age during the films, the hope that their sexual/criminal deviance is "just a phase" is implicit. Further, in the *reconstruction* of nonfictional events, the outcome—incarceration and separation—is safely predetermined (and often known before entering the cinema), so that the restoration of heterosexual "normality" with women in their so-called proper, nondesiring, nonaggressive places is never more than momentarily threatened.

Both cases are "atypical" of the ways in which women kill; that is, although the women concerned murdered familiars, they murdered women; the murderers in both cases acted in pairs; and years later, both cases continue to hold a grip on the popular imagination. Given the proliferation of "killer women" films during the 1990s, it is interesting to note that, although the crimes to which they refer were separated by more than twenty years, *Heavenly Creatures* and *Sister My Sister* were brought to the screen within months of each other. Furthermore, this fascination with the murderous desires of young women was reflected in two fictional movies—*Fun* and *Butterfly Kiss*—also released in the mid-1990s.

At this point, I want to map out the true events upon which each film is based. Retelling these events in such a brief account, there is always a danger of sensationalizing the murders and the murderers. My intention in the accounts offered here is quite the opposite. Too often, violence against women is eroticized and trivialized, and, though neither film shirks from the horror of violence, there is a danger that by focusing on the relationship between the protagonists, the violence and the victims become invisible.

The Parker-Hulme case, upon which *Heavenly Creatures* is based, is one of New Zealand's most notorious murder cases: "one of those landmark events, like the trial of O. J. Simpson in America or the James Bulger case in Britain, which makes an entire nation take stock of itself."[3] In June of 1954, sixteen-year-old Pauline Yvonne Parker and fifteen-year-old Juliet Marion Hulme were charged with the brutal murder of Honora Mary Parker, Pauline's mother. Honora's body was found on a deserted path in Victoria Park in Christchurch. She had died of shock after being brutally attacked, exhibiting forty-five separate wounds to her head, neck, face, and hands. Although Pauline and Juliet initially tried to pass Honora's death off as an accident, claiming that she had "slipped" while they were out walking and repeatedly banged her head, Honora's horrific injuries were inconsistent with the girls' explanation. The murder weapon—a half brick—was recovered close to Honora's body. Once in custody, Pauline confessed almost immediately to the murder of her mother but initially insisted that she had acted alone. It was not until the next day that Juliet was also arrested and later charged with the murder of Honora Parker.[4]

More shocking still, Pauline's diaries revealed that she and Juliet had *planned* the murder—referred to by Pauline as "the happy event"—to prevent their ensuing separation.[5] The diaries and the intense relationship between the girls caused a sensation at their trial, where they pleaded "not guilty" on the grounds of insanity. While the prosecution infamously claimed that the defendants were "precocious and dirty-minded little girls," in his opening speech for the defence, Mr. T. A. Gresson countered: "Our evidence will show that they are mentally ill. Their interest in sexual and homosexual matters will show that they are not ordinary, but ill."[6]

Contemporary press reports suggest that the girls' disputed (homo)sexuality was a major factor in the case, although Parker and Hulme always denied that there had been any physical relationship between them, a denial reiterated by Juliet Hulme/Anne Perry following her recent unmasking.[7] Dr. Francis Bennett, a psychiatrist who had examined Pauline before the murder and "diagnosed" homosexuality (a scene comically reprised in *Heavenly Creatures*), argued that the girls were *"folie à deux* homosexual paranoiacs of the elated type."[8] On the other hand, Dr. Kenneth Stallworthy, for the prosecution, argued: "There is in my opinion, no relation between active homosexuality and paranoia. I do not know of any practicing homosexual who is a paranoiac. I do not consider homosexuality, which is by no means uncommon, as any indication of insanity."[9] The active expression of sexuality was inextricably linked with the girls' violent agency. Given the prevailing attitudes of the time, "proving" homosexuality could also be interpreted as proving insanity, displacing the crime of murder with the illness induced by same-sex desire.

On 28 August 1954, an all-male jury found Parker and Hulme to be both sane and guilty, and the girls were sentenced to be detained "at Her Majesty's pleasure" in separate adult institutions. Both girls were released in 1959, having served five and a half years in prison. It was a condition of their release that they never meet again. Both women ultimately changed their identities and left New Zealand, remaining anonymous until press interest in the case was reignited with the release of *Heavenly Creatures*. This compulsion to locate the adult women seems to reflect contradictory fears that, on the one hand, they may have violated the conditions of their release and met again,[10] and, on the other, that they have *not* reoffended, but that, as adults, the women Parker and Hulme are living relatively normal lives. In this respect, the fact that neither woman has married or had children seems to be somewhat reassuring. They are still marked as deviant and hence visible but not dangerous.

The case on which *Sister My Sister* is based took place twenty-one years before the Parker-Hulme murder in Le Mans, a quiet rural town in France. In 1933—as Hart notes, the year "that Hitler became absolute dictator of Germany and Freud published 'On Femininity'"—sisters Christine and Lea Papin were found guilty of the murders of their mistresses, Madame Lancelin and her daughter, Geneviève.[11] Madame and Geneviève's bodies were found sprawled on the stairs of their home. They had been repeatedly battered, their exposed buttocks and thighs were covered in a deep crosshatch of slashes and their eyes had been torn from their sockets: "the only case in criminal history where eyeballs had been removed without the use of an instrument."[12]

Christine and Lea were found lying in each other's arms in their attic bedroom.[13] The sisters confessed to the murders. Christine, the elder sister, was sentenced to death, the death sentence was commuted, but she nevertheless "died of self-imposed malnutrition after a year in jail."[14] Lea served her sentence and upon her release returned to live with their mother.

"What mysterious alchemy changed model servants into 'enraged ewes'"?[15] This question gripped the imagination of commentators then as now. Ward Jouve argues: ". . . the fascination of murder cases is that they do not stop at the crime itself, the perpetrators, the victims, the immediate surroundings. Every representation or explanation that is offered becomes part of it."[16]

In 1930s France, the Papin sisters were championed by the left as icons of the class struggle, their victims, symbols of the oppressive regime. Lacan dubbed the murders "a social masterpiece."[17] It is difficult to imagine the predominately male French intelligentsia reacting in such a way had the maids murdered *Monsieur* Lancelin. Furthermore, returning to Ward Jouve, despite their fascination with the case, with the exception of Genet:[18] "Every man's account . . . seems to tend to one end: to guard against the unacceptable idea that women have killed. Either the act, or the sisters' gender, has to be suppressed."[19]

In turning to the recent filmic representations of both cases this fascination with *why* and *how* young women could commit such heinous crimes remains center stage. In both *Heavenly Creatures* and *Sister My Sister*, there is never any doubt about the identity of the killers. Neither film is concerned with "whodunit" (which is already known), nor even with *how* it was done, for these are not mysterious cases, the murders do not need to be solved, or the guilt of the murderers established. Similarly, although in both cases the build-up to the murder is tense, the violence does not come as a complete surprise. Indeed, in both films, the murder frames the narrative. Furthermore, from their opening sequences, both films offer up the relationship between the two women in each film as a possible explanation. This is best illustrated by example, and I will begin by discussing *Heavenly Creatures* before turning—more briefly—to *Sister My Sister*

Heavenly Creatures opens with a travelogue of "Christchurch: New Zealand's City of the Plains." Following an aerial establishing shot, the travelogue takes us into the heart of 1950s Christchurch, introducing locations that are featured in the film as in the original trial: the "woodland of Hagley Park" (prefiguring the murder scene),[20] Canterbury University College (where Juliet's father was Rector), the Girls High School in Cranmer Square (where Pauline and Juliet meet), Christchurch gardens (where they fantasize and play), and sporting venues (from which they are excluded by illness).[21] In setting the scene, the English male narrator uses the adjective *gay* on two occasions: the daffodils in the woodland of Hagley Park are "gay and golden,"[22] while Christchurch gardens are "gay and colourful." This "gaiety," illustrated here by heterosexual coupledom and families, provides a contrast both with the gaiety (joy) of Pauline and Juliet's exclusive friendship and their developing gay (same-sex) desire. It is this desire—as much as the crime with which Pauline and Juliet are charged—that disrupts and shocks the naively gay Christchurch of the travelogue and, within *Heavenly Creatures*, becomes a means of de-emphasizing the brutal murder.

From the archival travelogue footage, shot with a static camera and visually contained by a black border, the cut to the flight from the murder scene is both disorienting and dramatic, reflecting the impact of the original crime(s) on staid and conservative Christchurch. The prologue cuts between Pauline and Juliet's flight from the murder scene and a fantasy in which the girls run across the deck of a ship toward an unidentified "Mummy" and "Daddy." The sequence begins with a Stedicam shot from the perspective of an unidentified I/eye running along a wooded footpath from an undisclosed horror. This opening is reminiscent of the slasher film in contradictory ways (reflecting director Peter Jackson's horror credentials?) and sets up the ambivalent representation of Pauline and Juliet as both victims and perpetrators of violence. The unidentified I/eye chasing distressed and terrified women through a deserted wood-land is certainly a common enough feature of the slasher film.[23] How-ever, the shifting points of view within this sequence position the unidentified females as both the slashers and the slashed, perpetrators and vic-tims. A close-up of the girls' blood splattered legs adds to the impression that they are *victims* of a slasher-type attack. Even so, there is a certain ambivalence in this shot, given the fascination with the legs of the *femme fatale*.

The slasher sequence is intercut here with what appears to be roman-tic fantasy, the same legs—but clean and in black and white—running across the deck of the ship to a romantic score, the match cut suggesting that these worlds of horror and romantic fantasy are, in some way, linked.[24] Indeed, toward the end of this sequence, the slasher and fantasy worlds seem to merge, an audible zoom in toward the fantasy "Mummy" and "Daddy" mirroring the pursuit(s) of the slasher sequences. As Mummy and Daddy turn toward the pursuing "daughters," we cut back to the flight from the murder scene. As the girls stumble onto the road, a middle-aged woman comes running toward them, and we finally see the girls' bloody faces from her point of view. Crying and screaming the girls sob directly to the camera:

> (Pauline) It's Mummy, she's terribly hurt.
>
> (Juliet) Please help us.

Juliet's tearful, to camera plea, "Please help *us*" (not, "please help *her*"), positions the hysterical teenagers as the victims—not perpetrators—of Mummy's "hurt."[25] This focus on the girls, and the relationship between them, is emphasized as the screen fades to black, then we read:

> During 1953 and 1954, Pauline Yvonne Parker kept diaries recording her friendship with Juliet Marion Hulme.
>
> This is their story.
>
> All diary entries are in Pauline's words.

Whereas the printed prologue names the girls as the infamous Parker and Hulme, there is no direct reference to the murder, and "their story" is explicitly positioned as the story of their friendship. In director Peter Jackson's words, the film is a "murder story about love. A murder story with no villains."[26] Thus, although the filmmakers do not shirk from showing the horrific murder, the narrative works to explain and simultaneously deflect the violence that frames the film by telling the "tragic" love story instead.

From this explosive opening, Jackson develops the relationship between the girls from their first meeting at Christchurch Girls School in 1953. Pauline and Juliet share a sense of isolation and alienation, signified by their shared histories of childhood illnesses and prolonged periods of hospitalization that have prevented them from joining in many of the activities of their peers. Their fantasy worlds (Borovnia and the Fourth World of "music, art and enjoyment") influenced by a shared passion for music, literature, and art, provide them with the means to transcend the limits society would impose on them. Most obviously, it allows

Pauline and Juliet to bridge their class differences. Whereas in the real world, Pauline is ashamed to bring Juliet into her home, in their fantasies she and Juliet are aristocrats in a world of their own making from which the Riepers are notably excluded. The fantasy worlds enable the girls to transcend societal constraints concerning gender and sexuality as well as class. As Charles and Deborah, King and Queen of the mythical kingdom of Borovnia, Pauline and Juliet are able to express sexual attraction and affection for one another within a heterosexual(ized) framework. When Juliet is rehospitalized with tuberculosis, the girls continue to develop their fantasy kingdom in long and frequent love letters between their characters. Juliet's imagination is quite literally feverish, the worlds of Borovnia and New Zealand visually colliding on-screen for the first time as Juliet/Deborah summons "her" diabolical son, Diello, to dispose of the minister who interrupts her correspondence with Pauline/Charles with warnings of fire and damnation.

During Juliet's illness, Pauline develops a relationship with one of her mother's lodgers, and it is while John is having sex with her that we are first taken *into* Borovnia. The passive, disinterested Pauline is transformed into Gina, a beautiful gypsy girl (moulded by Juliet) who searches the fantasy kingdom, not for John's Borovnian alter ego Nicholas, but for Juliet/Deborah.[27] After Juliet/Deborah is released from the hospital, John/Nicholas has served his purpose and is executed by Diello in a set-up that foreshadows Honora's murder and signals the end of Pauline's only heterosexual relationship. When Pauline is later diagnosed as "ho-mo-sex-u-al," she similarly summons Diello to dispose of the male psychiatrist, Dr. Francis Bennett.

Whilst at one level this blurring of boundaries between reality and fantasy amusingly challenges contemporaneous religious and medical homophobia, as a measure of the increasing intensity of the girls' relationship, this boundary blurring also recalls the real-life defense team's claim that the girls' interest in "sexual and homosexual matters" was in itself indicative of insanity. As the *New Yorker* reviewer argues: "[W]hat happens to these imaginative girls is a real-life illustration of vampire bonding," the unhealthy, lesbian, vampiric bond necessitating a blood sacrifice.[28]

Significantly, then, the girls first discuss the plan to "moider Mother" as they share a bath immediately following their first night of lovemaking. Pauline and Juliet are soon to be separated, the result of events beyond their control. Juliet's parents have announced their intention to divorce, and Dr. Hulme is to leave New Zealand for England, taking Juliet as far as South Africa, once more "for the good of her health." Both sets of parents have rejected the girls' pleas to allow Pauline to accompany Juliet to South Africa but have arranged for the girls to spend their last weeks together at Ilam, the Hulmes' residence. Convinced that her mother is "the major obstacle" in the way of her continuing relationship with Juliet, Pauline has already struck on the idea of murder, but only discloses her plan to Juliet after their lovemaking, a sequence of events significantly altered from the diaries. As with the earlier fantasies of murder, the sex scene blurs the boundaries between fantasy and reality as the girls take on the roles of their favorite film and music stars ("Saints") and finally become immersed in a Borovnian orgy.

This change both medicalizes and criminalizes the sexual relationship as the girls simultaneously lose their grip on reality and turn to murder as the means of maintaining their newly found sexual relationship. Nothing is as it seems. The real gardens of Ilam merge with the fantastical Fourth World as Pauline and Juliet burn their Mario Lanza records, a last symbolic break with heterosexual fantasy on the eve of the murder. Mario Lanza's voice is replaced on the soundtrack with a tearful Juliet as tragic heroine singing "Soni Andati" from *La Bohème*. As Juliet sings, the ship fantasy of the opening sequence is reprised, resulting in what appears to be successful completion: The Hulmes turn around and embrace the girls, and the fantasy ends as Pauline and Juliet kiss. The ship, which in reality was to have taken Juliet from Pauline, thus becomes the fantasy means of leaving the repressive Christchurch society behind and setting sail for new, middle-class beginnings—together. However, Pauline and Juliet's kiss emphasizes that this is also a fantasy of acceptance ("coming out"?) in which the girls are positioned as lovers, not sisters.

The build-up to the "happy event" itself is excruciatingly rendered. Having taken us through the days leading up to the murder at breakneck speed, the narrative pace slows as the day of the murder dawns, emphasized by the relentless ticking of the clock that brings the murder ever closer. As in the trial itself, the apparently mundane details of the day of the murder must be rerecorded: Juliet selecting the murder weapon; the girls helping Honora in the kitchen; the brick put in the stocking; Pauline's family sharing their last meal together. As Honora, Pauline, and Juliet arrive at the Victoria Park tearooms, "The Humming Chorus" from *Madame Butterfly* conveys the sense of impending tragedy, continuing as the women walk through the woodland, lingering shots of their legs recalling the opening slasher sequence. However, in contrast to the frantic flight at the beginning of the film, the women move in solemn and silent slow motion. "The Humming Chorus," positioned in Puccini's opera before Madame Butterfly's *suicide*, again suggests that the murderers are their own victims, their brutal actions destroying what they set out to protect. The music stops just as the women turn to begin the walk back to the tearooms, a walk we already know only Pauline and Juliet will complete. In this revisiting of the slasher sequence, the viewer is sympathetic to both slasher(s) and victim, making the inevitable horror all the more unbearable. Although the murder is brutally and realistically rendered in real time, we only see seven blows (Honora was struck around 45 times). However horrific, this is only the beginning of Honora's murder.

As at the beginning of the film, the murder scene is intercut with the ship fantasy. Leaving the murder in progress, the film finishes with the ship fantasy; only this time Pauline is left behind on the shore as Juliet sails away, both girls screaming and reaching out to one another. Their fantasy was not a fantasy of the middle-class family, but a fantasy of desire between women and the *acceptance* of desire between women, which could only lead to murder and separation.[29] The film closes with Pauline's tearful face as she watches her lover leave her. As in the opening sequence, Jackson portrays the murderers as their own victims, de-emphasizing the brutal murder of Honora to underscore the tragedy of the girls' separation.

In an epilogue, we learn of the girls' arrest, trial, imprisonment, and eventual release. Like the tabloid newspapers covering the discovery of Juliet Hulme and Pauline Parker in 1995 and 1997, respectively, the final words of the film offer the reassurance that Parker and Hulme were—and are—separated: "It was," we are told, "a condition of their release that they never meet again." Clearly, the containment the film offers on this point is a reflection of "real" events and not an invention of the filmmakers. However, emphasizing Ward Jouve's assertion that every representation that is offered becomes a part of the murder case, when the film was released, renewed media interest led to an ultimately successful search to discover where Pauline and Juliet are now.[30]

As the real-life protagonists of *Sister My Sister* are both dead, their crime(s) arguably pose less of a threat to the contemporary audience. Even so, the framing of *Sister My Sister* performs a similar function, guarding against the unacceptable idea that women have killed by refiguring the crime as desire—here incestuous desire.

Similar to the structure described above, *Sister My Sister* begins with the relationship between two girls, the threat of separation and a bloody crime scene. The first images on screen are in black and white, presenting two young girls, one recognizably older than the other. In their interactions, the older sister plays a maternal role—mirrored by her sister's play with a doll—but is interrupted by the arrival of the mother, who picks up the younger girl and takes her away. Both look unhappy at the separation, and the younger girl waves back at her sister over the mother's shoulder.[31] Following the title credit, the scene, now in color, changes, and we begin a slow descent from an attic staircase to a haunting a capella tune, "Sleep my little sister sleep." On the first landing, dried flowers are strewn on the carpet and blood splattered on the wall. At the bottom of the stairs we see a woman's foot lying at a strange angle, then continue over the blood splattered tiles and up to a window. The song finishes and color fades from the scene, perhaps signifying the blood draining from the bodies, and tying the bloody spectacle to the black and white depiction of the separation of the sisters.

The lyrics of the song emphasize this bond between sisters, the singer imploring her "little sister" to sleep and dream *for* her, asking that when she dreams she dreams she is *with* her, and that when she sleeps she holds the hand of the sister who will never leave her side. The song recurs at various points in the film, and from this opening association of song, singer, and crime scene, whenever the song recurs, it implicates the relationship it depicts in the murder, warning where the desire of women will lead. As with the boat fantasy in *Heavenly Creatures*, the song provides a means whereby the film "makes sense of the crime." This opening sequence establishes the fact of the crime—the murders—and sets out the means by which the narrative will explain and contain them—the relationship between the two sisters.

The end prefigured, we can then return to the beginning to explain how we got there. However, when the film returns to the crime scene at the end of the film, as in *Heavenly Creatures,* a final reassurance is offered. Here we have a male voice-over recounting, from a court room, the horrendous injuries sustained by the Danzard women (the filmmakers have changed the names of the victims), imploring the sisters to explain their crime. Again, deflecting the crime of violence, the crime of desire is foregrounded. The male voice demands: "Was it simply sisterly love? Speak! You are here to defend yourselves. You will be judged." Immediately following this order, we hear Christine screaming Lea's name, as though in response to her interrogator. Judgment then, has to be passed on the crime of desire between women, emphasized by the use of the freeze frame image of two manic, naked women clinging to one another.

A postscript tells of the outcome of the trial, Lea's eventual release, and Christine's death in jail. The final words, as in *Heavenly Creatures*, provide assurance of the containment of homosexuality. Notably, it is not enough that Christine dies but that, in the period between incarceration and death, she never spoke Lea's name again. Here, the crime—the incestuous desire—is literally figured as unspeakable. Confronted by the crime of murder and desire, by the only male presence in the film, Christine is struck dumb.

Christine's inability to speak her sister's name provides a fitting conclusion to this chapter, through which I would like to relocate the crimes the films depict back in a wider discursive context. Despite all the representations of both cases—including the films, as well as my own fascination with, and analysis of, them—the fact that we must continually return to the murders and representations, in a search for *how* and *why*, emphasizes the extent to which these murders escape our attempts at containment. Thus, although the films work literally and metaphorically to contain the women within the time frame and structure of the film, the questions raised by the original acts of violence are, at best, partially answered. This is not to argue that we should not continue to return to these cases—in fact and in fiction—to attempt to learn their lessons, but to suggest that we need to be wary of any definitive answer. Further, in the context of commercial filmmaking, the interpretations that are offered reflect the questions that are asked, and, to return to where I began this essay, the cinematic fascination with the violent woman, and the erotic tradition of representing her is in itself a form of containing the original crimes, of telling the story from one perspective, foregrounding the erotic elements which lurked beneath the surface of the trials and subsequent representations.

Notes

1. Graham Fuller, "Shots in the Dark," *Interview* 24.11 (1994): 78.

2. Lynda Hart, *Fatal Women: Lesbian Sexuality and the Mark of Aggression* (Princeton: Princeton UP, 1994), x.

3. Christopher Tookey, "Deadlier Than the Male: Horror of Teenage Killers is Brought Brilliantly to Life," *Daily Mail,* 10 February 1995, 42.

4. This version of events is culled from several sources, including Julie Glamuzina and Alison J. Laurie, *Parker and Hulme: A Lesbian View* (1991; Ithaca, NY: Firebrand Books, 1995).

5. Although Pauline Parker's diaries no longer exist, extracts compiled from the trial-transcripts, police photographs and other published accounts, can be found on the *Heavenly Creatures* web site (address as below).

6. *The Times,* 26 August 1954, 5.

7. John Darnton, "Author Faces Up to a Long Dark Secret." *New York Times,* 14 Feruary 1995; Louise Chunn, Slaughter by the Innocents," *The Guardian* 2, 30 January 1995, 2–3.

8. *The Times,* 26 August 1954, 5.

9. *The Sydney Morning Herald,* 28 August 1954.

10. Articles in the British press following the "discovery" of Pauline concluded with a reassurance that Parker and Hulme had not seen each other since their release from prison and had no intention of seeing each other in the future (see British press, 6 January 1997, and Alison Daniels, "The Secret History," *The Guardian,* 9 January 1997).

11. Hart, 14.

12. Alix Kirsta, *Deadlier Than the Male: Violence and Aggression in Women* (London: Harper Collins, 1994), 129.

13. It is striking that in accounts of the Papin case the way the sisters *looked* upon their arrest is repeatedly—if inconsistently—stated, as though positioning the women as "objects" in this conventional way can contain their dangerous subjectivity. For a more detailed discussion of the Papin sisters, see Karen Boyle, "Revisiting the Papin Case: Gender, Sexuality, and Violence in *Sister My Sister,"* *South Central Review* (forthcoming).

14. Nicole Ward Jouve, "An Eye for an Eye: The Case of the Papin Sisters," in *Moving Targets: Women, Murder and Representation,* ed. Helen Birch (London: Virago, 1993), 22.

15. Ward Jouve, 12.

16. Ward Jouve, 12.

17. Hart, 146.

18. Genet's play *Les bonnes/The Maids* was inspired by the Papin case. See Ward Jouve, 25–31.

19. Ward Jouve, 20.

20. The murder took place in Victoria Park, not Hagley Park. However, the juxtaposition of the travelogue with the scenes of the girls' flight from the wooded murder scene suggests a horrific revisiting of the "gay and golden" woodland.

21. The girls' "unhealthy" exclusion from sport and physical recreation is also consistent with a view of lesbianism as "sickness."

22. On the *Heavenly Creatures* web site, Adam Abrams notes that there is a famous photograph of Juliet Hulme, taken the year before the murder, where she is posing in a bed of daffodils. This photograph, much reprinted at the time of the crime and since (see *The Guardian* 2, 30 January 1995, 3), also appears, alongside drawings and film star pin-ups, on Pauline's bedroom wall in the film. The use of this picture provides another means of linking the "gay and golden" space of the Christchurch park with Pauline and Juliet's crime(s). (http://www.geocities.com.Hollywood/ Studio/2194/creatures/html)

23. Carol Clover, *Men, Women and Chain Saws: Gender in the Modern Horror Film* (London: BFI, 1992), 182–91.

24. Watching the film again after Kate Winslet's success in *Titanic,* the cruise ship fantasy appears doubly doomed.

25. Given the fusion of the slasher and the romantic fantasy in the final ship scene, the "Mummy," who is so terribly hurt would initially appear to be Hilda Hulme. Indeed, in light of Hilda Hulme's adulterous affair, Glamuzina and Laurie document perceptions from the time of the trial that "the wrong mother got it," 57.

26. Luisa Ribeiro, *"Heavenly Creatures,"* *Film Quarterly* 49.1 (1995): 33–38.

27. Although Pauline plays the role of Charles in their correspondence and childish role play (as, for example, at the birth of Diello), in the Borovnian scenes Pauline appears as herself and/or Gina.

28. *The New Yorker,* 21 November 1994, 131. The lesbian vampire is an ambiguous if persistent image throughout film history, "at once an image of death and an object of desire, drawing on profound subconscious fears that the living have toward the dead and that men have toward women, while serving as a focus for repressed fantasies," (see Andrea Weiss, *Vampires and Violets: Lesbians in the Cinema* [London: Virago, 1992], 84). This idea is discussed in more detail by Weiss in chapter 4 of the same work, and by Barbara Creed in *The Monstrous Feminine: Film, Feminism, Psychoanalysis* (London: Routledge, 1993), chapter 5.

29. Although, interestingly, Juliet is comforted on board by *both* her parents, suggesting—falsely—that the murder achieved their reconciliation.

30. To their credit, the filmmakers did not try to track the women down.

31. There are similarities between this scene and the opening of *Single White Female*, in which two sisters—twins—are shown playing together, dressing up in front of a mirror, putting on make-up and brushing their hair. The scene is short and ends with one twin kissing the other at which point the scene fades to black. *Single White Female* is in many ways an interesting complement to the films discussed here, as in this film the *separation* (through death) from the sister/lover is the dark secret which Hedra keeps from her new flatmate, Allison. Hedra tries to mould herself into Allison's likeness to replace this earlier relationship. When Allison rejects her, Hedra's desire becomes aggression.

Bibliography

Boyle, Karen. "Revisiting the Papin Case: Gender, Sexuality, and Violence in *Sister My Sister.*" *South Central Review* (forthcoming).

Butterfly Kiss. Dir. Michael Winterbottom. Perf. Amanda Plummer, Saskia Reeves. First Run Features, 1994.

Chunn, Louise. "Slaughter by the Innocents." *The Guardian* 2, 30 January 1995, 2–3.

Clover, Carol. *Men, Women and Chain Saws: Gender in the Modern Horror Film*. London: BFI, 1992.

Creed, Barbara. *The Monstrous Feminine: Film, Feminism, Psychoanalysis*. London: Routledge, 1993.

Daniels, Alison. "The Secret History." *The Guardian* 2, 9 January 1997.

Darnton, John. "Author Faces Up to a Long Dark Secret." *New York Times*, 14 February 1995.

Fuller, Graham. "Shots in the Dark." *Interview* 24.11 (1994): 78.

Fun. Dir. Rafal Zielinski. Perf. Renee Humphrey, Alicia Witt, William R. Moses, 1994.

Glamuzina, Julie, and Alison J. Laurie. *Parker and Hulme: A Lesbian View*. 1991. Ithaca: New York: Firebrand Books 1995.

Hart, Lynda. *Fatal Women: Lesbian Sexuality and the Mark of Aggression*. Princeton, NJ: Princeton UP, 1994.

Heavenly Creatures. Dir. Peter Jackson. Perf. Melanie Lynskey and Kate Winslet. Roadshow/Miramax/Buena Vista, 1994.

Kirsta, Alix. *Deadlier Than the Male: Violence and Aggression in Women*. London: HarperCollins, 1994.

Ribeiro, Luisa. "*Heavenly Creatures*." *Film Quarterly* 49.1 (1995): 33–38.

Sister My Sister. Dir. Nancy Meckler. Perf. Julie Walters, Joely Richardson, Jodhi May, Sophie Thursfield. Arrow Film, 1994.

Titanic. Dir. James Cameron. Perf. Kate Winslet, Leonardo DiCaprio. Paramount, Twentieth Century Fox, and Lightstorm Entertainment, 1997.

Tookey, Christopher. "Deadlier Than the Male: Horror of Teenage Killers Is Brought Brilliantly to Life." *Daily Mail*, 10 February 1995.

Ward Jouve, Nicole. "An Eye for an Eye: The Case of the Papin Sisters." In *Moving Targets: Women, Murder and Representation*, edited by Helen Birch. London: Virago, 1993.

Weiss, Andrea. *Vampires and Violets: Lesbians in the Cinema*. London: Jonathan Cape, 1992.

Chapter 4

Executing the Commoners: Examining Class in *Heavenly Creatures*

Davinia Thornley

In 1954, New Zealand was rocked by a notorious matricide committed by two fifteen-year-old girls in the stately city of Christchurch. Pauline Rieper, a lower-class New Zealander, and Juliet Hulme, a British girl who came to New Zealand with her expatriate parents, met and formed an unshakable friendship based on shared interests and fantasies. Their parents—disturbed by the portrait of adolescent *amour fou* they saw developing—forced the girls to separate, and, in retaliation, Pauline and Juliet murdered Pauline's mother, Mrs. Rieper.

Forty years later Peter Jackson and Frances Walsh, director/writer and cowriter of *Heavenly Creatures*, revisited this real-life case that had been shelved and ignored almost immediately after the original furor had died down. Jackson stated: "For all the coverage in the newspapers ... there were few efforts to come up with a convincing explanation for why these two intelligent, imaginative teenagers were driven to such a horrible and senseless act."[1] Jackson and Walsh's answer to this question can be found in their representation of Pauline and Juliet's strange, intense attachment to each other and their frequent traverse between different levels of reality. Their interpretation of the story was based on many painstaking months of research using court transcripts, interviews with people involved in the case, and historical city records.[2] *Heavenly Creatures* has been lauded by several sources[3] as being particularly true to the original events.

Previous analyses of the film have tended to focus on the more obvious issues of gender and sexuality apparent in the narrative. Luisa Ribeiro's work on the film suggested that the girls' fantasy world and its manifestations were born of an uncurbable feminine desire that was shunned in the prosaic suburbs of Christchurch.[4] John Murray, writing for *Metro*, a well-known Auckland arts and current events magazine, again picks up on the excessiveness of Pauline and Juliet's tryst (as do the majority of reviews of the film). Murray is particularly interested in how their friendship flouts conventional understandings of the time regarding desire, sexuality, and feminine behavior.[5] Michelle Elleray frames Pauline's desire for Juliet as inseparable from her Anglophilia and suggests that "viewers' reception of New Zealandness in the film determines their reaction to the lesbianism."[6] Jennifer Henderson admirably attempts to locate the effects of class envy in "Pauline's 'lesbian' desire," but she stops short of any kind of sociohistorical examination, preferring instead to use psychoanalytical theories to make sense of the film.[7]

All of these authors focus their attention first and foremost on the gendered and sexualized aspects of the girls' relationship. They only briefly touch on other important elements, such as the relationship between history and ideology in New Zealand and how this connection brought about the social situation in which the girls found themselves. In addition, none of the above essays offers any sustained discussion or analysis of the impact of class within New Zealand and how this is represented in the film. In this essay, I want to begin to shift the discussion from this preoccupation with gender and sexuality into the field of national identity. I will also concentrate on the strong undercurrent of class as a divisive factor in the girls' relationship and its trajectory. More specifically, I am interested in historical connections: among the larger picture of New Zealand and its development as both a nation and a country of settlers, the social situation in New Zealand in the early 1950s, and the film itself. By anchoring the tale to the specificity of a New Zealand occurrence, I can begin to trace connections between Jackson's cinematic vision and the country's struggle for a tangible—rather than discourse-bound—form of equality and, implicit in this goal, cultural autonomy from Britain.

Heavenly Creatures is many things to many people. It has been called a love story, a murder story, a historical docudrama. Importantly, it is also a story that attempts to paint a picture of life in mid-century New Zealand. In doing so, Jackson taps into the nation's unconsciousness regarding long-held ideological myths of egalitarianism and the sanctity of empire, particularly the colonial relationship between New Zealand and her mother country, Britain. Taking the film as a starting point, I will break down these myths through historical reference to the founding of the country and the paths of social and economic development that led from there. Although New Zealand has a history of ideological adherence to the notion that "we are all equal"—that everyone in New Zealand begins with the same life chances and, in time, acquires relatively the same quality of living—the film's narrative highlights discrepancies in these beliefs. While it is always precarious to 'read' contemporary films as accurate representations of the actual period or events, Jackson's treatment of *Heavenly Creatures* does serve to shed light on the inevitability of class division throughout New Zealand's history, regardless of its reputation as "one of the most egalitarian countries in the world."[8]

New Zealanders have long prided themselves on their country and its public structures as being "the social crucible" of the world. By tracing the circumstances that initiated and structured New Zealand's early economic, political, and social development as a pacific outreach for/of England, the roots of the rhetoric of classlessness become apparent. New Zealand, in fact, continued to tie itself to Britain through this circumscribed path of development, becoming a "dominion capitalist society," never entirely free of both the favors and the strictures of its faraway parent.[9] Such close ties to the mother country meant that in actuality New Zealand's fortunes and the well-being of her citizens depended heavily on the good graces of Britain and the resulting assistance that was received. As I will show, the ideology of equality was maintained—and broken down—through this relationship.

There are two fissures running throughout *Heavenly Creatures*, forces that seem to act against each other, but which, in fact, perpetuate each other. The first is found in received British ideals of what constitutes "high" culture and, in addition, delineates high class from low class. The integration of another country's cultural norms and standards does not always sit easily with the egalitarian ideology of New Zealand. New Zealanders' understandings of this egalitarianism were predicated on the type of settler that came to the new country and how they came to travel there. In the aftermath of the Industrial Revolution, many disillusioned working people flocked to the promise held up by the New Zealand Company, a venture started by London capitalists in 1838, of virtually free land for settlement. Edward Gibbon Wakefield, founder of the company, stated: "Possess yourselves of the soil and you are secure."[10] These new arrivals were fleeing, not from religious persecution as in America, but from desperately poor backgrounds with almost no economic or political security. From the outset it is clear that, although these "laboring classes" wished to come to New Zealand to make a new life different from the kind they had experienced in England, the social conditioning that predicated class divisions and unequal living—if not the social conditions themselves—followed them across the long stretch of water between home and the new country.[11]

Eventually conditions did improve for all the settlers, facilitating the production of the egalitarianism myths that still hold purchase in New Zealand discourse. Through the implementation of large-scale sheep farming (which produced high returns in exchange for little capital output), capitalists increased their profitability. In turn it allowed them to pay wages that greatly reduced the impact of class.[12] Additionally, the agrarian nature of the work meant that landowner and worker often found themselves toiling side by side in order to turn a profit from the land. With all levels of classes earning substantially higher incomes than had been conceivable in Britain, the ideology of "mateship" served to smooth over *actual* class divisions, such as those inherent in the groups that constituted the first settlers to New Zealand.[13] However, it is imperative to recognize that class hierarchies did transfer in the migration from Britain to New Zealand—these hierarchies were simply structured differently in response to the conditions of the new country.

In addition, New Zealand's culture corroborates this insistence on equality at all costs by deploying a commonsense or ideological tack in regard to such diverse areas as welfare, social reform, race relations, and even to how New Zealanders are understood by the rest of the world.[14] These beliefs took root in the 1890s when New Zealand became known as the social laboratory of the world due to a spate of laws passed during that period; their intent was to improve the lot of working people. In reality, these laws functioned to first mask real social differences by providing a government sanctioned "safety net" for the less fortunate and secondly to curb possible organized unrest due to this classed inequality.

While these changes did provide some justification for the label of "social laboratory," on the whole they have failed to institute changes of the scale imagined, to this day, in average New Zealanders' minds and reproduced in everyday discourse. In this respect, the claim that New Zealanders left British class structures behind in Britain becomes necessarily modified and tempered.

Ideological acceptance of egalitarianism, however, has continued throughout the country's history. Values of thrift, modesty, neighborliness, and equal life chances were consolidated by political rhetoric, particularly after the trough of the Depression and World War II.[15] In historian Graeme Dunstall's article on the social scene of the 1950s, he refers to a quote from *Landfall*, one of New Zealand's longest standing literary magazines, in order to describe the ruling idea of the postwar society. He quotes the following: "[E]veryone acts the same, receives the same amount of the world's goods, everyone moves in the same direction."[16] To a large extent a double standard was created because the country was experiencing a surge of unexpected, but much welcomed, prosperity during this time.[17] Even as living conditions improved, however, Prime Minister Holland's National Government of 1949 to 1957 was busy undoing the work of the previous Labour Party, cutting funds for the arts and humanities and scaling back social welfare programs, while directing the excess overseas profits into consumption goods such as cars.[18]

This dichotomy translated into a continuation of the "we are all equal" myth in that New Zealanders could look around at their neighbors and the identical, neat quarter-acre sections, and feel contented—relieved even—to live in such a secure society. Such thinking glossed over the structural inequalities that ensure the difficulty of bridging the class divide in any permanent way; those with less are meant to be content with their lot and not blame larger social processes for their position within society. So it is with the Rieper family in *Heavenly Creatures*. Honora Rieper's struggle to navigate this divide is channeled into her treatment of and aspirations for her daughter, Pauline. Jennifer Henderson's examination of Honora and Pauline's relationship outlines the ways in which Honora attempts to employ the twin ideals of modesty and educational achievement in order to prevent Pauline from inheriting her "cheapness." Honora wears this label both because she is a working-class woman and because (we are informed during the credits) she was never legally married to Pauline's father, the amiable but dull Herbert Rieper.[19]

By enforcing a regime of protective surveillance and an emphasis on good grades, Honora hopes to simultaneously protect Pauline as a teenager and provide her with the means to advance her social status as she reaches independent adulthood.

The second fissure I will examine is precipitated by this clash between Britain and New Zealand's ideological understanding of the role of class(es) in society. Entrenched in—I would say *caused* by this—is the increasingly divisive symptom of class difference in Pauline and Juliet's relationship. We can see the chasm between the Hulme household, with its ties to intellectualism and the empire, and the Rieper household, mired in colonial suburban domesticity juxtaposed with the commercial, through the boarding facility Mrs. Rieper runs out of their small quarters. One particularly emblematic scene occurs when Juliet first comes to the Riepers' for afternoon tea (a longstanding British social ritual, transposed to New Zealand soil and partaken of just as reverently as at "home").[20]

Pauline and Honora excitedly prepare for Juliet's arrival: Honora by making plates of scones and pikelets and Pauline by shooing a boarder away upstairs after informing him that the event is a "private function" to which he is not invited. From the very beginning of this "function," there is a clear power differential between Juliet and Pauline's parents, the former of whom is possessed of significantly more knowledge on a variety of subjects from world travel to politics and the arts than Pauline's poor parents. The clash between supposed classlessness and the social inequity fostered through wholesale adaptation of British ideals is highlighted through a comparison of this afternoon event and an eerily similar setting, lunch with the Rieper family immediately before the murder.

During afternoon tea, Juliet informs Mr. Rieper that they have written a novel about their fantasy kingdom, Borovnia. Mr. Rieper cheerily suggests that perhaps the school newspaper—a suitably pedestrian affair for the work of these precocious schoolgirls—would accept their "novel." Mr. Rieper's comment makes it apparent that the girls should know their place (class?), although Juliet loftily informs him that, in fact, they will be sending the finished product to New York, where "all the best publishing houses are."

However, at the luncheon toward the end of the film, Mr. Rieper reproaches the girls for daring to make fun of the revered Sir Edmund Hillary (a New Zealander and the first white person to climb Mt. Ever-

est), stating, "That man is a credit to the nation." Sir Hillary's title acknowledges a subsequent knighthood from the Queen, thus making concrete the connection between New Zealand achievement and British recognition. Mr. Rieper's comment verbalizes the often unspoken understanding among New Zealanders that until Britain recognizes an
achievement, it is not an achievement of note. In addition, the disparity
between the leveling attitude shown in his early suggestion to the girls,
and his acceptance of British-sanctioned class divisions in his later comment, addresses the inherent conflict in New Zealand's national class
ideology.

New Zealand's lack of a national culture or indeed any kind of independent (read not British-derived) national identity has often been com-
mented on in sources as diverse as travel guides, colloquial jokes, government reports, literary criticism, and nationwide economic and historical accounts. A cursory glance through any mass market travel guide also
speaks volumes about how New Zealand's newfound cultural confidence, which has only gained strength over the last two decades, has
caught many authors unaware. Nick Hanna includes in his introduction
to *Fodor's Exploring New Zealand*: "A myth that is demolished as soon
as you hit a town or city of any size is that the country is a cultural
backwater; the sheer variety...on offer may come as something of a surprise.[21] In *Passport's Illustrated Guide to New Zealand* Hanna also
writes "The popular image about New Zealanders is that their interests
focus around just three things: beer, rugby, and racing. While there is a
good deal of truth to this statement, it belies a cultural sophistication that
is less well known."[22] Elizabeth B. Booz also mentions the country's
former reputation as an "intellectual backwater" and points to the frequent comparisons between New Zealand and "other parts of the world,
especially England."[23] Ironically, although these guides praise New Zealand's cultural growth, all three books still feature requisite shots of
sheep and scenery on their covers.

Mark Williams's discussion of national cultural movements shows
how the best recognized were inevitably founded in order to establish an
identity for New Zealand poetry, painting, and prose that was free from
"colonial deference [and] Georgian diction."[24] Providing another example is Gregory Waller's investigation of the founding of the New Zealand
Film Commission. His report highlights the two main justifications for
the film commission's establishment given in feasibility reports and re-

peated in replies to these reports from other public and private bodies, as well as during parliamentary debates and in funding logic. These were necessary to counter the largely "unrelieved diet of [films, media, foreign product] from foreign cultures" and, second, to provide an exportable product that would "do much to announce the existence of New Zealand to the world at large" and so begin to counter the country's notorious antipodean "cultural cringe."[25] The struggle for New Zealand to establish a separate identity from its founding influences can be seen in all aspects of national life: politics, religion, culture, the legal system.

We can see similar influences in the first few frames of *Heavenly Creatures*. Jackson dovetails from a staid travelogue on the city of Christchurch to the murder and back to the circumstances of Pauline and Juliet's first meeting. The clip highlights Christchurch's gardens, government buildings, universities, and monuments, all artifacts deemed "high" culture and without exception named after British towns and historic sites. When Canterbury University is shown, the voice-over narration enthuses about "the weathered graystone buildings" and "shadowed cloisters," attributing age to these buildings in order to build a connection of sorts between Britain's veritable academic institutions (the oldest of which date back many centuries) and New Zealand's which is, in actuality, only one century old. These references are interspersed with shots of girls in uniforms and hats walking to school and cricket games underway in Hagley Park.

The choice of what to *exclude*, as well as what to *include*, in this travelogue is telling. The focus is entirely on New Zealand's inherited traditions, how well the country can appear to approximate "home." We are not shown New Zealand's native environment, only those areas that have been transformed into English gardens. There is no mention of the country's indigenous groups. The only person mentioned is Lord Rutherford, a New Zealand scientist who spent the majority of his life living and working in Britain. These traditions also appear as we follow Pauline, running late to Christchurch Girls High School. The camera tracks scurrying legs clad in tartan kilts, sensible stockings, and uniform brown shoes as they pass over stone floors bearing the Latin motto *Sapientia et Veritas* (knowledge and truth). In the background we hear the strains of a girls' choir, dutifully singing "Just a Closer Walk with Thee." New Zealand's culture is shown as the first marker of the country's indebtedness to a colonial relationship that still holds strong ties, both economically and psychologically.

This notion of New Zealand's cultural positioning in relation to Britain—as smaller and inferior—is presented later in the film when the students are asked to write an essay about the Royal family. Pauline and Juliet take it upon themselves to construct a piece about the *Borovnian* Royal family, telling the irate teacher, "You didn't say it had to be about the Windsors!" as she proceeds to stop them in mid-performance. The fact that it was assumed that the students would know to follow this unmentioned guideline is interesting in and of itself. This scene in *Heavenly Creatures* accents the way in which the British curriculum—with its attendant ideology—overlays the New Zealand classroom. New Zealand's educational system is still modeled after a predominantly British-based plan, stressing European history and British literature over and above specifically New Zealand and/or Pacific studies. In addition, the teacher's horrified reaction to the girls' impertinence again stresses the need to accord Britain with the appropriate respect, given New Zealanders' position as exiles from the motherland.

The events of *Heavenly Creatures* occur only ten years before the country began to slowly separate itself from this colonial mentality—albeit not always willingly on the part of New Zealand. Britain's mid-1970s move to join the European Economic Community (EEC) ended the guaranteed market for New Zealand's primary products. This change produced a domino effect, with the country's farmers and the processing, packing, and transportation industries scrambling to fill the void with new forms of products and new markets. In the film, the strain of this future is already evident, in spite of the supposed bounty of the postwar period. Pauline's working-class family struggles to present a stiff upper lip to the outside world despite internal pressures and Mrs. Hulme's job as a marriage counselor shows her dealing with anxious couples faced with economic problems and subsequent social pressure.

Britain's departure for the EEC also marks the historical point when recognition of New Zealand's inherent class demarcation began to become widespread, precipitated by media denouncement of the country's political and welfare systems and foreshadowing a decade of economic stagnation. With this recognition came awareness of social problems such as juvenile crime, drug use, violence, and the breakup of the family unit.[26] In the Hulmes' and the Riepers' covert attempts to navigate their social situation—and attempt control over their daughters' interactions and manipulation of their differing social positions—we can see the vestiges of another era. In the 1950s, an understanding of one's social class was still a private matter, to be addressed individually or through familial bonds. The late 1960s slowly introduced New Zealanders to the reality of class as a concept with ideological underpinnings, as a public matter to be dealt with on a national scale.

These ideological understandings of class and cultural assimilation intersect in the girls' relationship and spark off their final terrifying murder. Juliet is first introduced into the narrative only after we have followed the path of her father's stately gray Rolls Royce to the front of the school. The sleek car leads the audience to wonder about which dignitary is arriving to grace the school with her presence. Juliet, in fact, does assume a commanding presence at the front of the room as she is introduced to the "geeels of 3A," casting a supercilious eye about her at the rows of scrubbed, uniformed, plain-faced girls and their well-meaning but obviously parochial headmistress. Juliet goes so far as to correct the headmistress when she proceeds to mention Juliet's time at two New Zealand schools, stating, "I am *actually* from England, Miss Stewart."

Miss Stewart proceeds to point out that Juliet's father is Rector at Canterbury University, impressing upon her charges both the literal and figurative gap between them and the veritable Miss Hulme. While these girls are being tutored in the history and heritage of the mother country, Juliet is a product of these traditions, a true imperial set down in the flesh at girls' high. We soon glean that Juliet is not afraid to express her own opinion as she corrects the French mistress's pronunciation and refuses to participate in still-life drawing during art class. She informs the fussing art teacher that she prefers to sketch "St. George (England's patron saint) slaying the dragon" and proceeds to do so with great aplomb, calling on Pauline's assistance and completely ignoring the guidelines of the exercise.

Pauline, on the other hand, is ill at ease in her regimented colonial existence. Her disgruntled nature is shown throughout the first few scenes of *Heavenly Creatures*, as we see her arrive late for school, resolutely refuse to sing in morning assembly, and fail to be paired up in art class, preferring to "go" by herself. Once co-opted into Juliet's world, however, she attempts to reposition herself by absorbing her mentor's more European interests, such as Mario Lanza records and medieval fantasy games with appropriately ornate costumes.[27] As the girls move through the narrative we see, respectively, through these activities and interests, Mr. Rieper's attempts to keep Pauline mindful of "her proper place," and the girls' refusal to accept the bland cultural landscape surrounding them, precipitating their invention of the fantasy Fourth World.

The audience can see the clash between Pauline's perceptions and actuality when she listens, hugging herself, to a Mario Lanza record after Juliet informs her (during the art class debacle) of Lanza's status as "the world's greatest tenor!" Immersed in the sheer beauty of the music and her new feelings for Juliet, she is rudely interrupted by her fish-store— "He *is* the manager!"—father, mouthing along with Mario as he pretends to croon to a smelly dead mackerel he insists on waving in front of her. Although Pauline swats him out of the room protesting, "Stop it! You're spoiling it. Go away," we are already aware of how out of place Pauline feels. Both Juliet and Pauline feel trapped in their respective situations: Juliet because she has been brought to such a colonial back post, and Pauline because she cannot get out of this supposed back post.

Ingeniously, the girls choose to turn their backs on this paltry reality and instead invent a world of their own, named the "Fourth World" and dedicated to "music, art, and pure enjoyment." By creating this world, the girls both remove themselves from the class-bound confines of their familial situations and the culturally deficient locale of provincial New Zealand society. Interestingly though, both the Fourth World and Borovnia appear to be modeled after a system not unlike the class-bound one that Juliet left behind. The Fourth World is stocked with well-tended English-style gardens and water fountains, and Borovnia boasts a royal lineage to rival Britain's Windsors. The difference in this case is that Pauline is able to assume her rightful place in *this* society through her appropriation of the character of the royal Borovnian, King Charles. Ultimately, at this stage in the narrative the distinction between Borovnia, where class shifting is both possible and accepted, and reality, where parental and societal structures ensure no such thing will occur, is beginning to blur—with horrifying consequences.

At the beginning of their relationship, Pauline and Juliet's involvement provides a site of liminality for the young women. Justine King defines this space as "a realm of possibility," suggesting that once the female protagonist enters this realm she is able to remove herself from "her initial narrative (and cultural) situation."[28] In the case of Pauline and

Juliet, the Fourth World and Borovnia act as boundary markers for this movement, while initiation occurs through ceremonies involving candle-lit shrines to their shared "saints" and movie induced quasi-lesbian encounters. In *Heavenly Creatures* there are two important connections with this model of liminality, one which expands the possibilities proposed by King and one which highlights the inevitability of reinscription via that same route of expansion.

First, rather than only tying liminal movement to gender as King does, my application of liminality to Jackson's film extends King's model to include class as well as gender. That is, while the Fourth World and Borovnia allow the girls to transcend the circumscribed feminine roles allotted to them in Christchurch's social milieu, including choosing a deviant sexuality, it also allows Pauline to move between social classes—facilitating her ascension to Juliet's level through the characters she assumes in their alternate realities. Through these rituals, Pauline and Juliet are able to reconcile the disparity between their differing lifestyles and social classes.[29] Pauline's class transgression(s) also serve(s) to dispute the ideologically agreed-on assumption of the *un*importance of class positioning in New Zealand society. The fact that Pauline feels it is necessary to assume a higher class status in her games with Juliet gives lie to the belief that "we are all equal," which was touted in political and social discourse throughout the film and, in parallel, during that historical period.

Second, whereas King argues that the notion of liminality must be understood as "a redefining and reempowering transformation of identity or rite of passage," she also goes on to show how this transformation often serves to "reconcile the protagonist (and spectator) to the inevitability of [the character's] prescribed position."[30] Indeed, in *Heavenly Creatures* the machinations of class difference are working to effect this reinscription long before the girls' actions become a matter for the police and the legal system. As the film's narrative progresses, the option of reestablishment in the real world begins to become less viable for Pauline. She has become more and more estranged from her parents, particularly Honora. Pauline is the first to suggest that they should consider "moidering" Mother, and she also remains calm and goal oriented throughout the final weeks, even though Juliet's resolve falters "on the day of the happy event" (as Pauline records it in her diary).

Simultaneously, however, Juliet is being recuperated into her rightful class and realigned to her subsequent life chances through her parents' actions. Henry and Hilda decide to return to Britain in the wake of their impending divorce, making plans to leave Juliet in South Africa en route "for the good of her health." It is the Hulmes who suggest Pauline should stay at their house for the final two weeks before they leave New Zealand—in effect softening the blow of permanent separation.[31] Just as Juliet arrived in New Zealand claiming her imperial "difference" from the society and surroundings she found herself in, now her parents intend for her to return, shedding the taint of colonial subjectivity (or subject-ness) through her return voyage home.[32] In effect, then, the girls' final plan is doubly reinscriptive: It not only ensures both Pauline and Juliet's violent return to their respective classed realities, it also severs forever the possibility of Pauline's accession to Juliet's socially superior British-based world.

Within the narrative of *Heavenly Creatures*, Pauline and Juliet find ways to circumnavigate their differing social positions through the liminal space of their fantasy worlds. However, in line with the continuing stratification present in New Zealand society, their attempts—violently conceived and executed—are ultimately just as violently negated. An end title informs us that Pauline and Juliet were released after spending five years in separate New Zealand prisons "detained at her Majesty's pleasure" on the condition that they never meet again.[33]

The weight of evidence suggests that issues regarding class and class divisions have been neglected in analyses of *Heavenly Creatures*. Whereas the film itself depicts the prevalence of class stratification in New Zealand through its portrayal of Christchurch in the 1950s, questions of gender and sexuality have tended to dominate discussions about the film. I have been unable to find any sustained discussion on whether Jackson's representation of class in *Heavenly Creatures* does or does not correlate with the dominant ideologies of the period. The relationship between reception and the film's treatment of class is significant work that needs to be investigated further.

By examining the connections between class, New Zealand society, and *Heavenly Creatures*, larger parallels can be drawn between history, ideology, and film. We can begin to understand how representations of history and ideology are frequently confused with one another, and how often films reproduce dominant ideologies that may provide misrepresentative, misleading, or even untrue versions of history or society. However, I believe that *Heavenly Creatures'* representation of class is indeed accurate to the times in New Zealand precisely because the film does allow that class divisions were a central influence, both in society as a whole and in the girls' friendship and their subsequent actions.

Notes

1. Jonathan Dennis and Jan Bieringa, eds., *Film in Aotearoa/New Zealand* (Wellington: Victoria UP), 156.

2. Because it was revealed during the subsequent trial that Pauline's parents were never legally married, Pauline was charged under her mother's maiden name of Parker.

3. See various *Heavenly Creatures* web sites; see also Dennis and Bieringa, eds., *Film in Aotearoa/New Zealand.*

4. Luisa Ribeiro, "Heavenly Creatures," *Film Quarterly* 49.1 (1995): 33–38.

5. John C. Murray, *"Heavenly Creatures:* An Appreciation," *Metro Magazine* (1995): 12–17.

6. Michelle Elleray, *"Heavenly Creatures* in Godzone," in *Outakes: Essays on Queer Theory and Film,* ed. Ellis Hanson (Durham, NC: Duke UP, 1999), 223.

7 Jennifer Henderson. "Hose Stalking: *Heavenly Creatures,"* *Canadian Journal of Film Studies* 6.1 (1997): 45.

8. David Bedggood, *Rich and Poor in New Zealand: A Critique of Class, Politics and Ideology* (Auckland: George Allen & Unwin, 1980), 7.

9. This phrase was coined by Warwick Armstrong and Philip Ehrensaft in their article "New Zealand: Imperialism, Class and Uneven Development," *Australian and New Zealand Journal of Sociology* 14.3 (1978): 298, to define the category of countries that emerged as the nineteenth-century "regions of recent settlement" supplying temperate foodstuffs and other staple products to the imperial center of the world system, Britain.

10. J. M. R. Owens, "New Zealand before Annexation," in *The Oxford History of New Zealand,* 2nd ed., ed. Geoffrey W. Rice (Auckland: Oxford UP, 1992), 50.

11. The majority of the settlers were "young persons of the laboring class," given free passage on the ships sailing to the new country through an emigration fund set up according to the terms of the purchase of land in the company's first and principal settlement, Wellington. However, these terms included preference given to workers who were contracted to labor for the people who had already acquired land titles, intending to emigrate, and then to those who possessed the skills to make the colony immediately productive: farm laborers, blacksmiths, seamstresses, domestic

servants, men of the building trade. See W. B. Sutch, *The Quest for Security in New Zealand: 1840 to 1966* (London: Oxford UP, 1966), 11.

12. Power in New Zealand rested in the hands of those that held land and would remain so for over a hundred years. In many respects, the class struggle in New Zealand continues to be the struggle between landowners (including those who serve their interests: banking and financial services, the church system, overseas traders and investors, government bodies) and those who wish to acquire their rightful share of this land. Equally, in the early years of the colony, specific laws, enacted in Britain and transposed onto New Zealand soil, insured the continuation of a system of poverty for those who could not "possess themselves of the soil," favoring property owners and providing little in the way of state-supported welfare. See Rob Steven, "Land and White Settler Colonialism: The Case of Aotearoa," in *Culture and Identity in New Zealand*, eds. David Novitz and Bill Willmott (New Zealand: GP Books, 1989), 30.

13. Michelle Elleray analyzed Pauline and Juliet's appropriation of mateship rituals in her essay "*Heavenly Creatures* in Godzone." Bev James and Kay Saville-Smith, *Gender, Culture, and Power: Challenging New Zealand's Gendered Culture* (Auckland: Oxford UP, 1989), as well as Jacqui True, "Fit Citizens for the British Empire? Classifying Racial and Gendered Subjects in 'Godzone (New Zealand)," in *Women Out of Place: The Gender of Agency and the Race of Nationality*, ed. Brackette F. Williams (London: Routledge, 1996), 103–28, have done substantial work on the leveling role of mateship rituals such as drinking, sports, and outdoor pursuits (fishing, hunting) in reproducing the idea of class as malleable or even irrelevant, while at the same time promoting and consolidating gender differences.

14. Common myths along traditional Protestant lines include: Everyone in New Zealand has the same opportunities; hard work will produce wealth; there is no real poverty in New Zealand; race relations between the dominant white settler majority and minority groups (such as Polynesian and Asian) are excellent, especially in comparison with other countries. See Bob Consedine, "Inequality and the Egalitarian Myth," in *Culture and Identity in New Zealand*, ed. David Novitz and Will Willmott (Wellington: GP Books, 1989), 174.

15. Where these myths differ from those immortalized in "The American Dream" is that there are sanctions on the accumulation and display of wealth. The rhetoric of equality works to bring the top down as well as the bottom up. That is, although it is everyone's right, and indeed responsibility, to acquire the same standard of living as one's neighbor, one should not move beyond this. I have addressed the "tall poppy syndrome" in relation to the acquisition of knowledge as one of the reasons given for the constant one-way flow of creative and intellectual talent from New Zealand to other countries providing greater resources and opportunities. See Davinia Thornley, "Duel or Duet? Gendered Nationalism in *The Piano.*" *Film Criticism* 24.3 (spring 2000): 61–76. In addition, the acquisition of economic and financial resources should be managed discreetly; conspicuous consumption is frowned upon. This value perpetuates the notion of egalitarianism, making it even more difficult to identify the rich from the poor, so to speak.

16. Graeme Dunstall, "The Social Pattern," in *The Oxford History of New Zealand,* 2nd edition, ed. Geoffrey W. Rice (Auckland: Oxford UP, 1992), 453.

17. Foreign exchange fluctuations moved in New Zealand's favor, causing New Zealand's exports in 1950 and 1951 in each year to buy 30 percent more imported goods than in 1949. See Sutch, 410.

18. Sutch, 408.

19. Henderson, 44.

20. It has only been since 1980 or so that many large New Zealand companies, particularly government bureaucracies, have stopped the time honored tradition of a half-hour break for all workers in the morning and afternoon for "tea service."

21. Nick Hanna, *Fodor's Exploring New Zealand* (New York: Fodor's Travel Publications, 1999), 8.

22. Nick Hanna, *Passport's Illustrated Guide to New Zealand* (Chicago: Passport Books, 1999), 78.

23. Elizabeth B. Booz, *Odyssey New Zealand* (Hong Kong: Odyssey Publications, 1999), 10–11.

24. Mark Williams, "Crippled by Geography? New Zealand Nationalisms," in *Not on Any Map: Essays on Post-Coloniality and Cultural Nationalism,* ed. Stuart Murray (Devon, UK: U of Exeter P, 1997), 23.

25. Gregory A. Waller, "The New Zealand Film Commission: Promoting an Industry, Forging a National Identity," *Historical Journal of Film, Radio and Television* 16.2 (1996): 249; "cultural cringe" refers to New Zealanders' habit of comparing themselves and their country unfavorably with Britain. An obvious example occurs with Mr. Rieper's comments about Sir Edmund Hillary.

26. Bedggood, 7.

27. Pauline's first recognition of difference between herself and Juliet is shown when she goes to play at Juliet's house after school. As she rounds the driveway on her bike, Juliet's large and imposing house is suddenly before her, and Pauline stops, confused as to how to approach such a mansion.

28. Justine King, "Crossing Thresholds: The Contemporary British Women's Film," in *Dissolving Views: Key Writings on British Cinema,* ed. Andrew Higson (New York: Cassell, 1996), 220.

29. Jennifer Henderson has analyzed Pauline's movement between identities and worlds in her article mentioned above.

30. King, 220.

31. This is in fact the underlying idea suggested by Mrs. Hulme when she comes to request permission for Pauline to stay. She tells Mr. and Mrs. Rieper that Juliet is "uncontrollable" as Mrs. Rieper bursts into tears, admitting that Pauline has not spoken to her in weeks.

32. Importantly, however, even Juliet's claim to "British-ness" is somewhat tenuous as Michelle Elleray outlines. She points out that Juliet has spent a great deal of her childhood in the colonies and will return to them again on this supposed trip "home." See Elleray, 228.

33. Immediately upon her release, Juliet left New Zealand in order to join her parents in Britain, while Pauline initially remained. She currently lives in North England.

Bibliography

Armstrong, Warwick, and Philip Ehrensaft. "New Zealand: Imperialism, Class and Uneven Development." *Australian and New Zealand Journal of Sociology* 14.3 (1978): 197–303.

Bedggood, David. *Rich and Poor in New Zealand: A Critique of Class, Politics, and Ideology.* Auckland: George Allen & Unwin, 1980.

Booz, Elizabeth B. *Odyssey New Zealand.* Hong Kong: Odyssey Publications, 1999.

Consedine, Bob. "Inequality and the Egalitarian Myth." In *Culture and Identity in New Zealand,* edited by David Novitz and Bill Willmott. Wellington: GP Books, 1989.

Dennis, Jonathan, and Jan Bieringa, eds. *Film in Aotearoa/New Zealand.* Wellington: Victoria UP, 1996.

Dunstall, Graeme. "The Social Pattern." In *The Oxford History of New Zealand.* 2nd ed., edited by Geoffrey W. Rice. Auckland: Oxford UP, 1992.

Elleray, Michelle. "*Heavenly Creatures* in Godzone." In *Outakes: Essays on Queer Theory and Film,* edited by Ellis Hanson. Durham, NC: Duke UP, 1999.

Hanna, Nick. *Fodor's Exploring New Zealand.* New York: Fodor's Travel Publications, 1999.

———. *Passport's Illustrated Guide to New Zealand.* Chicago: Passport Books, 1999.

Heavenly Creatures. Dir. Peter Jackson. Perf. Melanie Lynskey and Kate Winslet. Roadshow/Miramax/Buena Vista, 1994.

Henderson, Jennifer. "Hose Stalking: *Heavenly Creatures.*" *Canadian Journal of Film Studies* 6.1 (1997): 43–60.

James, Bev, and Kay Saville-Smith. *Gender, Culture, and Power: Challenging New Zealand's Gendered Culture.* Auckland: Oxford UP, 1989.

King, Justine. "Crossing Thresholds: The Contemporary British Women's Film." In *Dissolving Views: Key Writings on British Cinema,* edited by Andrew Higson. New York: Cassell, 1996.

Murray, John C. "*Heavenly Creatures:* An Appreciation." *Metro Magazine* 102 (1995): 12–17.

Owens, J. M. R. "New Zealand before Annexation." In *The Oxford History of New Zealand,* 2nd ed., edited by Geoffrey W. Rice. Auckland: Oxford UP, 1992.

Ribeiro, Luisa. "Heavenly Creatures." *Film Quarterly* 49.1 (1995): 33–38.

Steven, Rob. "Land and White Settler Colonialism: The Case of Aotearoa." In *Culture and Identity in New Zealand,* edited by David Novitz and Bill Willmott. Wellington: GP Books, 1989.

Thornley, Davinia. "Duel or Duet? Gendered Nationalism in *The Piano.*" *Film Criticism* 24.3 (spring 2000): 61–76.

True, Jacqui. "Fit Citizens for the British Empire? Classifying Racial and Gendered Subjects in 'Godzone' (New Zealand)." In *Women Out of Place: The Gender of Agency and the Race of Nationality,* edited by Brackette F. Williams. London: Routledge, 1996.

Waller, Gregory A. "The New Zealand Film Commission: Promoting an Industry, Forging a National Identity." *Historical Journal of Film, Radio and Television* 16.2 (1996): 243–63.

Williams, Mark. "Crippled by Geography? New Zealand Nationalisms." In *Not on Any Map: Essays on Post-Coloniality and Cultural Nationalism,* edited by Stuart Murray. Devon, UK: U of Exeter P, 1997.

Chapter 5

The Heroine's Journey? Women and Spiritual Questing in New Zealand Film and Television— A Production Study

Ann Hardy

For some time now it has been rare for films made in New Zealand to have as their protagonist a white, heterosexual, goal-directed, adult, male—that is, a traditional hero. Heroes make difficult decisions, provide community leadership, and fight battles against human enemies and the forces of nature. Most of all, however, they fight the imperfections in their own psyches, providing, as the doyen of hero mythology, Joseph Campbell has suggested, nothing less than a model of effective human spiritual development.[1]

During the twentieth century, such heroes were numerous, to the extent that discussions of representations of the New Zealand or Kiwi male, his relationships with the land, with his male friends, and occasionally with women, have become a staple of local film criticism.[2] Kiwi males, at least until *Hercules* came to be filmed on our shores, may have been built on a more modest scale than Hollywood heroes, but they still endured dangerous journeys and underwent titanic struggles for the cause of freedom in films such as *Runaway, Sleeping Dogs, Smash Palace, Utu* and *Goodbye Pork Pie*. However, since 1985 or so, the situation has changed with regard to both representation and criticism. In fact if one were to view all the films made in New Zealand since 1985, one would probably come to the conclusion that the white adult male is an endangered creature, or at least one with very little remaining cultural influence.

To a certain extent that impression is made possible because a good proportion of the output of films made in New Zealand over that time has been directed by women, who deliberately focus on female protagonists. In many of these, the white, adult males who do make an appearance are either exposed as brutal and dominating or are stressed, beleaguered, and somewhat pathetic—think of the vain, lost character of Stewart in *The Piano*, twitching Mr. Siemens in Merata Mita's film *Mauri*, or the ineffectual Colin in Maclean's *Crush*. On the evidence of their films, New Zealand women directors are clearly giving voice to an opinion that it is men, and not women, who are the site of *lack*—that it is males who need to reconstruct themselves and regain their spiritual credentials before they can apply to be thought of as heroes again.

Because that kind of stance is not unexpected as an outcome of a strong feminist movement, it is more interesting perhaps that some *male* film- and television-makers share similar views—they too have produced texts that suggest that being a white adult male in contemporary New Zealand is a positioning characterized by strong tensions, contradictions, and uncertainty about the nature and authority of that positioning. If, in some postulated golden past, western men ever felt secure in a social system guaranteed by the moral and spiritual power delegated by a male God, that security is now seen to have evaporated under the stresses of secularization and numerous other liberal forms of social change.

In terms of film history you can almost pick the moment when those tensions became visible. New Zealand film heroes have often been distinguished by an existential degree of self-reliance, but in a 1985 movie with a sci-fi premise, the loneliness of being male is presented at its most extreme. *The Quiet Earth* is about the end of the world as brought about by an international network of scientists. After the catastrophic "effect" occurs, the New Zealand scientist Zac believes himself to be the last man alive. For a while, like the newly immortal Phil in *Groundhog Day*, he has a wonderful time flouting all the laws that had previously constrained his behavior. However, complete self-indulgence is not satisfying for long, so, dressed in a woman's satin petticoat, carrying a shotgun, he goes to ask some hard questions of God. Here, in a huge, echoing, empty church, Zac is at his lowest ebb. Aiming his gun at a statue of Christ, he calls out to God, challenging him to explain his purpose. When he fails either to answer or to appear, Zac blasts apart the statue and declares that, he, Zac, is now the only God.

Although his hubristic response to the collapse of the possibility of belief is to place himself in the role of a deity, that arrogation of power proves to be unsustainable. By terminating his allegiance to the Christian "master narrative" that has legitimated so many social arrangements for so long, the tenuousness of his own situation is further underlined. As the last representative of mankind, his rejection of God has other implications—the idea of the end of the world is thus also the idea of a crisis of masculinity.[3] Ultimately Zac resolves this crisis by committing suicide, which both reverses the effect, and, in a maneuver also present in the other texts I will discuss, in fact restores the authority of both God and Man, by reproducing the sacrifice that instituted the original chain of legitimation. It is a maneuver reminiscent of that "fort da" game so appreciated by psychoanalytic critics: A child throws something away in order to have it returned. However, in the interval between the throwing away and the returning, there are time and space—in this case time for others, especially female seekers, to occupy the space the hero has vacated.

I have already mentioned some of the films made by female directors concurrent with, or since, the watershed marked by *The Quiet Earth*, all of which have female protagonists. Most male filmmakers have also set aside the white, adult male hero in favor of a diverse range of other cultural identities. These include a focus on young men who have not yet gained access to adult social and economic power, among them the protagonists of *The Navigator*, *The End of the Golden Weather*, *Bad Taste*, and *Braindead*. Significant numbers of Maori male protagonists feature in films such as *Kingpin*, *Te Rua*, *Once Were Warriors* and *Broken English*. *Flying Fox in a Freedom Tree* is a film about growing up in Samoa and *Illustrious Energy* is a historical narrative about a young Chinese gold miner. As most of these characters come from groups that are associated with marginality under current societal configurations, they do not fit exactly into the niche vacated by the white, male hero. For instance, in the case of young male and Maori protagonists, the texts are likely to be filtered through critiques of excessive rather than justified levels of violence.

A development of equal significance, however, is the deployment of female protagonists and female heroes by male writers and directors to carry the dramatic and moral thrusts of the narrative. Examples of this trend include two films about the New Zealand literary figures, Sylvia Ashton-Warner (*Sylvia*), and Katherine Mansfield (*Leave All Fair*), the female romantic couples in *Desperate Remedies*, and *Heavenly Creatures* and the elevation of Beth's character in the screen adaptation of *Once Were Warriors*. Not all such films feature a young female as the sole protagonist; she will often be balanced by a man, usually a male of Maori ethnicity. However, there is certainly a case to be made that there is something particularly attractive to male writers and directors in exploring strong female characterizations at this time. Is the use of female characters as heroes evidence of reflexive gender critique? Might it be a genuine exploration of alternatives to male models of power? Or remembering such traditional caveats as Jung's theories about the appeal of the *anima* figure for men, or Mulvey's generalization that movies are an illusion cut to the measure of (presumably, male) desire[4]—is it still just the same old shell-game, the pieces have moved into different places, but the underlying power dynamic hasn't really changed?

The Examples

The questions I am asking have arisen in the context not just of analyzing finished texts, but in undertaking longitudinal production studies of two recent local productions. One is a feature film called *Saving Grace*, the other a television miniseries called *The Chosen*. Both fit into an established Kiwi pattern of displaying negative, sceptical attitudes toward organized religion while leaving room for a positive appreciation of aspects of "spirituality." Male directors and producers headed both projects, which feature to varying degrees young female heroes whose lives are threatened because they are entangled with issues of religion and spirituality.[5] These characters, Grace and Sarah, take issue with the conventional arrangement whereby males relay either the Word of God or words of spiritual truth. Instead they try to search for formulations suited to their own experience and understanding.

Neither the choice of emphasis nor method of approach is accidental since this material is a gender analysis of a larger project looking at discourses about religion and spirituality within the New Zealand film and television industries.[6] The choice of method rests on the assumption that films and television programs are partial, flexible entities, made by groups and individuals operating from particular points of view under specific institutional constraints during an extended moment of time. Hence the model I have employed is the tripartite approach advocated by J. B. Thompson.[7] It balances the study of the context of production with analysis of the text itself and then of the responses of audiences on the grounds that no one method alone, and especially not the exclusive use of textual analysis, can determine the range of possible meanings that a piece can sustain. The advantage of studying examples of New Zealand film and television in this manner is that one can observe ideas, discourses, and relationships being constructed and challenged through a number of contexts. The film or program, finished and ready for distribution, is likely significantly different from the one envisaged at the beginning of the preproduction process. Moreover, it will probably be perceived differently at all stages by each of the many people involved in its production. These various assessments occur even before the film or TV show arrives in front of an audience; each of its members will then bring variant sets of experiences to its interpretation.

With each of the two projects, a series of interviews with key creative and production personnel was conducted before filming began, that is, at the preproduction stage, another set when filming was all but completed. Later, there were additional interviews related to postproduction to discuss editing, marketing, and distribution issues. The power structures of film and television production in New Zealand are not identical. In television the vision and control often rests with the producer or a chain of producers; the director carries out that vision and adds his or her own touches, but significant departures from the script will need to be negotiated with those further up the hierarchy.[8] The nature of all productions varies according to who comprises the production team, but in New Zealand film productions it has been common practice for directors—who are often also scriptwriters—to shape the film according to their personal vision. On *Saving Grace*, for example, the director's, Costa Botes, contract gave him creative control or "final cut" on the production.[9] On this occasion I have chosen to highlight and contrast the responses of two pairs of actors from each project with each pair containing a male and female respondent. It should be noted that other choices, highlighting other relationships would most likely produce different results.[10]

Project Descriptions

The Chosen consists of two two-hour episodes produced by a large, commercial private production company, Communicado. The series was made specifically to screen on the more populist of the state owned television channels, Channel Two, which is thought to have an audience of fourteen- to thirty-nine-year-olds. It was produced at a time when other local drama productions had not been attracting good ratings figures, and the network was anxious above all that this program rate well. For instance, the producer of the series, Chris Hampson, said that the subject matter and tone of *The Chosen* were calculated to take advantage of interest in cults and in the millennium. So, at the outset of the filming, articulating a division between elitist cinema and mass entertainment television, he was of the opinion any spiritual references in the program were not so much of intrinsic interest as a lure for viewers interested in the arcane. "It's designed as a commercially viable bit of television. It's not a piece of art-house material; it's aimed at a specific demographic audience on a particular channel. [It is] a slick and sleazy bit of TV. . . it is exploitative in that respect . . . it's deliberately using those spiritual elements to hook the audience."[11]

The Chosen is set in a small farming community in northern New Zealand with a murky past. In the nineteenth century it had played host to and then burned to death the leader of an unorthodox religious sect. A hundred years later, his great-great-grandson, Peter McAllister, and *his* followers have come back to carry out a plan of revenge. The cult leader's philosophies of complete self-acceptance and drug-assisted worship attract many young people from the town. Among them is a young woman, Sarah, the heroine of this piece, who is frustrated by the hypocrisy of the community in which she lives. Not least among its hypocrisies is the fact that the local priest, Father Albert Tahere, refuses to give himself permission to return the love she feels for him. For much of the program the character of Sarah is active, assertive, and trenchantly critical of those around her. She repudiates Catholicism, which is linked in her mind with repression of the human personality's natural and inherently innocent capacities for love, expressed both emotionally and physically.

TAHERE
…You've been brainwashed …

SARAH
Maybe I was. Brainwashed so I didn't know truth from lies.
Brainwashed so I didn't know my mind or my body. That's what being a
Catholic means.[12]
…

SARAH
I was taught I was born with Original Sin…my soul was stained before I was
born—I mean what kind of way was that to be brought into life?

TAHERE
Okay, so we were taught that, as children …

SARAH
And look at you, you haven't changed, you haven't progressed at all.
You're deprived of love and deprived of life![13]

Sarah's reasons for her dereliction to the cult, centrally, her assertion of
her right to free choice in matters of belief are unfortunately, however,
overshadowed by other events in an increasingly melodramatic program
which escalates through murder, incest, rape, fraud, and attempted mass
suicide in its attempts to connect with an audience. Finally, its resolution
is not so much in terms of church-based spirituality as romantic love, its
more common, earthly counterpart. In regard to gender positionings, it
also slips back into familiar patterns: Father Tahere saves Sarah from
burning at the stake at the hands of the cult leader and leaves the church
in order to live with her.

Despite some cynicism about the project among the production crew,
the series writers, both of whom had a lively personal interest in current
debates about spirituality, stated they had originally seen the character of
Sarah as a spiritual seeker. They had also planned a more sympathetic
treatment of the cult but had been required to make substantial
modifications to the script as the result of network input. For, in the
current climate, as Hampson had noted "it's not often television even
deals with morality so [the fact that the program is dealing with these
issues at all] it is significant by comparison."[14]

We are accustomed to judging the success of an audio-visual project
solely in terms of its reception as a finished public text. However, it can

be interesting to remember that it has also constituted a significant event in the lives of the people involved in making it. The activity of producing a film or television program draws on questions and confirms existing or incipient societal and professional discourses among participants in every field of technical and creative labor associated with it.

On this level the religious and spiritual issues touched on by the script were not unimportant to the two young Australian actors who played nineteen-year-old Sarah and the cult leader Peter McAllister. Commenting on her role as Sarah, Radha Mitchell agreed that the piece was ultimately very traditional in its treatment of gender in that her character, who at first had been the instigator of the action, became more reactive, more of a link between the two men, as the program progressed. That aspect of the project was a disappointment to her, but she had found a useful personal connection to the material through her own experiences of being raised by a mother who was a member of the Hare Krishna sect. She said she could see a lot of her mother in the character she was playing and found it helpful to imagine her in similar situations at the same age. . . .

> MITCHELL: I grew up in . . . I was involved in I guess what will be called a cult, but not totally in a way that that was the entire aspect of my life, it was just an element of it, and I think it was good because it showed me that our views of things are definitely constructed by the community that we're involved in and that we live in and that there's nothing that's given that's necessarily true.[15]

Radha has a tolerant, pragmatic attitude to religion. She is not overwhelmed by it, as her character Sarah was, because she relativizes its claims to truth. In her own life she now distinguishes between the institutional aspects of religion, which she feels she does not need, and spirituality, which she experiences through yoga and meditation practices. She finds the context of her job, including her work on *The Chosen*, conducive to providing space for that kind of practice.

> MITCHELL: I sort of meditate through my work I guess. . . it's like creative kind of space, which I think, is the same feeling. When you're actually acting, when you're actually in the scene, then that's great, you get lost, you don't know where you are anymore, but when you're waiting around getting your makeup done, you might be doing that [meditating]. . . .[16]

Radha is a confident actor who had already worked on numerous television series and three feature films. She went into *The Chosen* with her eyes open, knowing exactly the kind of material she was dealing with. From the evidence of the interviews it seems that the working relationships between the personnel on the project were respectful and productive, with opportunities for each to influence, to a limited degree, the content of the work. Although the overall nature of the piece remained fairly constant, individual scenes were workshopped and rewritten. This process provided Radha with a satisfying sense of control over her own performance, and as a result she offered an interpretation of her character that reinforces the description of her as a seeker after truth and implies many of the characteristics of the hero.

> MITCHELL: There were some scenes that we actually rewrote . . . it was these cabin scenes which were sort of like an ideological battle ground between Sarah and the priest. I don't think the writer really had a grip on what was going on, . . . but we invested that rewrite with some more. . . . Sarah having some kind of intelligent response to her experience with *The Chosen*. I think she gained a level of maturity, and she was quite naive before, you know. These series of events sort of landed upon her and I think at the end she remains innocent but not naive; she doesn't lose her sense of self but at the same time she gains a greater knowledge of the world. . . . So I guess that's kind of her journey.[17]

The Chosen, then, is a fragmented and in the end conservative, rather than a radical or liberatory text. The characterization of Sarah at first appears to be that of an independent self-directed seeker, finding her own way out of a constraining society by means of the cult as a site of bodily, emotional, sexual freedom. However, to the critical eye this characterization gradually loses both its dimensionality[18] and its internal coherence, becoming more obviously a function of the plot, where a female character is an object of sexual value exchanged by two rival males. Nevertheless, the actor who performed the role did manage to find some consistency and progression in it, and through the exercise of her professional skills, gained satisfaction and even a measure of spiritual nourishment from her involvement in the project—she did much more than just survive through the experience.

In terms of an interest in the intersection of film, religion, and gender, it seems that the character of Sarah is initially a spokesperson for common societal criticisms of the Church and of the clergy. They are both castigated by her for being inauthentic and out of touch with the needs of modern individuals. When the focus moves away from Sarah, to the battle between the Catholic priest and the cult leader, that sense of criticism doesn't lapse but changes its object and is *dispersed* throughout the narrative rather than being referred directly through Sarah's viewpoint. This dispersed discourse critiques notions of patriarchal power by drawing attention to the abusive practices of charismatic cult leaders positioned as "kings" over their earthly followers.

Jeremy Sims, the actor who plays the cult leader Peter McAllister, slips between discussing his character's motivations and his own opinions in his comments on this aspect of the program. He demonstrates both an awareness of the danger of power wielded on the basis of conventional social roles and paradoxically implies his own attraction to that power, when he talks about how McAllister judges the dynamics of the program's representation of institutional religion.

> SIMS: He's [the priest] the classic kind of person that annoys me too, someone that . . . is ostensibly good and preaches goodness without actually having made the personal sacrifices necessarily to have that authority. He [Peter McAllister] believes that . . . with organized religion most of the people running it are hypocrites with their own agendas. They're all ambitious people, they work within the structures they call their religion and within that structure they're just like everybody else and what gives them the right [to?] because it's religion to feel superior to other people, that's basically his premise . . . pretty much my premise as well.[19]

However, those principles of superiority are employed in Sims's own characterization of the cult leader, who subdues his opponents with hard-hitting analyses of the damage caused by blindly following moral dogmas. They were also evident in his particularly deft, assertive navigation of the interview situation itself. In fact, I think the quote above is a particularly interesting statement for a male actor to make at this time about playing the part of a charismatic yet abusive religious leader. It suggests the complexity of response that some men may feel about the issues of both religion and gender. It suggests how difficult it is to untangle any positive potentiality that spirituality might offer from the ideological baggage weighing down the contexts in which most religions now operate. To extrapolate further, it suggests why it may be difficult for men to entirely abandon mythological and representational systems, such as that of the Christian church, which have been such effective guarantors of male power. A second example makes similar points but with a different emphasis.

Whereas *The Chosen* was above all else commercial in its aims, the feature film, *Saving Grace* came out of a different background. A low-budget production, made for around $1.5 million, it was completely funded by a state organization, the New Zealand Film Commission. Although it was hoped that the project would make money, supporting it was also seen as a chance to develop new creative talent. The director, writer, and female lead were all novices at feature filmmaking while their inexperience was balanced by the experience of the producer and lead male actor, who were veterans of the film industry.

Saving Grace was based on an award winning play by a twenty-four-year-old playwright, Duncan Sarkies, and explicit interest in issues of spirituality is much more central to this production than it was to *The Chosen*. Sarkies is an agnostic, fascinated by twin themes of Death and the reactions of individuals in response to such an irresistible force.[20] He had decided that an exploration of the figure of Christ would be a suitable vehicle for these concerns, but because he was determined not to take sides on the issue of Christ's divinity, he wanted to make sure that the text remained ambiguous on the issue of belief. For both him and the director Costa Botes, a negative evaluation of the institutional aspects of religion was taken for granted, as was an understanding that the diverse beliefs of future audience members were not to be impinged on by means of a tyrannical text.

The film features just two characters. One is Gerald, an unemployed woodworker, who may or may not be a reincarnation of Christ, and the other is Grace, a fierce young female "street kid," a homeless person, who has probably existed in an environment of promiscuity and substance abuse. The two start to live together in a platonic relationship. When Gerald tells Grace about his "real" identity, she wants to leave but has nowhere else to go. Returning, she decides to accept his valuation of himself, they become sexually intimate, and she tries to help him make his identity known. However, the end of the story is implied by its premise and eventually, apparently at his request, Grace crucifies Gerald. Shortly after she is detained for his murder, which, as new visual diegetic evidence unexpectedly shows, was not requested by him after all. Grace feels betrayed by this turn of events and by her subsequent incarceration, but soon after Gerald's death she has a final encounter with him—where they both try to determine what and who it was they were really involved with.

Grace, another supposedly nineteen-year-old character, was played by twenty-six-year-old Kirsty Hamilton. Kirsty was drama school trained, had been in a short film, but had never acted in a feature before. Once she got the part, she threw herself into researching the role, interviewing street people and watching all the films she could find on poverty and homelessness.[21] From her point of view this was to be a film about a disadvantaged but determined young woman who goes through an agonizingly confusing set of circumstances to emerge from them with a new sense of her own spiritual strength—she was to be a heroine who, in the end, needed no one but herself. This view of her role also seemed to be shared by the scriptwriter, and similar comments were made by the director:

> SARKIES: It is Grace's movie effectively and Grace is our viewpoint to view Gerald. . . . Grace is pretty much the strong character in her own right. I'm not saying that the audience is necessarily going to identify completely with Grace, but they'll definitely be in terms of being a protagonist. . . . It is her story, he's an integral part of it, but at the end of the day we see it through her eyes.[22]

There were several factors that militated against these views being sustained into the edited version of the film, however. For instance, the emphasis on maintaining ambiguity in order not to foreclose on and impose meaning resulted in a production environment where nobody really seemed sure which of the competing interpretations of the film's meaning was to be preferred. Nobody, that is, except Jim Moriarty, who played Gerald. Moriarty is an actor of more than twenty years' experience, who is a powerful presence in everyday life as well. While the others, including Hamilton, might have been unsure as to whether or not Moriarty's character was Jesus—he had made up his mind.

> HARDY: So do you think he's Jesus Christ? I should ask that directly.
>
> MORIARTY: Well, as an actor, of course I do. I have to take on 100% commitment that the character believes he is. And I will. I'll play him to the utmost of my conviction that that's who he believes he is. And use all the clues in the script to carry out that purpose on behalf of him. Yep.[23]

While Moriarty was confident both in expressing his opinions in rehearsals, and taking what was useful out of the suggestions of others, Hamilton seemed to have been more diffident during that process.

> HAMILTON: I'm quite a quiet person, I tend to just sit back and listen to what everyone else has to say, rather than, bleat on. Cause sometimes you're saying the same things anyway. I know that Jim had a lot of standing up for his character, or the themes of the story, or was very concerned about the interpretation. Or what the audience would think. So it was mostly between Jim and Costa and

Duncan I think. And I was just interested to know what he had to say. But if I
didn't feel something was right I would say it. And usually they'd agree.[24]

Combining the general uncertainty about the preferred meaning of
the film, with Jim Moriarty and Kirsty Hamilton's differing levels of
confidence as performers, it is perhaps not surprising that the final scene
as first shot did not carry the overtones of the achievement of spiritual
self-sufficiency which Hamilton had intended. Grace is alone in a cell,
and the figure of Gerald enters (somehow) wearing the robes of a
Catholic-style statue of Christ. They engage in a slow litany of reproach
and explanation, which ends with Gerald's simple assertion of
presence—"I'm here."

This is how Kirsty Hamilton describes what happened for her when
she tried to deliver her intended performance of the scene.

HAMILTON: I think when you talked to us at the beginning we all had slightly
different versions of what we thought the film was and we needed to have the
same version. For me it's like I said about Grace finding her own spirituality
and there being some hope at the end, and when we came to shoot it— . . . I
thought "this guy is Jesus."

I guess in a way it was kind of like . . . embracing a security, yeah, but it was just
strange, yeah, the look in Jim's eyes was just really, really amazing, when he said
"I'm here" he really meant it . . . it was kind of a neat feeling.

HARDY: What was wrong with that, what's the problem from your point of
view?

HAMILTON: Because I thought it was a different story, I thought it was about
Grace finding herself, not about Grace finding Jesus, and it's perfectly
acceptable, that's one ending to the film, . . . but it's not the one I thought it
was going to be.[25]

Summary/Reinterpretation

In her wish that Grace had found a resolution that was "more for
herself," Hamilton is employing the language of what I would consider
to be a "psychological" discourse of spirituality[26] in which a state of
psychological health and maturity is indicated by a clear-sighted attitude
of individual self-reliance in the face of all obstacles. The attainment of
such a state that, because it is individualistic, limits no one else's
freedom of belief, would have met the criteria for anti-dogmatic
tolerance that was important to all the production team of *Saving Grace*.

It would also have constituted an effective alternative to the unattractive aspects of institutional religion with which the figure of Christ is now often linked. Instead, Hamilton felt that her reaction to the strength of Moriarty's performance meant that she lapsed into a discourse of dependency on a stronger power in the very form associated with Christianity. She used the word *security*—which carries gendered connotations of emotional and economic dependency, as well as an unwavering sense of trust in the other party's good will. The word also refers back to statements that Hamilton made in an earlier interview about her belief in God as a child: that she thought he and Jesus were one and the same and that she prayed to Him in order to feel safe and for other members of her family to be safe also.

However, she now felt she was a different person and was not at all happy that that juvenile view had reasserted itself when the scene was filmed. In fact the writer, director, and producer were not happy either. Instead of producing a new open, ambiguous, critical yet creative relationship to the spirit rather than the religion of Christianity, it appears that they had inadvertently worked together to reinforce an old relationship of unquestioning submission to the figure of Christ in, among other connotations, his form as the remover of doubt, the male embodiment of the guarantee that this world is ultimately well-organized. Indeed, audience research done for the producers by a market research company[27] showed that members of at least one of the focus groups thought the film was pro-Christian and was trying to persuade them to be sympathetic to a Christian worldview.

The production team went on to write, shoot, and edit two more endings to the film before they finally found one that placed the resolution of the narrative firmly in Grace's hands.[28]

Conclusion

Male heroes have often featured in narratives where the spiritual aspects of their searching have been obscured by their spectacular performance of feats of extreme physical courage. Success in these tasks is acknowledged and rewarded by an obligation to occupy the *proxime accessit* position in such mythologically based structures, that is the position of King, which has itself often been constructed as a delegation of power from God.

Heroines are much rarer, and so far, in productions made by men, their rewards have been modest, much more bittersweet. In the case of another New Zealand made film with arguably metaphysical concerns, *Heavenly Creatures*, the rewards were very bitter indeed.[29] (The 1998 production *Elizabeth* directed by Shekhar Kapur is an interesting variation on this dynamic, with a male direction and scriptwriting team presenting of a female character who, at the end of the film, takes on the form and lineaments of a god). The young female characters in the film and program that have been discussed, are by comparison, tentative searchers, whose quests for spiritual satisfaction may end in various ways. In *The Chosen*, the character of Sarah is rewarded merely with the conventional gift of a loving relationship, although the actor who played her, Radha Mitchell, seems to have gotten both more and less out of the experience than that. Kirsty Hamilton, who set out to play what she thought was a strong, self-referenced searcher in *Saving Grace* found herself instead confused and knocked off balance in the performance of an unstable script by the sudden reappearance/reassertion of childhood discourses about the power of a male god. As a result, in the first version of the film at least, her searching places her back in a position as a victimized female reliant upon the transcendental version of male authority for the solace of meaning.

I have tried to balance analysis of the textual characteristics of these works with information about the production contexts and professional experiences of the actors involved. The aim of that approach has been to suggest that participating in a conservative outcome is not always a disempowering experience, while even a supposedly challenging film cannot be accounted as such until it has actually been performed and seen by audiences. However, the central argument of this chapter relates to the use of young female protagonists to address male concerns about religion, spirituality, and power.

It is undeniable that there is a new interest in the representation of religion and spirituality in the entertainment media. Part of that interest involves individuals, both in production teams and in audiences, trying to sort out what those terms might mean to *them* and what impact a resolved understanding of those terms might have on their actions. Just as traditional gender oppositions between male and female are coming under continued pressure, with men also now exhibiting stronger awareness of that pressure in their representations, post-Enlightenment oppositions between material and spiritual views of existence are also coming into question. It is not surprising, therefore, that both sets of tensions may be linked and appear together in the representational arena of the mass media. In the description of *The Quiet Earth* that linkage was obvious, but few male filmmakers since then have had the inclination to represent that articulation of interests so forcefully.

Among the creative teams on the two projects studied there was certainly a stated intention to critique the hypocrisies underpinning much religious power. On both there was also acknowledgment that the female characters were given the bulk of the task of doing that. However, there was no acknowledgment of the probability that contemporary anxieties concerning male authority had also been projected onto the female characters. These characters initially seem to be given a great deal of leeway to investigate, challenge, and take decisive action. In other words, they undertake many of the tasks of a hero. In effect, though, they are on a very short leash which can be pulled back rapidly within the limits of conventional narrative and discursive structures. Their creators fantasize about and play at giving up their power and the belief structures that support it—all the way back to God—but can't quite let go—not yet.

To a certain extent the lack of attention paid to this dynamic may be because the terms needed to structure a public debate concerning conjunctions of gender and metaphysical concerns hover around the threshold of visibility (or audibility). While some discourses of spirituality[30] may provide what J. B. Thompson[31] calls an "incipient critique" of societal practices, they have not yet matured into effective discourses of public influence. Conversely, due to fashion, which in New Zealand at least currently seems to prioritize a feckless, ironic variety of hypermasculinity, explicit *gender* discourses, especially those informed by feminism, have gone into retreat. In the meantime what can be observed are chaotic, fragmented, ambivalent representations of the kind discussed here. Secularizing impulses, such as those demonstrated with such devastating effect by Zac, when he called God's bluff, may ostensibly have shattered the figure of Christ in his context as a symbol of organized religion, but out there in the darkness there are many people, with different motivations, still sifting through the pieces.

Appendix

Persons who worked in the following roles on the productions were interviewed for this research.

Saving Grace (film)	*The Chosen* (TV)
Scriptwriter	Scriptwriters
Director	Producer
Producer	Production Manager
Actors (x2)	Actors (x2)
Editor	Editor
Funding provider (NZFC)	Funding provider (NZOA)
Marketer (NZFC)	Director
Production Designer	
Public Relations Writer	

Notes

1. The concept of the hero most frequently referred to in the context of film production was systematized in the works of Joseph Campbell, specifically in *The Hero with a Thousand Faces* (London: Sphere Publications, 1975). He employed that model to provide an influential exegesis of the first *Star Wars* movie in the 1980s television series *The Power of Myth,* and it has since been systemized into a writing by Christopher Vogler, *The Writer's Journey: Mythic Structure for Screenwriters and Storytellers* (Studio City: Michael Wiese Productions, 1992).

2. Cf. Russell Campbell, "The Cinematic Redefinition of Pakeha Male Identity," *Illusions* 7 (1988); For discussions of Maori male identity see Peter Cleave "Native Voice—1981 and All That," *Illusions* 25 (winter 1996): 19–26; see also Peter Cleave, "Ten Years of Illusions," in *From the Depot-Takirua: Some Essays on Film and Theatre in Aotearoa* (Palmerston North: Campus Press, 1998).

3. The idea of a crisis of masculinity is of course not a new one. As Matthew Allen suggests, however, in "Masculinity-as-Masquerade: The Funny Business of Gender on *Man o Man,*" *Continuum* (1996): 2, this crisis is constructed in many different ways, most of which position feminism as its cause. *The Quiet Earth* differs in tracing that loss of confidence back through the chain of signification to the Ultimate Authority, although the fact that Zac is dressed in female garb when he challenges God, suggests that femininity is an unexplored component of his situation.

4. Laura Mulvey, "Visual Pleasure and Narrative Cinema," in *Visual and Other Pleasures,* by Laura Mulvey (Bloomington: Indiana UP, 1989), 25.

5. The terms *religious* and *spiritual* are notoriously difficult to define. Suffice it to say that in a predominantly secular country like New Zealand, religion has tended to have had a bad press in recent decades, attracting to itself connotations of institutionalization, dogmatism, authoritarianism, rigidity, even hypocrisy. Spirituality, on the other hand, although the term has a large range of usages, seems to be becoming exponentially more acceptable as a pointer to a revived interest in values that includes determining both the core of humanness and its limits.

6. Ann Hardy, "Sites of Value? The Construction and Reception of Religion and Spirituality in New Zealand Film and Television," (Ph.D. diss., University of Waikato, Hamilton, New Zealand, in progress).

7. John Thompson, *Ideology and Modern Culture: Social Theory in the Era of Mass Communication* (Cambridge: Polity Press, 1990).

8. Sally Campbell, production manager of *The Chosen,* interview by author, 3 February 1998.

9. Larry Parr, producer of *Saving Grace,* interview by author, 7 January 1997.

10. See the appendix for a list of interview subjects.

11. Chris Hampson, producer of *The Chosen,* interview by author, 26 November 1997.

12. Maxine Fleming and Gavin Strawhan, *The Chosen,* 2d hour, scene 87, Communicado Ltd., 1997–1998.

13. Maxine Fleming and Gavin Strawhan, *The Chosen,* 3d hour, scene 66, Communicado Ltd., 1997–1998.

14. Hampson, interview.

15. Radha Mitchell, interview by author, 2 February 1998.

16. Mitchell, interview.

17. Mitchell, interview.

18. For an institutional discussion of the concept of character "dimensionality," see Linda Segar, *Creating Unforgettable Characters* (New York: Henry Holt, 1990).

19. Jeremy Sims, interview by author, 2 February 1998.

20. Duncan Sarkies, writer of *Saving Grace,* interview by author, 22 February 1997.

21. Kirsty Hamilton, actor, interview by author, 9 January 1997.

22. Sarkies, interview.

23. Jim Moriarty, interview by author.

24. Hamilton, interview.

25. Hamilton, interview.

26. Janice Peck, "Psychologized Religion in a Mediated World," in *Rethinking Media, Religion and Culture,* ed. Stewart Hoover and Knut Lundby (Thousand Oaks, CA: Sage Publications, 1997).

27. Colmar Brunton Research, "*Saving Grace*—Test Screening: Audience Survey and Focus Group Research." Report for the New Zealand Film Commission (Wellington: Colmar Brunton, 1997).

28. These latter issues have proven to be important because, as Thompson has noted, one of the distinguishing characteristics of mass media texts is the absolute break which occurs between the context of production and the multiple contexts of that text's reception, which may be extended both over time and spread out over many locations. The text is likely to be interpreted differently in each context. *Saving Grace,* for example, has so far had three different endings and three separate sets of marketing materials, which give it the appearance of belonging to a different genre each time, which might therefore attract different audiences. When *The Chosen,* e.g., is screened on public television, this screening is likely to attract an older audience.

29. In *Heavenly Creatures*, a cruel God and his judgment are implied by his absence from the actions of the characters, which, despite attempts to establish their own spiritual realm on meaning, land them in a hell on earth.

30. Barbara Claire Freeman in *The Feminine Sublime: Gender and Excess in Women's Fiction* (Berkeley: U of California P, 1995), 10, makes the point that "there is no single, unchanging politics with which one can identify the sublime" that it has been aligned with conservative political views (e.g., in the writings of Edmund Burke) but has also been associated "with the possibility of liberty and freedom."

31. See Thompson, *Ideology and Modern Culture.*

Bibliography

Allen, Matthew. "Masculinity-as-Masquerade: The Funny Business of Gender in *Man o Man." Continuum* 10 (1996): 2.

Bad Taste. Dir. Peter Jackson. Perf. Peter Jackson, Peter O'Herne. Wingnut Films/New Zealand Film Commission, 1987.

Braindead. Dir. Peter Jackson. Perf. Tim Balme, Diana Penalver. Wingnut Films/New Zealand Film Commission, 1992.

Broken English. Dir. Gregor Nicholas. Perf. Rade Serbezija, Aleksandra Vujcic. Communicado Productions/New Zealand Film Commission/New Zealand on Air, 1996.

Campbell, Joseph. *The Hero with a Thousand Faces.* London: Sphere Publications, 1975.

Campbell, Russell. "The Cinematic Redefinition of Pakeha Male Identity." *Illusions* 7 (1988): 19–26.

The Chosen. TV program. Dir. Michael Smith. Perf. Cliff Curtis, Radha Mitchell. Communicado Productions, New Zealand, 1998.

Cleave, Peter. "Native Voice—1981 and All That." *Illusions* 25 (1996): 47–51.

———. "Ten Years of *Illusions.*" In *From the Depot-Takirua: Some Essays on Film and Theatre in Aotearoa—New Zealand.* Palmerston North: Campus Press, 1998.

Colmar Brunton Research. "*Saving Grace*—Test Screening: Audience Survey and Focus Group Research." For the New Zealand Film Commission. Wellington: Colmar Brunton, 1997.

Crush. Dir. Alison Maclean. Perf. Marcia Gay Harden, Donogh Rees, Caitlin Bossley. Hibiscus Films/New Zealand Film Commission, 1992.

Desperate Remedies. Dir. Stewart Main and Peter Wells. Perf. Jennifer Ward-Lealand, Kevin Smith, Lisa Chappell, Cliff Curtis. James Wallace Productions/New Zealand Film Commission, 1993.

Elizabeth. Dir. Shekar Kapur. Perf. Cate Blanchette, Christopher Eccleston, Joseph Fiennes. India/United Kingdom. Channel 4 Films, 1998.

The End of the Golden Weather. Dir. Ian Mune. Perf. Stephen Fulford, Stephen Papps. South Pacific Pictures, Blue Dolphin, 1991.

Fairclough, Norman. *Media Discourse.* London: Edward Arnold, 1995.

Flying Fox in a Freedom Tree. Dir. Martyn Sanderson. Perf. Faifua Amiga Jr., Richard von Sturmer. Graham McLean Associates/New Zealand Film Commission, 1989.

Freeman, Barbara. *The Feminine Sublime: Gender and Excess in Women's Fiction.* Berkeley: U of California P, 1995.

Goodbye Pork Pie. Dir. Geoff Murphy. Perf. Kelly Johnson, Claire Oberman, Bruno Lawrence. AMA Films/New Zealand Film Commission, 1980.

Groundhog Day. Dir. Harold Ramis. Perf. Andie MacDowell, Bill Murray. Columbia Pictures, 1993.

Hardy, Ann. "Sites of Value: The Construction and Reception of Religion and Spirituality in New Zealand Film and Television." Ph.D. diss., University of Waikato, Hamilton, New Zealand, in progress.

Heavenly Creatures. Dir. Peter Jackson. Perf. Kate Winslet, Melanie Lynskey. Wingnut Films/Fontana Film Productions/New Zealand Film Commission, 1994.

Hercules: The Legendary Journeys. Dir. Bill Norton, Doug Lefler, Josh Becker. Perf. Kevin Sorbo, Anthony Quinn. Renaissance Pictures for Universal City Studios, 1996.

Illustrious Energy. Dir. Leon Narbey. Perf. Shaun Bao, Harry Yip. Mirage Entertainment Corporation/New Zealand Film Commission, 1988.

Joseph Campbell's The Power of Myth: Vol. 1. The Hero's Adventure. Exec. Ed. Bill Moyers. Apostrophe Productions/PBS, 1998.

Kingpin. Dir. Mike Walker. Perf. Mitchell Manuel, Junior Amiga. Morrow Productions/The Film Investment Corporation of New Zealand, 1985.

Leave All Fair. Dir. John Reid. Perf. John Gielgud, Jane Birkin. Pacific Films, New Zealand, 1985.

Mauri. Dir. Merata Mita. Perf. Eva Rickard. Anzac Wallace, Susan D. Ramiri Paul. Awatea Films/New Zealand Film Commission, 1988.

Mulvey, Laura. "Visual Pleasure and Narrative Cinema." In *Visual and Other Pleasures,* by Laura Mulvey. Bloomington: Indiana UP, 1989.

The Navigator: A Medieval Odyssey. Dir. Vincent Ward. Arena Films/Film Investment Corp./Australian Film Commission/New Zealand Film Commission, 1988.

Once Were Warriors. Dir. Lee Tamahori. Perf. Rena Owen, Temuera Morrison. Communicado Productions, Fineline Features, New Zealand, 1994.

Peck, Janice. "Psychologized Religion in a Mediated World." In *Rethinking Media, Religion, and Culture,* edited by Stewart Hoover and Knut Lundby. Thousand Oaks, CA: Sage, 1997.

The Piano. Dir. Jane Campion. Perf. Holly Hunter, Sam Neill, Harvey Keitel, Anna Pacquin. CIBY 2000, Australia/New Zealand, 1993.

The Quiet Earth. Dir. Sam Pillsbury. Perf. Bruno Lawrence, Alison Routledge, Peter Smith. Cinepro/Pillsbury Productions, New Zealand, 1985.

Runaway. Dir. John O'Shea. Perf. Colin Broadley, Nadja Regin, Deidre McCarron, Kiri Te Kanawa. Pacific Films, New Zealand, 1964.

Saving Grace. Dir. Costa Botes. Perf. Jim Moriarty, Kirsty Hamilton. Kahukura Productions, New Zealand, 1997.

Segar, Linda. *Creating Unforgettable Characters.* New York: Henry Holt, 1990.

Sleeping Dogs. Dir. Roger Donaldson. Perf. Ken Blackburn, Deryn Cooper, Grant Tilly. Aardvark Films, New Zealand, 1977.

Smash Palace. Dir. Roger Donaldson. Perf. Brono Lawrence, Anna Jemison. Aardvark Films/New Zealand Film Commission, 1981.

Sylvia. Dir. Michael Firth. Perf. Eleanor David, Nigel Terry, Martyn Sanderson. Southern Light Pictures/Cinepro, 1985.

Te Rua. Dir. Barry Barclay. Perf. Wi Kuki Kaa, Donna Akersten, Marai Fitzi, Peter Kaa. Pacific Films/New Zealand Film Commission/Berlin Senate & Film Commission, New Zealand/Germany, 1991.

Thompson, John B. *Ideology and Modern Culture—Critical Social Theory in the Era of Mass Communication.* Cambridge: Polity Press, 1990.

Utu. Dir. Geoff Murphy. Perf. Bruno Lawrence, Kelly Johnson, Anzac Wallace. Utu Productions/New Zealand Film Commission, 1993.

Vogler, Christopher. *The Writer's Journey: Mythic Structure for Screenwriters and Storytellers.* Studio City: Michael Wiese Productions, 1992.

Chapter 6

La Femme Nikita: Violent Woman or Amenable Spectacle?

Paul Sutton

Luc Besson, the director of *La Femme Nikita* (1990), is known in France as an exponent of the so-called *cinéma du look*, a term that has generally been used pejoratively to describe a certain kind of filmmaking and certain kinds of films that are thought to privilege style over content. This genre of film is generally regarded as "youth-oriented" and is associated "with high production values," with the "look" of the *cinéma du look* referring to their "high investment in non-naturalistic, self-conscious aesthetics."[1] The main critical objections to these films center on their associations with postmodernity and consequently their perceived "lack of ideological or social substance."[2] Thus, Besson has been associated with "the aspirations and the anxieties . . . of the young" in France.[3] Bearing this in mind, it is certainly no coincidence that at the beginning of *La Femme Nikita,* its heroine is represented as a member—the only female member—of a doubly subcultural or marginal gang, both junky and punk. Speaking of the origins and style of the British punks in 1976 and 1977, Dick Hebdige in his influential *Subculture: The Meaning of Style*, argues that punk was a bricolage of "distorted reflections of all the major post-war subcultures."[4] He further suggests that punk was in fact a kind of masquerade, condemned to act out alienation, to mime its imagined condition, to manufacture a whole series of subjective correlatives for the official archetypes of the "crisis of modern life."

Thus, for Hebdige, the punks were not only directly responding to increased joblessness, changing moral standards, the rediscovery of poverty, the Depression, and so forth, they were dramatizing what had come to be called "Britain's decline."

Nikita (Anne Parillaud), then, is situated, at the very beginning of the film, as a member of a marginal social group that is associated with social deprivation, with difference, with otherness—signifiers of a subcultural style "which offends the 'silent majority,' which challenges the principle of unity and cohesion, which contradicts the myth of consensus."[5] What I want to stress in this chapter is the constructedness of Nikita as punk (and junky), as social "deviant" and to illustrate how this operates as a forerunner of her later incarnation as state assassin. Nikita, as we will see, is doubly constructed as violent and twice has her violence explained. In the first instance by the simple fact of being a punk/junky, and in the second through her employment; she is required to do the job so as to repay her debt to society. Detailing how subcultures become visible in the wider culture, Hebdige notes the following:

> In most cases, it is the subculture's stylistic innovations which first attract the media's attention. Subsequently deviant or "anti-social" acts—vandalism, swearing, fighting, "animal behaviour"—are "discovered" by the police, the judiciary, the press; and these acts are used to "explain" the subculture's original transgression of sartorial codes. . . . In the case of the punks, the media's sighting of punk style virtually coincided with the discovery or invention of punk deviance.[6]

The sartorial element functions in *La Femme Nikita* as the barometer for Nikita's status, but, as it will become clear, only within a male governed economy of value—she is devalued as punk/junky, valued as beautiful femme (fatale). In the case of Nikita then, her punkishness is used to "explain" her initial violence, just as her violence also explains punk. Her crime, the apparently motiveless murder of a policeman in cold blood, is explained by the identity she has assumed, and this explanation serves, perhaps, to contain this violence, to render her shocking act somehow comprehensible. The murder occurs only after the police have shot and killed the other gang members—Nikita has only survived because she is a woman. The policeman she shoots dies because he makes an assumption about gender; he dies because he has perceived her to be unthreatening. Nikita, in terms of her drug addiction is represented as the needy one of the gang. It is Nikita who whispers "I need it," who is situated as passive, both in relation to her need and in relation to her male counterparts, who actively attempt to supply that need.

It should be stressed, however, that during this opening sequence Nikita's gender appears indeterminate. She is, as one critic has suggested, "woman, child, boy, man" and it is only when Nikita is seen in a classically fetishistic close-up that it becomes clear that she is indeed a woman.[7] Now this is partly a function of her punkishness with its denial of conventional notions of beauty, and its "blank robotics" of bodily expression or deportment that sets her up as a woman who requires "feminization," i.e., the mythical transformation from beast to beauty.[8] Nikita's becoming woman, and specifically a French woman, as one commentator has noted, is a double process.[9] As Amande (Jeanne Moreau) remarks when Nikita comes to her as part of her government training: "My dear girl, you don't look much now, but if we work hard together and if fortune smiles on us, we'll be able to make you into a human being. An intermediary but necessary step before becoming man's perfect complement: a woman."[10]

However, despite her accommodating transformation, Nikita's gender remains ambiguous and thus requires the continued use of various cultural and sartorial signifiers to render it stable, primarily through her position as femme fatale. There is a certain irony here, for as the phallic woman Nikita does indeed become "man's perfect complement," a fetishized fantasy object—a phallus—that affirms, whilst it also threatens, his masculinity.

So punk, then, in Besson's film, signifies both style and anti-style, a certain transgression and a certain conformity—it is fundamentally spectacular, as are Besson's films themselves, which might lead one to argue, with Hebdige, that ultimately Besson's films are stylized masquerades.[11] Similarly, it is clear that Nikita herself is simply spectacular, simply spectacle. Essentially, both Besson's film and its protagonist may be read as instances of "style over content," where style ultimately becomes content. Nikita is constructed, as a woman and as violent, as much through style—cinematic and sartorial—as through the agency of patriarchy and the state.

Thus far a number of associative links between Besson's film style, punk as a sartorial and cultural style, femininity as masquerade, and gender as performance have been proposed. In what follows, notions of masquerade will be examined in more detail.

Nikita is twice constructed as violent—once, as already argued, as a punk/drug addict, and once as a state sponsored assassin. She is further doubly constructed, as intimated earlier, as a woman: first, as beautiful object and, second, through the sanction of a heterosexual relationship.[12] Nikita is both contained and not contained within the diegesis of the film. In other words while one can argue perhaps for either, she nonetheless remains an ambiguous figure.[13] Fundamental to this question of containment is the dynamic of spectatorial relations vis-à-vis *La Femme Nikita*, both the film and the character, and I will address this central question in the context of Nikita's narrative manufacture and containment.

Generally, readings of *La Femme Nikita* have hinged on the question of Nikita's transgressive behavior, on whether she represents a positive or negative image for women.[14] She is often regarded in the opening sequence of the film as 'wild, disorderly—what is outside the law, what is uncontrollable,' more specifically, what cannot be contained.[15] However, this violent and transgressive behavior is already contained by the punk trope that explains it. Nikita is further contained in the narrative through her arrest and subsequent life imprisonment; she is also quite literally framed because having killed one policeman, her imprisonment, for a minimum of thirty years, is for the murder of three. She is then given what appears to her, and to the viewer, to be a lethal injection. When she later wakes up, she learns that she has officially committed "suicide" and is given a "choice" to either work for the state and Bob (its representative, her "boss," played by Tcheky Karyo), or become a so-called suicide for real. Here, then, Nikita finds herself contained by death (her family have attended her funeral) and by the threat of death.

Once "dead," Nikita undergoes an intensive training period, three years, which transforms her both into a woman and an assassin. She is trained in the use of computers, guns, and fists and also in "the construction of a new and feminine identity."[16] This process of transformation culminates in the construction of a new Nikita. We see her metaphorically reborn on the completion of a trial mission, after which she is put to work, code-named Joséphine, and using a job as a nurse—the ultimate feminine ideal—as a cover. Thus, as Susan Hayward has noted, "In order to stay alive, she [Nikita] has to deal out death on orders from the state, on orders from Bob the father; in other words she is no longer the agent of violence she was in the opening sequence. She has become the vehicle for and the embodiment of state violence, the sadistic outcome of containment."[17]

This trial mission takes place on Nikita's twenty-third birthday. She is taken out to a restaurant by Bob and given a gun as a present. She is instructed to carry out an execution. However, the information that Nikita is given by Bob is misleading, and her escape route (via the men's restroom) is blocked—she thus has to shoot her way out and eventually escapes by jumping into a waste chute. From trainee to assassin, Nikita is literally reborn during this mission, the chute a metaphorical birth canal.

The rebirth of Nikita functions, then, on a number of representational levels. Nikita is first shown to have become *une femme*, the perfect dinner partner. However, she is also visually coded, her costume indicating her embodiment of the femme fatale. On receipt of the pistol from Bob, she also becomes a literally fatal woman: a state controlled killer. She has been reduced to a stereotypical image: "little black dress, great big gun." Nikita, dressed in classic fetishist apparel—high heels, second-skin dress, gun—has become a literal fetish, the means by which the state and Bob who have created her can both disavow and represent their fear of female difference, their fear of castration. As fetish, Nikita is contained as the projection of a mental construct, an image behind which the "real" woman disappears. Guy Austin has argued that this fetishized Nikita is also contained at the level of the cinematic image. In contrast to her earlier punk incarnation, this Nikita "no longer spills out of the frame" but "fits the screen as an amenable spectacle."[18]

Susan Hayward, who views the early Nikita as only contained at the point of her arrest and incarceration, argues that this newly born Nikita "embodies a male construction of the femme fatale as deceptive masquerade." Given Nikita's gender ambiguity, she is both the "male made female" and a woman constructed by a man, Bob, and by the male, patriarchal, state. Nikita, as a state assassin, as the "site of state violence [she] masquerades, because she is already a male construct. . . . She is fetishised and then obliged to act phallically. She is the phallus masquerading as the phallus."[19]

Nikita is contained, then, through her construction, as a phallic woman, by a man, Bob, and the state under whose heteropatriarchal control he operates. As Hayward asserts, the female body is being fixed both as object and "is also being used as a displaced figure of masculinity."

However, as the rebirth sequence attests, Nikita is also continually positioned as female, primarily in order to disavow any potential same-sex
desire on the part of the male spectator. Thus Nikita's escape route is via
the men's restroom, allowing for a shot that situates her male pursuers in
relation to the legend "Hommes/Gents," followed immediately by a shot
of the fetishized *femme* Nikita herself.

Now before moving on to discuss issues of containment in relation to
male and female spectatorship, I would like to cite a number of brief extracts from an interview (remarkable for the convergence it reveals between the film and real life), given by Anne Parillaud, the actress who
plays Nikita, at the time of the film's release. Conducted by Richard
Cannavo and entitled "Birth of an Actress," the interview, parallelling
the central theme of *La Femme Nikita* itself, refers to the rebirth of Parillaud, her metamorphosis from "ex-starlette" to "real actress."[20] In Cannavo's words: "She [Parillaud] returns, and this return is a shock, for in
[La Femme] Nikita, she is simply amazing, a revelation" (p. 86).

Cannavo continues, stressing, through a series of violent images,
what he surmises must have been Besson's role in this transformation:

> It required the audacity and quiet confidence of someone like Besson—this
> mercenary of the cinema—to risk backing this disembodied creature, this
> empty carcass, this broken doll. It can't have been easy for him, alone, to over-
> come the reservations or to ignore the sniggers of laughter. (p. 86)

Here we have exactly the structure that I have delineated so far in relation to the diegesis of the film itself, but in this instance in terms of a
privileged spectator (Cannavo) and the actress playing the role. Cannavo
sets up Parillaud in exactly the same way that Besson sets up or contains
Nikita in his film. Besson, it should be noted, is also Parillaud's partner,
and it would appear that she was the inspiration or template for the character of Nikita. Cannavo asks: "Were you surprised when you read the
screenplay by what Besson wanted to make you act?" Parillaud replies:
"I was really very surprised by what I had inspired in him, or at least by
what he had wanted to show of me" (p. 87). Parillaud explains how she
began acting at age sixteen and believed in her elders, rather than in herself; she says: "[W]hen these elders transform you, when they decide
your personality and your image for you, you let them, because at this
age of uncertainty and research, they answer the questions that you are
asking yourself" (p. 86). Parillaud recounts how she became uncomfort-
able with this world and resolved to leave it: "I decided . . . that stopping

everything was the only way that I might enable myself to reappear one day, different" (p. 86). It would appear that this filmic reappearance is attributable *to La Femme Nikita*'s director. In a later question, Parillaud is asked whether she "owe[s] Besson everything?" This is her response:

> I owe him the most important thing—his belief in me. To have noticed what others, including me; hadn't seen. I will always be conscious of his belief in me for such a role, no doubt in the face of opposition. Because it was him (sic), and him (sic) alone who allowed me to realize one of my greatest dreams. (p. 89)

As illustrated, the interdiegetic containment of Nikita shares an uncanny relationship with the containment of Anne Parillaud, and the extracts from this interview certainly appear to lend extradiegetic evidence to the assertion that Nikita reflects in fact a negative rather than a positive image for women.

With reference to the extra- as opposed to interdiegetic, I would like to address the question of spectatorship in relation to *La Femme Nikita*, focusing specifically on the female spectator, as opposed to the fetishistic, Mulveyean male spectator already briefly examined. A study conducted by Susan Hayward noted that many, especially young, women viewers of the film regard Nikita as representing a positive image for women; a character on a "trajectory towards freedom."[21] However, it has been argued that the visual pleasure of the film leads to an identificatory position, on the part of male and female spectators, with the position of the state, and that viewers of the film survey Nikita just as she is placed under surveillance by this state.[22] Thus one might ask where the female spectator is located in this male economy of visual pleasure? Susan Hayward argues that ultimately any reading of *La Femme Nikita,* i.e., the character and the film, from a position of female spectatorship is problematic and that the film, as suggested earlier, used the female body "as a displaced figure of masculinity."[23] Female spectators of *Nikita* are confronted by a set of limited spectatorial positions that ultimately contain them. Thus, they can either identify with the positive, powerful Nikita but suffer with her the consequences of her transgression of patriarchy. Such a position is a masochistic one, in which, as Hayward notes, "we [women spectators] view our own subjection and approve of it." Alternatively, female spectators of the film can view Nikita negatively, occupying the sadistic and voyeuristic position of the traditional male spectator. As Hayward points out this "is. . . a trope of the film noir, one that makes the female body safe by fetishising it."[24]

In conclusion I would like to focus briefly on the issue of containment in *La Femme Nikita* and its Hollywood remake *Point of No Return*. With reference to the final sequence of each film I wonder whether either Nikita or Maggie (Bridget Fonda) can be seen to escape containment interdiegetically and whether there might also be a relationship of containment between the French film and its American remake. *Point of No Return* duplicates *La Femme Nikita* more or less scene for scene. However, the film's final scene demonstrates clearly that Maggie has escaped the clutches of the government—Bob (Gabriel Byrne) lies to his bosses, telling them that she is dead—and is therefore free. *La Femme Nikita*, by contrast, ends on an ambiguous note with Bob and Marco (Jean-Hugues Anglade) mourning Nikita's disappearance: "We'll miss her."

In *Point of No Return*, it is clear that Maggie escapes government control, and hence containment. In the case of *La Femme Nikita* it is difficult to be sure that she escapes, although it is certainly a possibility. However, here it remains more a function of a particular reading of the film: Nikita as "on a trajectory to freedom" or not. In the case of Maggie, while there is no question that she has eluded the state, her escape has in fact been engineered by Bob and thus in a sense she remains contained by the state and by patriarchy. The closing image of *Point of No Return* is the photo that J. P. (Dermot Mulroney) has taken of Maggie, an image that ultimately also illustrates Maggie's spectatorial containment as fetish.

The potentially open-ended *La Femme Nikita* is, therefore closed or contained by the final sequence of *Point of No Return*. Furthermore, Badham's film contains and remakes the cinematic violence of Besson's film in an act of metaphorical violence. In other words, the Hollywood remake controls the hyperactivity of the French film, much as Nikita is controlled by the state. Thus just as Nikita is herself contained, as a violent woman, by the government, patriarchy, Bob, so Badham's film contains the potential open-endedness of Besson's film and defuses its final ambiguity through its hegemonic Hollywood happy ending.

Notes

1. Ginette Vincendeau, ed. *Encyclopedia of European Cinema* (London: Cassell and the British Film Institute, 1995), 82.

2. Vincendeau., 82.

3. Laurent Bachet, "Poisson Pilote," *Premiere*, April 1990, 83. My translation, P. S.

4. Dick Hebdige, *Subculture: The Meaning of Style* (London: Routledge, 1989), 26.

5. Hebdige, 26.

6. Hebdige, 93.

7. Susan Hayward, "*Nikita*: Sex, Violence, Surveillance," paper presented at the conference "Violence and Gender: Representation and Containment," London, 9 December 1995. Hayward has since published an excellent extended study of Luc Besson and his films. See Susan Hayward, *Luc Besson* (Manchester: Manchester UP, 1998).

8. Hebdige, 108. Nikita's manner of walking, before her transformation would appear to owe much to Hebdige's description of punk dance as "blank robotics."

9. "One way of reading Nikita is as the transformation of an androgynous transnational youth—gum-chewing and virtually indistinguishable from her male friends . . . —into a French woman, with all the accoutrements of the part from Degas posters to couture clothes and the ability to decorate a Parisian apartment." Ginette Vincendeau, "Hijacked," *Sight and Sound* (July 1993): 25.

10. *Nikita,* dir. Luc Besson, France 1990. Original French version with English subtitles. VHS PAL. Distributed by Fox Video. Implicit in this remark is the idea that woman, unless beautiful, does not exist; and if beauty, as Francette Pacteau suggests, requires the absence of "real" woman, then woman can only exist for the hetrerosexual male, as beautiful image. Francette Pacteau notes: "The fantasmatic production of woman as image bespeaks the desire for a presence, a fullness of the seen which would preclude ambiguity, disjunction, loss and lack." See Francette Pacteau, *The Symptom of Beauty* (London: Reaktion Books, 1994), 110.

11. The punk in Besson's film is, of course, an appropriation of punk as cinematic style in that it forms part of the look of the film. Postmodernity has been described as an "aesthetic of recycling," and one might want to think of Nikita in similar terms, as a kind of recycled male fantasy.

12. As Francette Pacteau notes in *The Symptom of Beauty*, "beauty subsists," on "misrecognition and undecidability," and requires the "absence of the real woman that is the necessary support of the attribution of beauty," 12.

13. Hayward notes the importance of containment for this film when she remarks that, "containment . . . is the deep rooted meaning of this film." See "*Nikita.*"

14. See for example, Guy Austin, *Contemporary French Cinema: An Introduction* (Manchester: Manchester UP, 1996), 130–31; and Susan Hayward, *French National Cinema* (London: Routledge, 1993), 293.

15. Hayward, "*Nikita.*"

16. Austin, 130.

17. Hayward, "*Nikita.*"

18. Austin, 130.

19. Hayward, *"Nikita."*

20. Richard Cannavo, "Naissance d'une actrice," *Premiere*, April 1990, 86. This and subsequent translations are mine, P.S.

21. Hayward, *"Nikita."* Hayward's study refers to the responses to the film of female students in her film classes.

22. Hayward, *"Nikita."*

23. Hayward, *"Nikita."*

24. Hayward, *"Nikita."*

Bibliography

Austin, Guy. *Contemporary French Cinema: An Introduction.* Manchester: Manchester UP, 1996.

Bachet, Laurent. "Poisson Pilote." *Premiere,* April 1990, 83.

Cannavo, Richard. "Naissance d'une actrice." *Premiere,* April 1990, 86.

Hayward, Susan. *French National Cinema.* London: Routledge, 1993.

———. *Luc Besson.* Manchester: Manchester UP, 1998.

———. *"Nikita*: Sex, Violence, Surveillance." Paper presented at the conference "Violence and Gender: Representation and Containment." London, 9 December 1995.

Hebdige, Dick. *Subculture: The Meaning of Style.* London: Routledge, 1989.

La Femme Nikita. Dir. Luc Besson. Perf. Anne Parillaud, Jean-Hugues Anglade, Jeanne Moreau. Palace Pictures, Gaumont, Cecci, Tiger, 1990.

Pacteau, Francette. *The Sympton of Beauty.* London: Reaktion Books, 1994.

Point of No Return. Dir. John Badham. Perf. Bridget Fonda, Dermot Mulroney, Gabriel Byrne. Warner Bros., 1993.

Vincendeau, Ginette. "Hijacked." *Sight and Sound* (July 1993): 25.

———, ed. *Encyclopedia of European Cinema.* London: Cassell and the British Film Institute, 1995.

Chapter 7

The Myth of Beauty and Eroticism: Female Icons in Recent Russian Film, Advertising, and Popular Journals

Jane Knox-Voina

Moscow has recently gained the reputation of being "a competitive city filled with the world's most beautiful and available women... [c]ommonly called *dostupniye dyevochki* or 'accessible young ladies.'"[1] Billboard ads, new women's magazines, television shows, and postglasnost films are filled with new female icons. The sensual, smart, successful model, now sexually liberated, has replaced the old Soviet type, i.e., the mannish, asexual Stakhanovite tractor driver, kolkhoz manager or plant worker. This born again "It-girl" celebrates her new found "feminine beauty."[2] In order to understand the transformation of female icons from kitchen-maid-turned-tractor-drivers into winners of "Miss Russia" or "Miss Bikini," one must see the change as a rejection of the prior puritan Soviet attitude toward beauty and sexuality. A look at this reigning attitude during the Soviet era will help explain, for example, why Russian readers reacted negatively to an extract from Naomi Wolf's popular *Beauty Myth* (1991), published in the 1993 woman's issue of the Russian journal, *Innostrannaia literatura* (*Foreign Literature*).[3]

Wolf's "polemics against the traditional concept of beauty as a higher value" is now more than ever alien to the Russian public. According to Nadezhda Azghikhina and Helena Goscilo (1997), negative criticism came mostly from women themselves in the form of "antifemininst articles that appeared in [Moscow] mass press from . . . *Komsomol* to *Capital* (Stolitsa)."[4] This chapter contrasts western feminists' attack on the beauty myth with the rehabilitation of the flesh movement apparent now in Russian advertising, journalism, and "sexually liberated" glasnost and postglasnost films, such as P. Todorovsky's *International Girl* (1989), Balayan's *Lady MacBeth of the Mtsensk District* (1989), and V. Todorovsky's *Moscow Nights* (1994).

An analysis of female images in popular media culture shows that this sexual emancipation has given rise not to real eroticism or mutual sharing of sexual pleasure, but to an increase in violence, domination, and self-assertion and not only by men, but also by women against women and against themselves! With the emergence of new *femmes fatales*, the camera lens no longer represents solely the eye of the male spectator, for whom the woman is the passive object of his gaze and the camera operator's sexual pleasure. In such films as Kira Muratova's *Three Stories* (1997) or even P. Todorovsky's *Land of the Deaf* (1997) an inversion occurs. Sexual aggression by strong independent women replaces the opposite experience by men who, more often than not, are not-too-intelligent brutish mutants, psychologically disturbed misfits or impotent weaklings, such as the husband in P. Todorovsky's *Moscow Nights*, or the Chekhovian madman in the first narrative of Muratova's killer thriller trilogy *Three Stories*, "Boiler Number Nine," (a play on Chekhov's well known short story "Ward Number Six"), the doctor in the second novella, "Ophelia," or several of the jockeys in Muratova's *Obsessions* (1994). To understand the negative reaction to American feminists' condemnation of "beauty," we must see with the eyes of Russian spectators; we must understand their political and social history that determined this reaction. According to Azhgikhina and Goscilo in "Getting under their Skin: The Beauty Salon in Russian Women's Lives," the resounding criticism of female beauty by American feminists reminds their Russian counterparts of the seventy years of Stalinist prohibition of female attractiveness or overt female sexuality, the prohibition of stylish dress, the use of make-up and fashionable hair-dos, because that all smacked of decadence, of "kowtowing to Western fashions and perfume."[5] As a result, Russian women today recoil from anything resembling such preaching. As Azhgikhina and Goscilo tell us, "Russian critics view these prohibitions as an encroachment on what little area of 'comfort' Russian women have finally begun enjoying in the last few years."[6]

More than a decade after the demise of the Soviet Union, women in Russia are still recovering from the 70 years of sexual politics stemming from their "liberation" in 1917. The sexual politics preached by Trotsky in *Women and the Family* or Aleksandra Kollontai in *The Autobiography of a Sexually Emancipated Communist Woman* urged "the new Soviet woman" to renounce former traditional roles of mother and wife and to become workers on a par with men in the labor force.[7] Gender roles were deemphasized as were gender-distinctive clothes and behavior. Soon in film and on political posters women appeared with freshly cropped hair or with a scarf (or braid) hiding it. The new Soviet poster girls had cleanly scrubbed faces and bodies covered with bulky overalls. Such was the accepted female icon for decades. Even as late as 1979 we find the heroine of V. Menshov's *Moscow Doesn't Believe in Tears* still in factory overalls at the beginning of the film.

There were those difficult decades of Stalin's campaign against long, loose tresses, cosmetics, perfume, or anything that would stimulate energies along other channels than the politically correct path at work or war. Women were not allowed to express their sexuality. Instead they were "mannish, monumental, strong, progressive and capable of doing anything," as described by Rebecca Bridger and Kathryn Pinnick, who examine the heroines of the Soviet era in their 1997 book, *No More Heroines. Russia, Women and the Market.*[8]

Images of "Red women on the silver screen" became monumental, deglamorized, and desexed. Their main role was that of the good worker and builder of the state. All personal pleasure had to be sacrificed for the good of the whole. Not only were the physical and psychological differences of gender played down, but so too was sexual activity between men and women. Sexuality was suppressed under the guise of an ideology that stressed the morality of the common good, decency, practical sense and devotion to one's country. With Stalin, films, particularly the musicals of G. Aleksandrov, essentially became utopian fairy tales with oversimplified happy endings. Maya Turovskaya and other Russian film scholars have already pointed out the fairy-tale qualities of both narratives and characters of Stalin-era films.[9] Still by comparison with American film stars, Soviet heroines were tightly laced up in sexual straight jackets, as Ernst Lubitsch suggests in his 1939 American film parody of a Soviet woman, *Ninotchka* (based on the screen play by Charles Bracket, Billy Wilder, and Walter Reisch).

In general, along her path to the bright shining future, the Soviet film icon had too much to do to be distracted by sexual encounters. She had to overcome a villain, complete some unachievable task, and transcend her personal life (guided by a wise, usually male and therefore fatherly, party ideologue!) so that she could ascend the great heights that Trotsky and Kollontai had prescribed for her. Moreover, she had to be young—for the future common good—healthy, physically fit, strong, slightly attractive but not alluringly so, sociable, and so forth.

Foucault's main idea of sexuality as a social construct with men dominating women was to a certain degree reversed in the early Soviet period when women began dominating men in many spheres of society. Moreover, as the Bolsheviks tried to "desexualize" sexuality, they went to great extremes to erase personal differences in class, race, and gender, at least in theory. As Aleksandra Kollontai explained, "[T]he followers of historical materialism fully accept the natural specificities of each sex [but] demand only that each person, whether man or woman, have a real opportunity for the fullest and freest self-determination, and the widest scope for the development and application of all natural inclinations."[10] For Kollontai and others, emphasis on gender differences was seen as a bourgeois construct; for her and psychologists of the time, expectations were derived from cultural stereotypes and were amenable to resocialization. The psychologist T. G. Khashchenko played down sex differences in mental problem solving, stating, "Women's activity in the decision-making process would also release hitherto undeveloped potentialities and transform them in abilities."[11] This more recent view held by the Soviet school of developmental psychology was foreshadowed sixty years earlier by Lenin's often quoted statement, "Every kitchen maid can lead her government, if summoned." With that began the exodus of women out of the home into public space, into the workforce, into the party, into the ministries. The traditional prerevolutionary role of women as guardians of private, domestic space, as wives and child-bearers, sinks into a diminished background. Until the Thaws, in public, on posters, in Soviet art, in film, men and women stand out as genderless, dress-alike worker warriors, the new proletariat of desexed bodies, hard as steel and monumental in size.

With ideological and stylistic restrictions firmly in place, it became impossible to address personal or intimate issues in women's lives, issues that might excite or challenge the audience. Any frank and direct treatment of sexual experience was deemed "pornographic." Sex itself was seen as something taboo, something indecent and not to be talked about. With some exceptions in socialist realist art of the late 1930s and 1940s, a woman's naked body that had yielded to the sexual act in order to have children was depicted as aged, deformed, and ugly, even more so than in the dark ages of the *Domostroi* (the rules set down by the Russian Orthodox Church for Russian households in the time of Ivan the Terrible). Moreover, without access to appropriate birth control devices, a woman's body was submitted to multiple abortions, averaging six per woman, which further degraded and abused her body.

Even as late as 1986, sex still meant pornography: When a question about the "it" word was raised by an American during a Donahue-Pozner *telemost* (televised link up) between audiences in Boston and in Leningrad, an indignant elderly Soviet woman jumped up to defend her country with the long remembered statement, "We have no sex in the Soviet Union."[12] One can only assume that sex was both too distracting from the social, political tasks at hand, too private, too noncollective, and therefore, not fit for the Soviet screen or political posters.

Kissing was all but absent from Soviet films. If free expression and sex were generally repressed, how did sexuality actually appear in the movies? Films rechanneled sexual energy into the service of the dominant ideology. It was redirected to further the revolutionary struggle, to rebuild the nation, or to fight the enemy during World War II. In films like the Vasileev brothers' *Chapaev*, a 1934 reenactment of the heroism of the Russian Civil War, or F. Ermler's *No Greater Love,* a 1943 World War II movie, the main hero or heroine could have no real sexual attachments. The task of showing the audience the appropriate revolutionary sexual relationship is given to secondary, younger characters. These relationships are stunningly similar in meaning and in depiction. In *Chapaev* two young revolutionaries first meet when she, Anya, is assigned to him for machine-gun training. An unwanted advance on his part is hidden in a discussion of proper machine-gun maintenance. Their relationship evolves and revolves around weapons. It comes to a head just as Anya, bundled up in a heavy, awkward soldier's coat, hair pinned back under her cap, seizes the sexualized gun and releases all the sexual tension that she is not allowed to express elsewhere in the film.

In *No Greater Love (She Defends the Motherland)*, the heroine loses her child and husband at the hands of the barbarous Germans. Once the role of wife and mother is denied her, she dons a dark, shapeless, bulky dress and ties back her long, suddenly gray hair, hiding it under a shawl. Subverting her personal needs, she transforms into a tough, merciless, partisan "Comrade P" who now, rifle in hand, leads the cowering peasants in an attack on the German invaders. For one young pair, however, romance is initiated in a moonlit forest glade, but their attention is soon turned to the successful slaughter of the enemy. Then, having confiscated a pistol from a slain German soldier, our young romantic hero gives it to her, his fellow partisan, as a proposal of love. Immediately, the film's heroine, Pasha, proposes that she as commander has the right to marry them. All the while the young woman tenderly fondles the pistol, shyly looking up at her newly betrothed. Their love never comes to fruition, for he is soon killed in battle. His heroic death leaves her alone for a life of glorious self-sacrifice. In short, these films take sex out of the bedroom where it is a private matter between just two people and convert it to the adrenal flow of soldiers in the trenches. Passion is turned into devotion to the Motherland. This sublimation of actual physical passion into patriotism reaches its grim apex in the adoration of Stalin in such postwar movies as Chiurelli's *The Fall of Berlin* (1949).

Obviously, the way Russian women saw themselves and the way their bodies were depicted by the mythical images of the new Soviet woman did not fully coincide, even if they wished to be like these film icons. As Mikhail Bakhtin argues in *Art and Answerability*, "The outward boundary of the body is expressed *in the self-consciousness* in an essentially different way from the way it is experienced in relation to another human being"[13] The result is a duality of "an inner body" and "an outer body." Outward boundaries of the body are constructed by society, and in the case of the visual arts, by the artist, the film director, the fashion designer. The image created publicly differs from the way women see themselves in relation to those others. If these two constructions of the body (outward or social and inner, personal) differ too greatly, the discrepancy results in a feeling of marginalization, detachment, discomfort, and rejection, and it may lead to one of the many psychological illnesses afflicting women today.

It is not surprising, then, that in the second half of the 1980s with *glasnost* and in the 1990s with the demise of the Soviet Union a sexual revolution burst upon the scene. After years of taboos and restrictions, Russian women want to reclaim their physical image, their bodies! This rehabilitation of the flesh is a natural "reaction to the asceticism of the still recent past," writes Attwood in *Red Women on the Silver Screen*.[14] In her words, sex as a pastime has become for the new younger generation, "a way of alleviating boredom, an act of rebellion, . . . a blatant example of iconoclasm, a way of ridiculing the old communist reality."[15]

After decades of Soviet public abstinence and prudence, the nude, or almost nude, female body is now everywhere present, in magazine ads and billboards selling products, in the glut of new books and newspapers about sex, and in the ever-present sex scenes in new Russian cinema. As we learn in *No More Heroines*, "Now in place of woman workers in overalls and hard hats [comes] the scantily-clad glamour model draped over a gleaming and usually foreign car bonnet, inviting the onlooker not to produce but to consume."[16] Such advertising objectifies the female body, equating it with the commodity being sold. For example, one such recent Moscow billboard, advertising a prestigious foreign-made automobile and featuring a glamorous model, appeared everywhere with the words, "Could you possibly forget her?" In Russian, the pronoun "her" (*eë*) may refer to either "the car" or "the woman" and, as many onlookers joked, the reference was definitely to the shining new "foreign car."

Consider also the image of the woman in a 1998 billboard ad for RayBan sunglasses (on the hot summer streets of Moscow): Dressed in a low-cut black bathing suit, the female model is thrown up over the shoulder of a muscle-bound male model as he carries her at the beach. Both wear the consumer product, the dark sunglasses. He looks straight at the viewer through the glasses, holding her by a very visible tanned thigh, while she gazes down at him seductively, mouth opened. Her scantily clad upper torso curls around his head and shoulder, and her extremely long cat-like, artificial fingernails stroke his hair and neck. Leaning over his shoulder to look down at him she reveals a full view of her breast line popping out of the black suit.[17]

After a dearth of cosmetic goods, Russian women crave products that beautify and glamorize, products that make them into modern Barbie dolls with healthy, shining long hair. All this in their minds returns to them the essence of femininity scorned by the Soviet ideologues. It gives them self-confidence and badly needed self-esteem. A rash of beauty contests such as "Miss Bust," "Miss Erotica," "Miss Photo," "Miss Charm," "Miss USSR" promoted the new look and "rapidly spread from Moscow to provincial towns across the USSR in the late 1980s." For example, *Vzglyad* (Gaze, [*sic*]), a television show from the former Lenin-grad, televised a broadcast with "a row of aspiring Miss Lvov-disco dancing girls in bikinis."[18] Azhgikhina and Goscilo tell us that the public attitude accepted this as "normal day dreaming of girls wanting to be beautiful. Freely cascading hair, once anathematized during the Stalin era [is] now popularized by an imitation of 1970s [American] fad . . . set by Farrah Fawcett in *Charlie's Angels*."[19]

Even during the Soviet period, the beauty parlor was for Russian women what the psychiatrist's office was for American women: A place where you can feel good while talking about your problems.[20] Preoccupa-tion with female beauty and looks was, as Azhgikhina and Goscilo point out, " . . . a Russian woman's sole means of self-expression, a demon-stration of possible independence from the bleak deprivations of every-day life, an unsuccessful marriage, dissatisfaction with the job, politics and much else."[21] An even more important observation by Azhgikhina and Goscilo is that "women in Soviet Russia strove to be beautiful not only for men, and not only because men demanded that they do so . . . but because they wished to prove to themselves that despite the grueling demands of . . . life, they still look pretty good."[22] This tendency has be-come even stronger today, particularly for those who have the money to keep up with the latest European fashions and cosmetics.

Add to these factors the new policy of "choice" which Gorbachev pushed for women in the late 1980s: Either go back into the kitchen, the home, or become a professional woman, but don't mix roles as before. This tendency accelerated during the 1990s. According to sociologist Olga Zdravomyslova, "one-third of the respondents [for her 1992 study of current women's roles] clearly expressed the desire to leave work al-together and become a housewife, while only 6% opted for a career, if that meant going against the interests of family."[23]

Catering to the majority of women today, the new journal *Materin-stvo* (Motherhood) appeared with a present distribution of fifty thousand copies; its mission is "to help women become better mothers," states Ir-ina Karchagina, one of the contributing authors.[24] For example, the July issue 1998 features a story about a natural childbirth course for young pregnant women *and* their husbands. This issue, replete with glowing pictures of mothers and babies, includes a provocative photograph: a side shot of a late-term pregnant woman nude, basking under the streaming shower water.[25] Water drips down her face, long hair, and breasts, her extended stomach aglow in warm light. This image is followed by an aftershot as the child-expecting madonna applies a white cream to her glowing body. These beautiful images of full nudity, entitled "Hygiene of a Pregnant Woman," would be shocking for earlier Soviet readers but obviously sell the magazine today and return to women a sense of beauty and pleasure in the female body.

Another best-seller for the new generation is the very expensive "glossy" Russian edition of *Domashnii ochag* (Good Housekeeping). (Former Soviet journals were on cheap paper with poor quality photographs or drawings. Now the popular Russian magazines have caught up, if not surpassed the West with their high-quality, glossy photographs!) Along with Russian translations of American features, *Domashnii ochag* offers tips on how to become a "goddess of seduction" in order to please your husband and build a happy family nest.

While many young women today may finish institutions of design or schools of economics, they dream of marrying a "new Russian" (*novyi russkii*) who, unlike previous generations of men, prides himself on being able to become the sole provider in the family. This new rich Russian wants his woman to remain at home, be a loving wife, and raise children. Nearly 89% of all women polled by Zdravomyslova saw "family as the center of their lives."[26] Larisa Sadilova, director of the prize winning 1998 film *Happy Birthday*, promises a new trend, "We've given birth, we are giving birth and we plan to keep on doing so."

By contrast, a second smaller group of women have chosen the career path to become business partners, bankers, entrepreneurs. Because their numbers are so small, the magazine *Delovye zhenshchiny* (Business Women) has folded. The 1992 sociological studies conducted by Zdravomyslova revealed that only 11 percent of the women polled indicated they would choose a career over family. There is growing public skepticism of a woman who becomes too independent, too powerful. This skepticism is conveyed in the caricatures of the tall or fat Amazon-like business women in black business suits, or long black dresses but marred by a black patch over one eye, women who usually play secondary roles in the latest Russian films directed by men.

Above and beyond this small but visible group of *delovye zhenshchiny*, there is still another larger group of very young women who have not yet chosen the home hearth. Zdravomyslova reports, "Neither family, love, nor children stand higher than self-realization on the scale of personal values" for these young women.[27] Profits soar from new journals catering to them, showing them images with which they wish to identify. For example, the Russian edition of *NRS* provides the latest fashion information from Europe and America. *Krestyanka* (The Peasant Girl) is very popular among young girls, particularly those from the countryside. The June 1997 issue featured articles about a teenage "circus princess" who has already achieved stardom and about "a funny girl," an American "who grew up in poverty but became one of the richest women in the world with her voice even though she never studied singing," referring to Barbra Streisand.[28] *Cosmopolitan* tells its readers about "the adult life of young female stars," about "shopping as the public equivalent to sex" or about the new beauty contest, "Cosmo-Maybelline."[29] Because of the promise of travel, new clothes, and other items of luxury in the new market economy, these readers seek jobs as models and hostesses in new discos: "Women flocked [and still do] into advertising to appear nude in photo features promoting new rock bands, commercial outfits, [and] other advertising agencies."[30] These, often "pornographic representations of women merely represent an extreme version of something women actually wanted. Beauty contests and glamour modelling, though providing money, travel and genuine escape only for the few, served as symbols to many of a different way of life. For so many women it was a breath of fresh air, a relief from the moralizing and hypocrisy of the past."[31] Such films as Vasily Pichul's *Little Vera* (1988), Pyotr Todorovsky's *International Girl* (1989) and his son's film *Land of the Deaf* (Valery Todorovsky, 1998) give us examples of young women who have made choices that represent a radical departure from those of their mothers: Prostitution in the latter two cases. They reject the former path of education and honest hard work that led women of previous generations to lives of severe economic limitations (by today's standards, abject poverty) and to the suppression of physical pleasure in their own bodies.

Prostitution and with it the nightlife in expensive hotels and restaurants, fur coats, and foreign cars provide a lifestyle that is more glamorous and luxurious than the one the Soviet working woman could afford. The reasons for prostitution are very real today. According to Attwood (1993), women turn to this oldest of the professions because they "can't find a way of obtaining a reasonable life by any other means . . . [they] want to have a nice place to live, a car, to go to a seaside resort."[32]

P. Todorovsky's *International Girl*, like the American film *Pretty Woman*, directed by Garry Marshall one year later (1990), is basically a Cinderella tale of the 1980s. The *perestroika* generation of Russian filmmakers no longer seeks their Cinderella among "cooks who are learning to govern," as did their forefathers of the past.[33] Unlike *Pretty Woman*, however, Todorovsky's film does not have a happy fairy-tale ending; true, his international prostitute (working in a respectable hospital by day) does marry a rich client, a Swedish businessman, and goes off with him to live happily ever after in Sweden. There, however, she finds a life totally alien to her, and dies in a car crash as she drives in reckless desperation back to cherished Russia.

The end of the 1980s witnessed a backlash and rising criticism of the independent "new woman." Polls indicate that the public felt "women were paying too little attention to family responsibility." The movement to push women back into the home has accelerated and, as we saw above, is expressed in many new journals for women, journals that are filled with articles about how to be a better wife and mother. In spite of *glasnost*, Attwood writes, "Efforts which began in the 1970s to establish a more domestic mode of life for women have not ceased."[34]

This backlash is also expressed in recent Russian films where the viewer witnesses an increase of violent acts against women in what basically amounts to rape: The sexual act is forced by a male character who experiences a sensation of pleasure and power that causes the woman anguish, pain, even death, as we will see below. The message is that the male-dominated society of Russia today punishes women for stepping over boundaries.

This backlash is in part a form of public retaliation for the "feminization of men" during the Soviet regime, which, according to some Russian women, turned men into the weaker sex and women into the stronger one, often placing them as high, if not higher, in the workforce in formerly "male" professions. Such were the majority of heroines on the Soviet screen, as portrayed in the films *Tractor Drivers, Shining Path, No Greater Love, Commissar, Brief Encounters, Wings, Moscow Doesn't Believe in Tears*, and others. In the words of film scholar Vida Johnson, "Sexual violence symbolizes . . . the political and social impotence of men in a system which has systematically stripped them of power: they do to women what the state had been doing to them for years."[35] This view is reiterated, of course, by many Russian feminist film critics.

Marina Drozdova states in "Sublimation from Socialism, New Images of Women in Soviet Cinematography in the Era of *Perestroika*," Russian cinema does not offer us "real erotic images."[36] According to Drozdova, it does not convey real sexual energy, equal sexual relations or a mutual sharing of pleasure between the two genders, but instead shows the classical male-female sexual politics where the male attempts to assert power and dominance over the woman in order to build up a badly damaged identity. This is the result of a new tendency in Postglasnost film: the masculinization of men and the search to create a strong new Russian hero.

Sexual scenes in recent Russian films are devoid of any sensitivity, spirituality, or real pleasure. Sex is rather a sublimation of other urges: boredom or frustration with the growing obstacles and demands of the new market society, where everything has become a commodity, particularly sex. Sex has become a way of escaping an unsatisfactory marriage to an older impotent husband long since burned out or ground down by the hardships of Russian life. As Drozdova points out, the new sexual frontier allows the heroine a way of "breaking out of her conventional, but thoroughly false relationship with her husband. It's a way of gaining control over her life."[37]

Such is the motivation behind the narrative of two recent screen adaptations of Nikolai Leskov's nineteenth-century novel *Lady MacBeth of the Mtsensk District*,[38] R. Balayan's 1989 film by the same title and Valery Todorovsky's 1994 *Moscow Nights*. Leskov's novel originally appeared at the time of an imported "George Sandism." In Russia this western feminism was equated with "the emancipation of the flesh" for women and preached by certain progressive (male and female) members of the Russian intelligentsia in the mid-nineteenth century. Coming at a time when everything is imported from the West (capitalism, free market economy and, most importantly, freer mores), these two film versions are based on the story of a woman who, trapped in her conventional marriage, seeks to use her sexual powers to flee her stifling cage. This plot speaks to those Russian women who are ready to go to extremes to find self-realization through newly found passions or freedoms. However, the outcome of this novel does not bode well for the sexually emancipated "Amazon," who, according to the narrative, will resort to murder to achieve her power. The male hero breaks away from her control and goes on to another more vulnerable, younger woman. Ultimately, the latter-day Ophelia has no recourse but self-destruction with a plunge into murky waters while taking her rival with her.

The narrative of Balayan's *Lady MacBeth from the Mtsensk District* more or less faithfully plays out Leskov's plot. With exquisite taste he reproduces the costumes and luxury of the idle life which has swallowed up the strong-willed, buxom young mistress Katya (Natalya Andrei-chenko). She is married to a wealthy merchant at least twice her age who leaves her inside the manor house to languish in a state of passivity while he goes off to tend to his commercial affairs. With nothing to do but stare into mirrors, she wanders from room to room, window to window (a spatial metaphor commonly used to convey the enclosed domestic space of nineteenth-century wealthy Russian women). The gender roles in this film correspond to the world which the respondents in Zdravomyslova's sociological study envisioned as real or desirable today:

> ...a world similar to life on the summer estate of the gentry in the 19th century, a world divided into two halves. In one the men are busy with serious affairs: the struggle for power, for victory in some competitive battle, for quest of income. In the other quietly live women, who raise children, comfort their husbands, support them, accept compromise.[39]

However, for the group of 205 female students questioned by Zdravo-myslova in 1996, it became clear that a constant inner battle existed between two models of self-realization, two systems of values, on the one hand, "freedom, profession, sex, money," and on the other, "family, love, children, marriage, devotion, submission."[40]

This conflict is reflected in Katya, the heroine of Balayan's film. Initially subdued by her married life, she seeks freedom and sexual fulfillment. She is inevitably attracted to and seduced by the head serf in the courtyard below. He, a strapping, handsome but heartless egoist (played by Aleksandr Abdulov), knows a good thing when he sees it. While the master is away, their passionate affair blooms, releasing Katya from stifling boredom and providing him access to the manor house, and with it, prestige and power over the other serfs. When the master returns, the lovers murder not only him, but also a young boy in line to receive the estate's wealth once he comes of age. After their arrest and sentencing to Siberian exile, a tragic drama unfolds. Sergei moves on to another, younger, prettier inmate, whom Katya, out of revenge and despair, hurls together with herself into an icy Siberian river.

The title of Leskov's story conveys the ardent passions and fate of Shakespeare's strong heroes (male and female) who try to control fate with bold deeds, including murder. In the novella, the main characters have no sense of morality or remorse for their barbaric deeds. Initially the reader feels compassion for Katya in her gilded cage, but ultimately the author makes the reader condemn her for stepping over boundaries.

Leskov's apparent condemnation of the heroine seems to be missing from Balayan's modern-day film version. Such is the view of film critic Valentin Mikhalkovich:

> In contrast to the author of the novella, Balayan does not judge the sensibility from a Christian position, but creates a tragedy around the impossibility of returning to the initial pure and natural state [of this young free country girl before marriage]. Scenes on the meadow under the tree are but moments of joy in the heroine's otherwise cheerless existence. For the sake of returning to purity, she is forced to become boundlessly evil, to shoulder all the blame for the interminable weight of the pollution and crimes.[41]

Mikhalkovich's interpretation of this film, as well as Balayan's choice of the narrative script, provide insight about Russian life in general and the attitude toward sex and eroticism in particular. Certainly the director's choice itself is a commentary on the contemporary scene, on the effect new money has had on Russian society, and the increase of barbaric crimes. Amorality has become more and more visible with the very wealthy scrambling to regain, even outdo, the luxurious life of their prerevolutionary ancestors.

In contrast to the obsession with power through money, witnessed in the men (Sergei and the master), the heroine seeks fulfillment through sheer sexual pleasure. There are several scenes, as Mikhalkovich correctly indicates, where Katya positively glows with the sensual pleasure that she feels not only from sexual interaction with Sergei, but also from the sense of her own body lying in the meadow in the voluptuous warmth of the sunlit grass, or as she eats cherries, bosom heaving. We have made a gigantic leap from the tentative fondling of the pistol in the 1943 film *No Greater Love*. In the 1989 movie, the open display of soft feminine skin, shoulders, and breasts are pleasing to the eye of both the female and male viewer. What is less positive, although perhaps titillating, dangerous and stimulating, is the display of physical force when Sergei takes her for the first time. This, together with the hints of physical abuse as Sergei pretends to imitate the master beating his wife before their next sexual encounter, indicates that the sexual act remains one of dominance by the male and complete subordination by the woman. This casts a dark shadow on the new sexual liberation for Russian women.

Five years later in the postglasnost period the younger Todorovsky (Valery) paints a far more shocking picture in his 1995 *Moscow Nights* that places this same narrative in the modern setting of a dacha (summer house) of new Russians. The thirty-year-old Katya Izmailova, a lowly typist, discovering real passion for the first time, is ready to destroy all who might prevent her newfound happiness. This initially shy, insignificant, cowed creature sits hours on end typing for and taking verbal abuse from a middle-aged novelist, the domineering mother of her rather dull husband. Katya turns into a cold murderer once she is seduced by her mother-in-law's lover, the young gardener, played by the rising star Vladimir Mashkov. She causes the mother-in-law's death by refusing to bring her heart medication and then, convincing Sergei to kill her husband, believes that she has cleared the way for uninterrupted fulfillment of her passion. However, once his conquest is successful, the womanizing gardener, Sergei, moves on to greener pastures, forcing Katya to drive herself and his new mistress off a bridge to their death.

E. Plakhova says the following about this screen rendition of the nineteenth-century classic:

> Everything is foreordained from the start. Typing away on the keys of her old Underwood typewriter in a convulsive rhythm, and then spread on the wooden floor, her back arched [from the pain caused by hours at the keyboard], this deeply traumatized Beauty, downtrodden and forced to take a back seat in life, is capable only of self destruction."[42]

The sexual scenes are full of reminders of her entrapment and passivity. Her seductor gazes at her back through the window from the garden outside. We see his face, but not hers. The binary opposition of spatial images is at play here: Her space is inside, his outside.

Once inside, his gaze dissects her into body parts as he stares at her barefoot. During the first seduction, he forces Katya into the window frame, which she grasps and claws in a frenzy. During this long scene, which would certainly be termed rape by western standards, the camera zooms in on her almost inhuman, terrorized face, focusing on her wild dilated eyes and gaping mouth. She stares back at us through the black net of the sweater in which she is caught like a trapped animal ensnared and fighting back. The second encounter is even more sexually explicit, as she is shown with frontal nudity sitting, groaning, legs spread, face paralyzed by her strong emotions, as he lies face down on the bed before her. Passion has given her more courage and defiance: She barely turns her head when the mother-in-law suddenly looks in on them in horror.

In spite of Katya's defiance and total abandonment to her desires, she in fact readily accepts a new subservience in place of the old. Her seducer, not easily distinguishable from a rapist, is an arrogant and brutish man who is invariably glorified. He gains total control over his object. His power is enhanced by the camera angle and movement. Katya continues to be shot passively sitting at the typewriter while the despots in her life (first the mother-in-law and now the gardener) tower over and move around her. This is particularly clear in the shot where she types completely naked, as Sergei walks around her, dictating his revised ending to the novel by the murdered mother-in-law. He is naked only to the waist; we are allowed to gaze only at her as an object of sexual pleasure for the male character, the viewer, and camera operator.

Sexual energy long suppressed in the Soviet era and now liberated has burst out in the most distorted ways: The two genders have not been brought up witnessing normal sexual relationships between loving adults. Instead, in Soviet society men and women gradually have become estranged and alienated from one another. Similarly, in films of the 1990s, like Todorovsky's *Moscow Nights*, sexual activity shows no signs of the love, tenderness or mutual respect which the couples in early Soviet film displayed. On the Russian screen, as well as in advertising and journalism, the female body has been reduced to her voluptuous body parts. Obsession with sex is not surprising, given the years of abstinence: A spark in a dry tender box explodes quite naturally into a raging fire. Nor should it surprise us that, instead of opening in the country of its creation, "the new movie version of *Lolita* [played] without any particular controversy in Moscow, the former capital of hopelessly square Soviet socialist morality."[43]

The reaction of Russian women to these visual icons is clearly as complex and ambiguous as they are for many American women. Joke Hermes's overview of the effects that images of popular culture can have on female viewers fits the Russian scene. These visual representations can seduce women "into a false consciousness with which they can go along uncritically . . . . [T]hey can accommodate the position of women," and they can offer "appeal of that which is thrilling, exciting and dangerous."[44] Russian women still need to develop a critical perspective in relation to what they see in popular culture. They may indeed heed some of the latest advances made by American women.

As American feminist Winifred Woodhull points out, "taking control of our bodies became a watchword and a central effect in the women's movement."[44] This movement is still ahead for Russia, but it has been initiated by female directors such as Kira Muratova, Natasha Pinkova, and Larisa Sadilova. Perhaps only with their continued success will the stereotypical behavior of Russian women begin to be deconstructed. More films like Sadilova's *Happy Birthday* (1998) may help women seek more natural and wholesome ways to rediscover their sexuality and reclaim their bodies, so badly bruised by the physical and psychological abuse mirrored in recent Russian cinema.

Notes

The research for this article was completed from resources gathered at Bowdoin College, at the Davis Center for Russian Studies, Harvard University, at the Sochi International Film Festivals, and the Institute of Film Art with the support of the International Research and Exchanges Board (IREX) Short Term Travel Grants.

1. Michael Spector, "Moscow on the Make," *The New York Times Magazine,* 1 June 1997, 51.

2. Spector, 51.

3. Naomi Wolf, *The Beauty Myth: How Images of Women Are Used Against Women* (New York: Anchor Books, 1992).

4. Nadezhda Azhgikhina and Helena Goscilo, "Getting under Their Skin: The Beauty Salon in Russian Women's Lives," in *Russia, Women, Culture*, Pt. I, ed., Helena Goscilo and Beth Holmgren, (Bloomington, Indiana UP, 1996), 106.

5. Azhgikhina and Goscilo, "Getting under Their Skin," 99.

6. Azhgikhina and Goscilo, 107.

7. Leon Trotsky, *Women and Family* (New York: Pathfinder, 1970); Alexandra Kollontai, *The Autobiography of a Sexually Emancipated Communist Woman* (New York: Herder and Herder, 1971).

8. Rebecca Kay Bridger and Kathryn Pinnick, *No More Heroines: Russian Women and the Market* (London: Zed Books, 1993).

9. One could make a comparison with the female icons in American films that were influenced by the Production Code and later the McCarthy trials. However, this type of analysis is beyond the scope of this essay.

10. As quoted in Lynne Attwood, *The New Soviet Man and Woman: Sex-Role Socialization in the USSR* (Bloomington: Indiana UP, 1990), 1.

11. Attwood, *The New Soviet Man and Woman,* 74, 221.

12. This statement made on public television in the 1986 telebridge became immediate public knowledge and was quoted in the streets.

13. Mikhail Bakhtin, *Art and Answerability,* ed. M. Holquist and Vadim Liapunov (Austin: U of Texas P, 1990), 36.

14. Lynne Attwood, ed., *Red Women on the Silver Screen* (London: Pandora Press, 1993), 110.

15. Attwood, *Red Women,* 110–11.

16. Bridger and Pinnick, 28.

17. For a picture of this billboard, see "Advertising" on www.bowdoin.edu/dept/russian/.

18. Bridger and Pinnick, 29.

19. Azhgikhina and Goscilo, 163.

20. See, for example, I. Grekova's "Ladies' Hairdresser," *Russian Literature Triquarterly,* 5 (1973): 223–65, translated by L. Gregg. I. Grekova is the pseudonym of Elena Sergeevna Ventsel.

21. Azhgikhina and Goscilo, 107.

22. Azhgikhina and Goscilo, 108.

23. Olga Zdravomyslova, "Values," *Itogi* (Results), 3 March 1998, 44.

24. Irina Karchagina, *Materinstvo* (Motherhood), July 1998, 21. This statement is from a personal interview with the author on 20 April 1998 in Moscow.

25. Alina Dalskaya, "So That There Will Be Joy in Childbirth," *Materinstuo* (Motherhood), July 1998, 44.

26. Zdravomyslova, 43.

27. Zdravomyslova, 44.

28. Elena Averina, "From a Funny Girl to a Woman in Love," *Krestyanka* (Peasant Girl), June 1997, 42–43.

29. Marianna Orlinkova, "Shopping = Sex," *Cosmopolitan,* June 1997, 64–67.

30. Bridger and Pinnick, 36.

31. Bridger and Pinnick, 31.

32. Attwood, *Red Women,* 118.

33. Attwood, *Red Women,* 118.

34. Attwood, *The New Soviet Man and Woman,* x.

35. Quoted in Attwood, *Red Women,* 115.

36. Marina Drozdova, "Sublimations from Socialism: New Images of Women in Soviet Cinematography in the Era of *Perestroika,*" in *Red Women on the Silver Screen,* ed. Lynne Attwood (London: Pandora, 1993), 198.

37. Drozdova, 199.

38. Nikolai Leskov, *Lady MacBeth of the Mtsensk District.*

39. Zdravomyslova, 44.

40. Zdravomyslova, 45.

41. Valentin Mikhalkovich, "Lady Makbet mtsenskogo uezda. Tragedia chuvstvennosti," *Mneniya* 3 (1989): 18, translation by Jane Knox-Voina.

42. Elena Plakhova, "Esli b znali vy, kak mne dorogi...." *Film Art* 8 (1994), 30, translation by Jane-Knox-Voina.

43. Richard Schickel, "Taking a Peek at *Lolita,*" *Time,* 23 March 1998, 91.

44. Joke Hermes, "A Perfect Fit: Feminist Media Studies," in *Women's Studies and Culture,* ed. Rosemarie Buikema and Anneke Smelik (London: Zed Books, 1993), 60.

45. Winifred Woodhull, "Sexuality, Power, and the Questions of Rape," in *Feminism and Foucault: Reflections and Resistance,* ed. Irene Diamond and Lee Quinby (Boston: Northeastern UP, 1988), 173.

Bibliography

Attwood, Lynne. *The New Soviet Man and Woman: Sex-Role Socialization in the USSR,* Bloomington: Indiana UP, 1990.

Attwood, Lynne, ed. *Red Women on the Silver Screen.* London: Pandora Press, 1993.

Averina, Elena. "From a Funny Girl to a Woman in Love." *Krestyanka* (Peasant Girl), June 1997, 42–45.

Azhgikhina, Nadezhada, and Helena Goscilo. "Getting under Their Skin: The Beauty Salon in Russian Women's Lives," in *Russia, Women, Culture,* Pt. I, edited by Helena Goscilo and Beth Holmgren, Bloomington: Indiana UP, 1996.

Bakhtin, Mikhail. *Art and Answerability,* edited by M. Holquist and Vadim Liapunov. Austin: U of Texas P, 1990.

Bridger, Rebecca Kay, and Kathryn Pinnick. *No More Heroines: Russian Women and the Market.* London: Zed Books, 1993.

Chapaev. Dir. Sergei and Georgii Vasiliev. Perf. Boris Babochkin, Leonid Kmit, Varvara Myasnikova. Lenfilm, 1934.

Dalskaya, Alina. "So That There Will Be Joy in Childbirth." *Materinstvo* (Motherhood), June 1998, 38–92.

Drozdova, Marina. "Sublimations from Socialism: New Images of Women in Soviet Cinematography in the Era of *Perestroika.* " In *Red Women on the Silver Screen,* edited by Lynne Attwood. London: Pandora, 1993.

The Fall of Berlin. Dir. Mikhail Chiaurelli. Perf. Mikhail Chiaureli, Maksim Shtraukh, Aleksei Gribov, Marina Kovaleva. Mosfilm, 1949.

Goscilo, Helena, and Beth Holmgren, ed. *Russia, Women, Culture*. Bloomington: Indiana UP, 1996.

Grekhova, I. [Elena Sergeevna Ventsel] "Ladies' Hairdresser." *Russian Literature Triquarterly* 5 (1973): 223–65.

Happy Birthday. Dir. Larisa Sadilova. Perf. Gul'nara Mkhitaryan, Irina Proshina, Evgeniya Turkina, Rano Kubaeva, Natal'ya Pinkova. State Committee of the Russian Federation for Cinematography, 1998.

Hermes, Joke. "A Perfect Fit: Feminist Media Studies." In *Women's Studies and Culture*, edited by Rosemarie Buikema and Anneke Smelik. London: Zed Books, 1993.

International Girl. Dir. Pyotr Todorovsky. Perf. Elena Yakovleva, Tomas Laustiola. Mosfilm, Filmstallet AB (Sweden), 1989.

Karchagina, Irina, ed. *Materinstvo* (Motherhood) July 1998.

Knox-Voina, Jane. Unpublished interview with Irina Karchagina, 20 April 1998 in Moscow. Karchagina, Irina, ed. *Materinstvo* (Motherhood) July 1998.

Kollontai, Aleksandra. *The Autobiography of a Sexually Emancipated Communist Woman*. New York: Herder and Herder, 1971.

Lady MacBeth of the Mtsensk District. Dir. Roman Balayan. Perf. Natal'ya Andreichenko, Aleksandr Abdulov. Mosfilm, 1989.

Land of the Deaf. Dir. Valery Todorovsky. Perf. Chulpan Khamatova, Dina Korzun. Gorky Studio, 1997.

Little Vera. Dir. Vasily Pichul. Perf. Natal'ya Negoda, Andrei Sokolov. Gorky Studio, 1988.

Mikhalkovich, Valentin, "Lady Makbet mtsenskogo uezda. Tragedia chuvstvennosti," *Mneniya* 3 (1989): 18.

Moscow Doesn't Believe in Tears. Dir. Vladimir Menshov. Perf. Vera Alentova, Aleksei Batalov. Mosfilm, 1979.

Moscow Nights. Dir. Valery Todorovsky. Perf. Ingeborga Dapkunaite, Vladimir Mashkov. TTL, Les Films du Rivage, Roskomkino, Ostankino, 1994.

Ninotchka. Dir. Ernst Lubitsch. Perf. Greta Garbo, Melvyn Douglas, Bela Lugosi. Metro-Goldwyn-Mayer, 1939.

No Greater Love (Russian title: *She Defends the Motherland*). Dir. Friedrich Ermler. Perf. Vera Maretskaya, Nikolai Bogolyubov. TSOKS, 1943.

Obsessions. Dir. Kira Muratova. Perf. Svetlana Kolenda, Renata Litvinova. Roskomkino, Nikola Film and RTV, 1994.

Orlinkova, Marianna. "Shopping = Sex." *Cosmopolitan,* June 1997, 64–67.

Plakhova, Elena, "V. Todorovsky's Rendition of Lady MacBeth," *Film Art* 8 (1994): 22–23.

Pretty Woman. Dir. Garry Marshall. Perf. Julia Roberts, Richard Gere. Touchstone, 1990.

Schickel, Richard. "Taking a Peek at *Lolita*." *Time,* 23 March 1998, 91.

Spector, Michael. "Moscow on the Make." *The New York Times Magazine,* 1 June 1997, 51.

Three Stories. Dir. Kira Muratova. Perf. Renata Litvinova, Sergei Makovetsky, Oleg Tabakov. Firm of Tolstunov, NTV Profit, Odessa Studio, 1997.

Trotsky, Leon. *Women and the Family*. New York: Pathfinder, 1970.

Wolf, Naomi. *The Beauty Myth: How Images of Women Are Used Against Women*. New York: Anchor Books, 1992.

Woodhull, Winifred. "Sexuality, Power, and the Questions of Rape." In *Feminism and Foucault: Reflections and Resistance,* edited by Irene Diamond and Lee Quinby. Boston: Northeastern UP, 1988, 167–176.

Zaichik, Irina. "The Circus Girl." *Itogi* (Results), 3 March 1998, 14–15.

Zdravomyslova, Olga. "Values." *Itogi* (Results), 3 March 1998, 43–45.

Zemlyanukhin, Segei, and Miroslava Segida. *The Home Handbook of Cinema: Films of the Fatherland: 1918–1996.* Moscow: Double-D, 1996.

Chapter 8

Women Behind the Grave
Margaret Allison

John Fiske in his book *Media Matters: Everyday Culture and Political Change* likens culture to "a river of discourses," saying:

> There are deep, powerful currents carrying meanings of race, of gender and sexuality, of class and age: these intermix in different proportions and bubble up to the surface as discursive "topics," such as "family values" or "abortion" or "Black masculinity," and these discursive topics swirl into each other—each is muddied with the silt of the others, none can flow in unsullied purity or isolation. Media events are sites of maximum visibility and maximum turbulence.[1]

Fiske exemplifies his metaphor with, among others, case studies of the Murphy Brown/Dan Quayle debacle, which highlighted issues of single motherhood, welfare scrounging and associated racial connotations, and the case of *Anita Hill v. Clarence Thomas,* where a case involving two African Americans raised issues of race and predicated on the assumptions of white discourse. The cross-referencing between media formats and the new options, perceptions, and discourses they have generated are the focus in this chapter. The cases and stories to be treated here are chosen not just because they have many features in common, but as exemplars of the interplay between genres and real life and of the dynamic for change they can collectively produce.

This chapter is an investigation into representations of women as killers and into the implications of these representations for media practice and "real-world" responses. Fiske's metaphor will prove most pertinent here, making it possible to uncover links where on the surface none may be apparent, to show how the cross-referencing from one format to another produces a shift in discourse, which in turn raises new issues.

The three events or formats, fictitious, factitious, and real, all located in Britain, are:

1. The film *Shallow Grave* (released in 1994; director Danny Boyle);

2. The murder of Trevor, abusive husband and father in the British television Channel 4 soap, *Brookside;*

3. The case of Fred and Rosemary West, living in Gloucestershire, who murdered twelve girls and women together.

The sleeve on the videocassette of *Shallow Grave*, filmed in Edinburgh, Scotland, tells us: "Alex, David and Juliet are looking for a flatmate. They want someone like themselves—young, charming and affluent. Hugo moves in and soon proves to be as cool as his new flatmates had hoped—colder in fact, as the day after he moves in the others find him dead, locked in his room with a suitcase full of loot under the bed! What to do—keep the money and dispose of the corpse or turn the cash in?" In fact, they do the former; otherwise there would be no story. Our trio, journalist, accountant, and doctor, respectively, go for the loot and thereby, progressively undo themselves. This results in four dead, one gravely injured (possibly dying) and one put to flight. The original corpse is buried in a shallow grave in the woods, as later, are two further bodies, killed by David.

Brookside is a soap on the politically aware GB TV Channel 4, in existence since 1983. A mother and two daughters appear in Brookside Close, Liverpool, the scene of the soap, on the run from a violent husband and father, currently in prison for battering his wife, Mandy, and abusing his elder daughter, Beth. His release from prison and contrived return to the family home prove disastrous: History repeats itself, this time involving the younger daughter, Rachel, and culminating in his murder by Mandy and Beth. These two construct a patio, with a neighbor's help, and there they bury the body.

Fred and Rosemary West, married in 1972 and, living in Gloucestershire,[2] were arrested twenty years later on suspicion of murdering at least twelve people, mostly young girls they had jointly or separately abused physically and sexually, including their own daughter, Heather, and Rose's stepdaughter, Charmaine. All but two of the twelve bodies were found buried under floors, cellars, and patios around their home.

The following brief, but not exhaustive, chronology indicates the potential temporal influence of the above three narratives.

6 August 1992:	A raid on the home at 25 Cromwell Street of Fred and Rose West about the sexual abuse of their daughter finds no proof.
January 1993:	In real life, there is a campaign to free women, including Emma Humphries and Sarah Thornton,[3] convicted of murdering partners.
17 June 1993:	In a subsequent court case against Fred and Rose West their daughter refuses to testify. Fred and Rose West go free. Their children are taken into care.
May 1993:	In *Brookside* Mandy and Beth Jordache kill Trevor Jordache (husband and father) and bury him under the patio.
24 February 1994:	Police enter 25 Cromwell Street with a warrant to search for the remains of Heather, the Wests' daughter. The Wests are arrested.
Autumn 1994:	*Shallow Grave* is released.
1 January 1995:	Fred West hangs himself in prison before he can be tried.
30 Jan-3 Feb 1995:	In *Brookside*, Trevor's body is discovered under the patio.
10 February 1995:	*Heavenly Creatures* is released.[4]
Mid May 1995:	In the Jordache trial in *Brookside*, Mandy and Beth are found guilty of murder and conspiracy to murder and receive life and five years imprisonment, respectively.
26 July 1995:	In *Brookside* Beth dies in prison.
28 July 1995:	Sara Thornton is released from prison.
August 1995:	In *Brookside* Mandy Jordache is released from prison.
22 November 1995:	Rose West is convicted of ten murders and given ten life sentences.

It is clear from the above that there is close overlap and a high level of fade-ins and fade-outs with regard to the cases of the Wests and the Jordaches, together with actual cases coming to court at that time. There are parallels, too, with elements of *Shallow Grave*, which will serve as a paradigm for a range of features that will be examined in all three case studies. These features include:

a)   The relationship of women to space, allied to the notions of enemy and friend;

b)   The collusion to kill and the need to dispose of the bodies;

c) Implications for the outcomes and rights of those abused in the domestic environment.

Women and Space: Friends and Enemies

Whatever one thinks of the old adage "a woman's place is in the home," we know full well that there are all too many instances where a woman's home is not *her* place. We know, also, that the term *domestic violence* is a misnomer and a euphemism for legitimized male violence against women, and *not* for the domestic woman's violence against her male partner, much as "family man" has positive connotations of stability linked to virility, contrasting with the nonexistent equivalent, "family woman." Here we shall examine the different ways in which the three main protagonists, Juliet (SG), Mandy (Brook), Rosemary (Wests) relate to their domestic space and the violence that occurs within it.

Juliet (SG), a hospital doctor, resides in a large Edinburgh apartment whose huge ceilings, bold colors, and spacious rooms provide the perfect backdrop for a group of three seemingly unattached people, two male and one female, free-wheeling individuals very much in control of their lives. Juliet regularly fends off male outsiders,[5] not because they are a threat, but because they are a bore: The standard response to the telephone is, "She's not here!" Philip Kemp in his review of the film refers to their "hermetically sealed living space."[6] Hugo, interviewed alone by Juliet as a candidate for the fourth room in their flat, will become the dead intruder in their midst and push their brittle bonding to its limits.

She is ambivalent about her availability to the two men with whom she shares the flat, and the viewer is left to guess at an eternal triangle syndrome and its tensions, with Juliet the key player, as is implied by Alex's remark to her about herself and David: "God, you two are just so sensitive. All I'm doing is implying some sort of ugly, sexual liaison. Why, I'd be proud of that sort of thing." David, with whom she blows hot and cold as a lover, spies on her voyeuristically from his paranoid hideaway in the attic. Later, realizing he has been double-crossed, he bruises her face as he gags her while Alex, her accomplice at this point, hunts for the money: Like the typical battered wife, she is unable to go to work the following day. David to Juliet: "I thought you'd gone to work" Juliet: "With a face like this?" The filmic domestic space and its pressure cooker atmosphere become hostile to all three of its members who violently turn in on each other, and the seemingly confident Juliet ultimately flees it, a loser and a murderer.

The narrative of *Brookside* is located in Brookside Close, a neatly set out cul-de-sac, looking as if butter would not melt in its tidy suburban mouth. However, this soap has gained a reputation for treating thorny issues in a serious, nonsensational way. Compared with other British soaps, it has the distinction of providing more extended dialogue and fewer disruptive scene changes: This approach, added to the fact that the soap format provides us with a useful vehicle for entering domestic space and witnessing what takes place there, meant that Brookside was particularly well placed, via the traditionally eked out narrative soap techniques, to deal with the question of domestic violence and murder. Coincidentally, as the plot unfolded, so did that of the West case in a domestic space the prying eyes of the world were not able to enter. The closure and containment of the house in Brookside Close and that at No. 25 Cromwell Street are crucial to and symptomatic of the easy categorizing and removal from the sphere of public responsibility, of violence meted out by men to women and children behind closed doors. In fictional Brookside Close there is, as always, neighborly inquiry and even concern, but in the real-life version of Cromwell Street for many years there was a certain ignorance of events taking place there.

In Brookside Close, then, we find a threesome of newcomers, this time all female, whose domestic space is literally designated as "safe" because this is the "safe house" to which they have come to escape the violence and abuse of Trevor Jordache. He is the husband of Mandy, whom he has violently attacked, and he is the father of Beth, whom he has sexually abused. He is also the father of Rachel, as yet untouched by him and the one member of the household who still holds him in affection. Here the intruder into the domestic space, following his release from prison, is a known enemy, who uses cunning (he meets Beth coming out of college) and wiles (he plays on Mandy's sympathy when his flat is burgled). Finally, he takes advantage of his younger daughter, Rachel, an unwitting Red Riding Hood figure (he later gets into bed with her ostensibly to get warm), to regain access and even set up home in the very space meant to exclude him. The bonding between mother and elder daughter in their oppression by Trevor and Beth's spirited rejection of him are fractured by Mandy's "habit of having a man around," which leads to her relenting and taking him back into the household once more.

His renewed admission to the family circle is compounded by Rachel's innocent lack of awareness, and it is only when she, too, has been sexually abused that Mandy and Beth are driven to kill Trevor. There is an interesting parallel here between the fictional character of Rachel and that of Anne-Marie West in real life: In court neither was prepared to give crucial evidence against their respective fathers. In *Brookside*, what for female members of the Jordache family should have been fortress Brookside became an open door to their imprisonment by the state justice system, following from their patriarchal domestic oppression. The social services system, designed to protect them, had miserably failed to do so.

The social services also failed, in real life, fully to identify the situation at No. 25 Cromwell Street in the West case: Various proceedings brought against Fred West failed to stick. The eventual national outrage and media hype surrounding the West case highlight some inconsistencies between the so-called cooperation between the authorities and the general public with the media acting as go-between. On the one hand, the British media have encouraged a public familiarity with the world of crime and crime detection with interactive programs such as *Crimewatch UK* and *Crimewatch Update*[7] such that every member of the public is not only a potential detective, but also a potential *witness*. Interestingly, the majority of crimes featured are usually *sexy* rather than *sexual*, falling into the *public* domain rather than the *private*: bank robberies, burglaries, violent hold-ups, with murders indoors usually perpetrated by an intruder rather than a resident. Paradoxically, on the other hand, we find ourselves tied into the jargon of police and other public services referring to incidents tokenly as "a domestic," or "a fatal," convenient means of distancing those who are formally in charge from the grim realities of life, death and violence, a neat discursive containment.

Public awareness, then, of activities at No. 25 Cromwell Street was slow to take effect. The net-curtain syndrome is evident here as it is in the Jordache story: What goes on behind it is not really the business of those on the outside.[8] However, the prim and apparently closed facade of No. 25 Cromwell Street as of 24 February 1994 was to become a familiar image for GB news viewers, and an icon for fantasy and speculation as to what had taken place behind, and eventually, beneath it. Compared with the relative self-containedness of the apartment in *Shallow Grave*, and with the intended impermeability of the semi-detached house in Brookside Close, the terraced house (row house) at No. 25 Cromwell Street was both open and closed: Closed in that from beyond the doors and curtains little that escaped was really noted and acted upon. Various attempts to pin guilt on Rose and Fred West failed, and in one instance, it was even considered that Fred was "the most stable influence" on his daughter Anne-Marie whom he had long been abusing; closed in that, in the French sense it was a *maison close*, a venue for Rose to act as a prostitute; it was open in that many people had access to it—clients of Rose, temporary lodgers and foster children. However, there is a sense in which, in spite of a certain tight-lipped aspect of the house,[9] Fred and Rose West had extended their domestic space, operating in a car to pick up young girls, and drew people in from outside, many of whom were never to leave. Whereas Mandy and Beth acted as joint *defenders* within, attempting to bar their door, the Wests constituted a joint *enemy* within, both to those "born into the home," their own children, but also to those lured through the front door. By contrast with the Jordaches, following Fred West's arrest on 24 February 1994, Rose and her two children were allocated to three "safe houses" in succession, but in this case to avoid the violence of the public rather than domestic violence.

Motivation and Collusion:
The Decision to Kill and to Dispose

We have looked above at some of the domestic configurations in the three cases under consideration, from the shifting trio with its built-in duos in *Shallow Grave* to the duo/trio of the Jordache women in *Brookside*, to the concerted duo of the Wests. However, how did they all reach the decision to kill, in some cases to dismember,[10] and in all cases to bury their victims? More specifically, what is the role of the women behind the grave?

In *Shallow Grave,* Alex, the journalist always ready for a story—later, ironically his newspaper will detail him to cover this story—and who regards Hugo's corpse as nothing more than that, initially, is keen to keep the money and face the consequences. David, the safe accountant is reluctant. Juliet at first has scruples and, indeed, is already phoning the police when Alex finds and shows her the caseful of money. It is the duo of Juliet and David who finally decide to "do it":—Visiting him at his workplace, she eyes him intently, and David says: "OK. Let's do it." They incite each other to action, something which in their yuppie culture will be perceived as "sexy." "It" at this stage is not in fact a case of killing but of disfiguring and dismembering an already dead and rotting corpse, resulting from a drug overdose. For Juliet, a hospital doctor, a dead body is nothing new, but she is squeamish on this occasion, responding to Alex's jibe that as a doctor she "kills people every day," she says: "I still don't want to. It's different." Nevertheless, as "one of the boys" she goes along with the venture.

As individuals no single one of them would alone have had the guts or the physical strength to do the deed. Alex dictates what implements will be required, Juliet strides around in the Do It Yourself center (DIY will be a feature of all three case studies) with a shopping trolley resembling a mobile hospital bed, and David has the jitters. There ensues the tragi-comic descent from the fourth-floor flat of the now stiff body wrapped in black polythene and, once in the woods, the drawing of lots to decide who saws off hands and feet and disfigures the face of Hugo. David draws the short straw, and the violence to the corpse, which will eventually turn into violence against himself, begins.[11] David, having coped with this (incidentally it is practical Juliet who takes the hands and feet and disposes of them in the hospital incineration skip), although it affects him mentally and forces him to take up residence in the attic, he is nonetheless highly competent at killing two further men—ostensibly in self-defense—who come in search of the dead and buried Hugo.[12] These also find themselves in shallow graves, too shallow as time will prove.

What was originally collusion for mutual material gain becomes collusion to cover one's tracks and subsequently save one's individual skin while also walking off with the loot. Here it could be argued that Juliet's implicit sexual two-timing with Alex and David contributes to the crescendo of violence at the end of the film, along with the realization that, thinking *she* was hoodwinking the pair of them, both men have, in different ways double-crossed *her*. Having killed David—her scruples desert her on this occasion—and left Alex probably dying, she strides away from the scene of *her* crime(s), saves her skin but loses the game, to the background song of "Friends," while Alex, pinned to the floorboards with a carving knife, his blood dripping onto the banknotes beneath, has the last laugh. Juliet has been routed by her accomplice. Throughout we see a progressive preparedness to do violence, from the initial repugnance of premeditated dismembering of an already dead corpse, to the instinctive killing in self-defense by David, plus his severe maiming of

Alex, culminating in Juliet's swift decision to make a killing in more ways than one. Finally, it is the woman who makes the coolest decision.

From shallow graves in the woods to suburban patio. As a headline from the *Guardian* made clear,[13] the word *patio* has taken on a life of its own, implying a banalization of murder and domestic burial, enshrining it as an ingredient of soap opera. The Jordache case, *cause célèbre* as it came to be, although extraordinary in that it rose to the heights of fictional drama and brought about a wave of bonding and fellow-feeling among women nationwide, was per se, as evidenced by this response, not so out of the ordinary. Compared with the more self-seeking attitude of Juliet and friends, Mandy and Beth were driven to fight for their own survival and the protection of the younger daughter, Rachel: *Their* gain would be freedom from oppression and violence. There are, however, certain parallels between the two scenarios: In *Shallow Grave*, to cover their tracks David is obliged to kill two more men; Mandy and Beth, having first failed to kill Trevor with weed killer, need, in order not to be found out, to try a concoction with ground-up paracetamol (Beth is a medical student and so, like Juliet, should know what has the potential to kill). As with David and his "friends," realization dawns on Trevor Jordache. "His women" are double-crossing him, and even in his poisoned state he summons up enough energy to throw Beth to the floor and begin beating her. In a scene reminiscent of that at the end of *Shallow Grave* where Juliet puts a knife through David's neck as he stabs Alex, Mandy knifes Trevor in the back, and he slumps to the floor. There are, however differences: Juliet, in spite of anger and the heat of the moment, is still in control, using her shoe (a feminine touch?) to drive the knife more firmly into Alex's chest saying: "You did the right thing, but I can't take you with me"; whereas Mandy (still in the mode of wife?) is immediately hysterical, crying: "I murdered him! I'm a murderer!"

This moment in May 1993 presages a soap opera courtcase two years later, following the discovery of the body, wrapped in black bin-liners, à la *Shallow Grave*, exhumed (for the second time—the first was to retrieve Trevor's ring) following drainage problems next door. The case would echo and ricochet through the media, women's support groups and the justice system itself. Fictional the Jordache case may be, it is the tip of a factual iceberg. One of many newspaper articles to appear on the subject is to be found in the *Observer* of Sunday, 29 January 1995, under the headline "When DIY Turns out to Mean 'Dead in Yard'":

Leaving aside the late Frederick West, with his penchant for turning his
Gloucester house into a mausoleum, real killers and diggers like the fictional
Beth and Mandy Jordache are legion. And claims that Brookside was cashing
in on the West case are wide of the mark: the story was planned in detail three
years ago as a dramatic way of highlighting the issue of domestic violence, and
whether women who kill after long provocation should be convicted of murder
or manslaughter.

The same article concludes, to illustrate the longtime commonality of
such occurrences:

Four skeletons were unearthed under a patio in Belgravia, central London, next
door to the home of former MP Enoch Powell. Because the bones were more
than 75 years old no inquest took place. But Det Supt Guy Mills told reporters:
"It is a fascinating inquiry because there are all sorts of possible scenarios. Is it
the chambermaid? Is it the mistress? Is it the wife?"[14]

We are not told whether these bones were male or female, but the gloss
on domestic violence is somewhat at variance with that in the Jordache
case: Or should we conclude that had Mandy and Beth not taken the law
into their own hands it might have been they who were found under the
patio, since male violence toward women is a more common occurrence?
It was, in the event, Beth, the stronger of the two, who was the force behind the murder, acting perhaps as an unnatural daughter, both in relation
to her father and to her mother, who, albeit at her wits' end, was more
hesitant. It was Beth who slapped her hysterical mother immediately
after the killing. Any perception of unnatural behavior on her part was
compounded by the press in January 1995 with coverage of Beth's lesbianism. In an article headlined: "Brookside backs down over lesbian
kiss," *The Guardian*, 7 January 1995, reports the fact that a teatime re-
peat of the show would cut out the kiss since at that time more children
would be likely to be watching:

The Independent Television Commission which has received 14 complaints about
the lesbian storyline in the past, has not upheld any of them. Its code makes no
reference to lesbianism, although it covers taste and decency issues. However the
commission issued a formal warning to Channel 4 in October 1993, when Brookside showed a knife being used as a murder weapon in the omnibus edition. It
said a large number of children were likely to be watching.[15]

The more sensational *Sunday Mirror* (22 January 1995) carried a
front cover picture of Beth in an inviting pose, entitled *"Brookside,* Beth
and That Body."[16] The double entendre is explained in the three-page
spread of a prone, provocative Beth, carrying the caption: "Confessions

of a lesbian killer."[17] Whatever release they may have found via the death of Trevor, both Mandy and Beth will be contained by their perceived unnaturalness and deviancy, either because of their murderous act, or because of the threat that Beth is purported to pose to heterosexuality, a heterosexuality that has behaved extremely unnaturally and violently to her. Beth is placed on the margins, as is Juliet, a woman medic in what is still largely a man's world, a woman in a flat with two men. What is *her* real sexuality? Rose West would also be subjected to similar suppositions.

The cross-referencing in the above *Observer* article between the Jordache and the West case is telling. The two became interwoven in public perceptions, *Brookside* allowing us a glimpse of what life might have been like in 25 Cromwell Street, regularly dubbed "house of horrors" by the media. The crucial difference, though, was that, as far as it can be estimated, Fred and Rose West were operating as a duo, together with others from time to time. It should be noted, however, that Fred's brother also committed suicide while on bail accused of incest with his niece and of other sexual offenses. The *folie à deux* syndrome would seem to be operating here, whereby two people, once the boundaries of what is acceptable and what is taboo behavior are irretrievably broken down, take delight in each other's mutual transgression, without any compunction. This can be compared with the early elation of Juliet and friends as they realize they are rich and with the squandering of money on a video camera by the Juliet/Alex duo: A moment of folly, accompanied by Alex's cross-dressing and making himself up like a tart. Is the breaking of one taboo inevitably compounded by another? In the case of Beth can it be construed as making one doubly guilty?

Fred and Rose West did indeed accumulate a whole string of broken taboos: violence, abuse, incest, joint abuse of young persons, abductions and, inevitably, murders, dismemberings, and burials. All the crimes were committed against females. Unlike *Brookside*, the observer, or even spectator, since the whole affair became spectacle and was followed in the news media[18] much as a serial or soap, has no firsthand knowledge of the collusion and collaboration between Rose and Fred West, just reports of insatiable sexual appetites and a very high tolerance of violence. Their children, Stephen and Mae, recount in *Inside 25 Cromwell Street*[19] how, as they began to suspect their parents of having murdered their daughter, Heather, they tried to "trap" them by watching together the mirror image episodes of *Brookside*, and a further TV drama *Prime Suspect*, in which a woman was buried under a *patio*—but to no avail. Although this whole affair drew reprobation from the public, it was the joint nature of the atrocities that caused the most horror: How could a *woman* collude in and do such a thing? Moreover, because the abusive sexual activities concerned girls and women exclusively, the implication was that Rose, in spite of her known prostitution activities, was also a lesbian, making her all the more deviant in the eyes of the public. Maggie Wykes in *A Family Affair: The British Press, Sex and the Wests* (1998) has provided a comprehensive analysis of the role of perceived female deviance in this case, against a backdrop of Thatcherite morality, the glorification of the family as "safe" and "normal," and the patriarchally dominated press reporting.[20]

The serial nature of the killings also aroused the ghoulish imagination of the public and drew comparisons with the child murders by Ian Brady and Myra Hindley[21] in the 1960s, one of whose victims still lies undiscovered. In this duo Brady has refused for some time to talk to the media or cooperate with the police, whereas Hindley has tried, unsuccessfully, to obtain her own release after more than thirty years in prison. In fact, such a long sentence had not been initially intended. Moreover, it certainly does not take into account her avowed remorse and change of character. Her specter remains as a caveat to all others who may imitate her, illustrating the double standards in the sentencing of men and women: If women murder, it is doubly unnatural, incurring double punishment. The state has effectively silenced her.[22]

Silence, too, for Beth Jordache in *Brookside* who, on beginning her prison sentence, died a TV death on Wednesday 26 July 1995 from a congenital heart defect inherited from her father: Comparable to Alex *vis-à-vis* Juliet, Trevor Jordache has the last word over his daughter. Similarly, by committing suicide on 1 January 1995 Fred West took secrets with him to the grave and virtually sealed Rose's fate: Once she had been convicted of two murders, others were imputed to her, and she is now serving a life sentence for the perpetration of ten murders. Mandy, released from prison within a few months of being convicted, left Brookside Close and set up a new life elsewhere (soap plot oblige?). Juliet, penniless, flew off to Rio.

Outcomes and Implications

Let us in conclusion look at some of the issues pointing above the eddies and swirls referred to by Fiske in our opening quotation. We have examined three media artifacts, ranging from entertainment with violence (*Shallow Grave*) to a real-life serial murder case transformed by the media into ghoulish entertainment (The West case), with, somewhere between the two, soap opera entertainment (*Brookside*). The latter became a documentary drama intertwined with media coverage of real-life murder cases in which women had been convicted of killing violent partners. What emerges from this juxtaposition set in the context of 1990s Britain?

First, the power of the media across their various formats to capture the general imagination speaks directly to individuals and effects a sea change in perceptions. However, the cases of Jordache and West were also good television, sexual as well as sexy and as such were both commercial successes. *Brookside* has become a reference point for issues of domestic violence, as has *Crimewatch* for civic duty and police/public relations. It must be noted, too, that Channel 4, home of *Brookside*, was also joint partner in the production of *Shallow Grave*.

Second, yet equally important, there is a new understanding of women's violence in response to maltreatment and abuse: The arguments have moved on a stage from the PMT (or senile dementia) leads-to-petty-theft syndrome and the biologizing of women to their immediate environment, thus in some measure deflecting attention away from the woman offender. Women are still problematized in relation to violence, but there has also been a shift from the assumption that a woman could only be exonerated if she killed in self-defense "in hot blood," to a more comprehending approach to the element of premeditation peculiar to such cases. There is increased criticism of the discrepancies between the lenient sentencing of violent male murderers, provoked by "the nagging wife" and the much heavier sentences incurred by women for similar offenses against their male partners.

Furthermore, the boundaries between the public and private domains in relation to so-called domestic violence are perhaps being breached as a result of notorious fictitious and real-life cases. The by-product of this trend is that the beleaguered social services, so criticized for having failed to prevent the deaths of so many young girls at the hands of the Wests, had already begun to exercise increasing rights to have access to children whom they supposed to be at risk. The Jordache and West cases took place against a backdrop of increasing concern for the physical and moral safety of young children. In this climate the terms *child sex abuse*, and frequently *pedophilia*, were part of daily discourse. The development was in some measure the result of long-running affairs regarding sexual abuse investigated by the social services as in Cleveland (a region in the North East of England) in the mid-eighties and alleged ritual child abuse in the Scottish Isles: It was only after five years separation that the Scottish children were returned to their families, without the cases having ever been conclusively proven.[23]

Moreover, mistrust of males in positions of responsibility for young boys has grown together with an increased suspicion of male members of the clergy, given the number of abuse cases. While, on the one hand, the level of homophobia has been raised, on the other, the emphasis in the majority of these instances has been on the safety of *boys* rather than *girls,* thus deemphasizing the many acts of violence against females in the average domestic situation. Simultaneously, though, there is still heavier public reprobation for women who kill or abuse children, as was seen in the Louise Woodward affair and her conviction for the murder of Matthew Eapen in 1997 and in the earlier case in Britain of nurse Beverley Allitt (1991–93).[24]

Finally, while the Jordache story in *Brookside* may well have foregrounded strong women and to some extent legitimized their violence in the face of abuse and aggression, the fact that Mandy and Beth, too, are silenced and "disposed of" must also be seen in the context of postfeminism and the backlash against women. Women may also be the ultimate losers because of increased awareness and media treatment of the cycle of domestic and sexual violence and the acute need to break this cycle. More precisely, the Labour Government, elected in May 1997, has introduced initiatives to recreate stable home environments, while accepting less "traditional" households than those revered by the Thatcher Governments. These initiatives include, for example, parenting courses for young men and women, but also an introduction of these into the school curriculum. This approach is certainly laudable. However, care needs to be taken that increased government involvement does not recreate the cycle of female dependency.

Notes

1. John Fiske, *Media Matters: Everyday Culture and Political Change* (Minneapolis: U of Minnesota P, 1994), 7.

2. The popular image of Gloucestershire is of an idealized sleepy, rural county in southern England, home to aristocracy and royalty and not the kind of area in which such horrors would take place.

3. Humphries, imprisoned for an indefinite period in 1985 for having murdered her violent partner, was released In June 1995. Thornton, jailed for life in 1990 having killed her violent husband, was released in July 1995; her case had similarities with that of the Jordaches in that Thornton stabbed her policeman husband with a kitchen knife while he slept after a bout of drinking.

4. This film recounts a real-life story of two teenage girls, Pauline Parker and Juliet Hulme who carried out the premeditated murder of Parker's mother in New Zealand in 1954. The *Guardian* review of the film, (30 January 1995, G2 supplement, 2–3), "Slaughter by Innocents," foregrounds the sedate nature of this model colonial country at that period, the shock waves it sent through society, and the inevitable innuendoes of sexual deviance as some kind of explanation. The reviewer, Louise Chunn, says of the news story: "Its potent mixture of sex, family, youth and violence was a gift for the media and the public has never tired of it." Karen Boyle and Davinia Thornley in chapters 3 and 4 of this book, respectively, discuss *Heavenly Creatures* in detail.

5. Danny Boyle, the director of *Shallow Grave*, said of Juliet: "The female character was always an outsider, and we decided she didn't have to be Scottish, so we asked Kerry Fox, who is a New Zealander . . . she's very chameleon . . . ." See Danny Boyle, interview, *Sight and Sound*, January 1995, 34.

6. Philip Kemp, review of *Shallow Grave, Sight and Sound*, January 1995, 57.

7. *Crimewatch*, a monthly program on BBC investigating unsolved crimes, combines reassuring male and female presenters with real-life police officers to establish a rapport with the general public. While not seeking to sensationalize crime, it nonetheless harnesses the viewers' curiosity, civic sense, and taste for drama, and has become a respected extra "arm" of the law. On 25 November 1993 the newspaper *Today* displayed not only CCTV stills of the two young boys who abducted and murdered child James Bulger, but those stills "as shown on *Crimewatch*."

8. The review article "Torment Behind Net Curtains," *The Guardian,* 29 July 1993, of the book *Murder in the Heart* by Angela Artley (London: Hamish Hamilton, 1993) gives an account of 40 years of sadism and incest in a seemingly "upright" home in Lancashire, where two daughters, June and Hilda Thompson, shot their abusive father, were convicted of murder, and were given a two years' suspended sentence. Their case was "one of the first in which prolonged suffering was accepted legally as provocation," 37.

9. Two children of the Wests, Stephen and Mae, give a graphic account of events in the household in *Inside 25 Cromwell St* (London: Peter Grose, 1995). Neither they nor their mother were allowed to invite real friends to the house: "We were never allowed any friends to stay with us and we weren't allowed to stay with them. They wanted the family kept really tight . . . . I didn't have many friends for the simple reason Mum told them to fuck off when they came to the door" (Mae, 38). "Mum didn't really have any friends because Dad wouldn't allow it. And if she found someone to have a cup of tea with Dad would throw them out of the house . . . . He wanted complete power over the house" (Mae, 69).

10. "Eight of the nine victims found in Cromwell Street had been buried in small graves with their heads and limbs stuffed into tiny spaces—West said that he only dismembered the bodies to bury them. But Linda Gough had been buried in an area large enough to keep her in one piece. That she had been dismembered suggested that West found sexual excitement in cutting up, and disposing of, the bodies." See *Murder in Mind, the Killers, Their Crimes, Their Psychology: Fred and Rosemary West* (London: Marshall Cavendish, 1997), 22. In one case West had removed the fetus from his pregnant victim.

11. Philip Kemp believes *Shallow Grave* "relishes the ghoulish details of death and dismemberment. The sound of a saw rasping on human wristbone comes over with scalp-crawling immediacy." *Sight and Sound*, January 1995, 57–58.

12. In this case CCTV cameras provide a flashback effect: The viewer is placed inside the cash distributing machine being raided by the two men.

13. "No hitmen, no plane crashes, no bodies under the patio. Channel 5's flagship soap promises to be realistic. And they think we'll watch it?" *The Guardian, Friday Review*, 21 March 1997, 4.

14. "When DIY Turns out to Mean 'Dead in Yard," *The Observer*, 29 January 1995, 10.

15. "Brookside Backs Down over Lesbian Kiss," *The Guardian*, 7 January 1995.

16. "Brookside, Beth, and That Body," *Sunday Mirror*, 22 January 1995, 1.

17. "Confessions of a Lesbian Killer," *Sunday Mirror*, 22 January 1995, color magazine, 10–12.

18. The exhumation of the twelve bodies continued from 25 February to 7 June 1995.

19. Stephen West and Mae West, *Inside 25 Cromwell Street.*

20. Maggie Wykes, "A Family Affair: The British Press, Sex and the Wests," in *News, Gender and Power*, ed. Cynthia Carter, Gill Branston, and Stuart Allen (London: Routledge, 1998), 233–47.

21. Myra Hindley, for her part in the "Moors murders," so-called because she and her accomplice, Ian Brady, buried their child victims on the Lancashire/Yorkshire moors, has become a cult hate figure and an icon for "unnatural" female violence. A recent wall-sized portrait of her (corresponding to the photograph of her blond image of thirty years ago which regularly appears in the media) by Marcus Harvey,

composed of plaster cast imprints of a child's hand, caused an outcry when it was shown at the Royal Academy of Arts *Sensations* exhibition in London in autumn 1997, but was not withdrawn. Maggie Wykes, "A Family Affair," reminds us of the popular notion of female deviance and quotes *The Daily Mail* of 23 November 1995: "Rose West and Myra Hindley have formed a macabre friendship in jail . . . . [T]he two most evil women in Britain, both openly bi-sexual—have been seen holding hands in Durham prison."

22. In 1966 Hindley was given two life sentences for her part in at least five murders of young children. A number of campaigns for her release have been turned down by a succession of Home Secretaries, including an appeal in October 1998.

23. In 1994, as 25 Cromwell Street was being dismantled, a case of child abuse in a nursery in Newcastle (North Eastern England) was dismissed for lack of adequate evidence. Much as in the West case, the authorities took four more years to uncover a pedophile ring involving many children, some as young as two, and it was not until a three-year-long investigation concluded that a man and a woman, Christopher Lillie and Dawn Reid "did *probably* conspire with others unknown."

24. In 1991 Beverley Allitt murdered four babies and children and seriously harmed several others while working as a hospital nurse in Grantham (central England) and was subsequently diagnosed as suffering from Münchhausen syndrome by proxy. The title of the feature on her in *The Guardian* of 22 May 1993: "Childhood of a Child-Killer," foreshadows the front page headline later that year in the tabloid *Today*, 25 November 1993: "Born to Murder, (Shades of *Natural Born Killers?*)." This reference was to the two eleven-year-old murderers of the toddler James Bulger: Here again the debate was very much centered around the notion of "unnatural," and these two boys became just as much hate figures as other, adult, murderers.

Bibliography

"Born to Murder, (Shades of *Natural Born Killers?*)" *Today,* 25 November 1993, 1, 2–11, 28–29.

Boyle, Danny. Interview. *Sight and Sound,* January 1995, 57.

Brookside. One of Britain's three top soap operas, with *Coronation Street* and *Eastenders*, running on ITV, Channel 4, UK.

"Brookside Backs Down over Lesbian Kiss." *The Guardian,* 7 January 1995, 1.

"Brookside, Beth and That Body." *Sunday Mirror,* 22 January 1995, 1.

"Childhood of a Child-Killer." *The Guardian*, W/E Supplement, 22 May 1993, 1.

Chunn, Louise, "Slaughter by Innocents." Review of *Heavenly Creatures. The Guardian,* 30 January 1995, G 2 supplement, 2–3.

"Confessions of a Lesbian Killer." *Sunday Mirror,* color magazine, 22 January 1995, 10–12.

Crimewatch. A running series on BBC, UK.

Fiske, John. *Media Matters: Everyday Culture and Political Change.* Minneapolis: U of Minnesota P, 1994.

Heavenly Creatures. Dir. Peter Jackson. Perf. Melanie Lynskey and Kate Winslet. Road-show/Miramax/ Buena Vista, 1994.

Kemp, Philip. Review of *Shallow Grave. Sight and Sound,* January 1995, 57–58.

"The Making of a Murderer," *The Guardian*, W/E Supplement, 22 May 1993, 6–16.

Murder in Mind, The Killers, Their Crimes, Their Psychology: Fred and Rosemary West. No author. Duncan Campbell, Brian Masters, Dr. Raj Persaud, Colin Wilson, consultants. London: Marshall Cavendish, 1997.

"No Hitmen." *The Guardian, Friday Review,* 21 March 1997, 4.

Shallow Grave. Dir. Danny Boyle. Perf. Kerry Fox, Christopher Eccleston, Ewan McGregor. Rank, 1994.

"Torment Behind Net Curtains." Review of *Murder in the Heart,* by Angela Artley. *The Guardian,* 29 July 1993, 37.

West, Stephen, and Mae West. *Inside 25 Cromwell Street.* London: Peter Grose, 1995.

"When DIY Turns out to Mean 'Dead in Yard.'" *The Observer,* 29 January 1995, 10.

Wykes, Maggie. "A Family Affair: The British Press, Sex and the Wests." In *News, Gender and Power,* edited by Cynthia Carter, Gill Branston, and Stuart Allen. London: Routledge, 1998.

Chapter 9

The Quest for External Validation in Female Coming-of-Age Films

Amanda L. Maxfield

So, I cry and I pray and I beg:
Love me, love me, say that you love me

—"Lovefool," The Cardigans

Sung in the breathy babydoll tones of Nina Persson, the lyrics of "Love-fool"—which so appropriately anchored the soundtrack of Baz Luhr-man's splashy, ultra-hip 1996 remake of *Romeo and Juliet*, starring "su-per teens" Leonardo DiCaprio and Claire Danes—summarize the rela-tionship of adolescent girls first to society and then to the mainstream film industry. For adolescents of either gender, the process of coming-of-age, of successfully navigating that broad and choppy channel that sepa-rates childhood from adulthood, is of first priority. Surviving and getting out of the teenage years as quickly as possible is often the only consistent interest in an adolescent's life. For psychologist Erik Erikson, "establish-ing a sense of identity is the major task of adolescence. By identity, he means a coherent sense of self, based on a commitment to present and future roles, ideology, and values regarding future relationships."[1] How-ever, for girls specifically, the notion of love is inextricably intertwined with maturation. As social psychologist Carol Gilligan has shown, "while boys traditionally use acts of separation to develop identity, girls traditionally use acts of attachment."[2] Similarly, Erikson claims that "identity formation for boys centers largely on career and ideological issues, whereas for girls the emphasis is on interpersonal matters."[3] It is gaining the love and acceptance of males, peers, teachers, parents, and society at large that signals to girls that development is progressing and that soon the awkwardness of feeling unloved, unaccepted, and out of place will be over, and the end of adolescence is in sight. In this way, girls beg those around them to "love me, love me."

However, the film industry has prompted girls also to beg "fool me, fool me." The production of film after film depicting fictional, glamorized, simplistic, unrealistic, and unattainable images of not only adult life but also of the methods by which one may pass through adolescence to adulthood has served to influence young girls' attitudes, values, and behavior. Millions of girls each year flock to the theaters willing to consume the on-screen images and unknowingly to be "fooled" and manipulated by teen fairy tales that preserve archetypal stereotypes and paradigms. So enamored are they with seeing characters their own age in familiar situations—but far larger than life and in brilliant Technicolor and choreographed with a soundtrack in the latest music fad—that they are led to conform to what they see. Far from being mere entertainment or escape for adolescent girls, films that feature their contemporaries serve as guide books through the teen years. Girls are seen *en masse* to emulate their heroines in fashion, speech, views, and actions as they search for a mold to fit into or a pattern to follow. "Both social learning theory and cultivation theory postulate that [media] messages and models . . . have repercussions on the beliefs, attitudes, and perhaps the behaviors of the viewers."[4] Of particular concern are the advice and instructions that teen films provide with regard to those ever-elusive methods of coming-of-age.

Adolescents are the largest demographic group at the box office, and the film industry is diligent in producing subject matter to meet teen interests in exchange for their six dollars. According to sociologist Bradley S. Greenberg, "teenagers spend a considerable portion of their time . . . going to the movies, [and] they are a prime target and audience for movie makers."[5] He reports that in one study "half the youngsters had been out to a movie at least twice in the past thirty days, and twenty percent of them had been to a movie four or more times in that period."[6] Moreover, perhaps as problematic as the values, stereotypes, and expectations with which society raises children, is the notion that the media, specifically films, do not merely reflect that actual society, but create one of their own—a society with unique values, stereotypes, and expectations that can be made to seem as authentic as or even more authentic than reality. "Contemporary film theorists argue that, for a number of reasons, the cinematic image appears to the spectators as if it were reality, . . .[and] that the spectator's response to cinematic discourse illuminates the manner in which the human being in general is constructed in discourse."[7] Also, sociologists Nancy L. Buerkel-Rothfuss and Jeremiah Strauss report that "late adolescents and young adults describe the real world as being similar to portrayals in the media they consume."[8]

In *The Road to Romance and Ruin*, Jon Lewis states that specifically "[teen] films provide at best the principal artifacts of youth culture; at worst they offer proof positive of the hegemonic effect of the 'culture industry' (the argument that the media not only produce texts for consumption but ideology as well)."[9] In the adolescent race to fit in as quickly and neatly as possible, the ideology of world reality and the ideology of cinematic reality become a blur, and youths are left grasping at whatever comes at them loudest, brightest, and most persistently. In contemporary media-saturated society, rife with broken or breaking traditional social institutions, film is very often the winner. Moreover, it is the particular age and stage of development of the adolescent viewer that causes him or her to be especially vulnerable to cinematic messages. In *The Cinema of Adolescence,* David M. Considine argues that "unlike the adult, the adolescent is still in a stage of identity development, still formulating basic values and attitudes. Therefore, film must be regarded as one in a range of forces potentially capable of shaping either positively or negatively the young person's visions of himself and his society."[10] With going to the movies as one of the most prevalent activities of teenagers and with the teen insistence on pushing away from adults and traditional institutions in order to establish a pseudo-independence, it is easy to see where one of the greatest influences on the teen understanding of society lies. "In Britain, [sociologists] Wall and Simson reported that the motion picture played an important part in the life of the young, filling a knowledge vacuum and serving in many cases as the adolescent's only source of information in regard to such matters as social intercourse and human relationships. 'The emotional and social education of the growing youth,' they concluded, 'is left to the vivid realism of the screen.'"[11] It is the material that is fed into the "knowledge vacuum" of adolescent and preadolescent females that is of particular concern in this chapter.

Although it is my goal to discuss the representation of coming-of-age themes for adolescent female characters, I believe it is helpful to contextualize those themes in relation to some general observations about adolescent male characters. Boys on film are frequently shown to have maturation experiences by means of literal and figurative journeys of self-discovery and introspection that correspond with Gilligan's notion of separation and Erikson's notion of ideology in boys' identity formation. On these quests for manhood, physical and mental obstacles are encountered and overcome, and by the end of the film the male protagonists achieve a higher sense of self-awareness and of the male position in adult society. For example, both *Stand By Me* (1986) and *White Water Summer* (1987) involve literal journeys through the wilderness within which young boys must face and overcome their fears and their physical inadequacies in order to return to civilization more mature, more confident, more capable, and therefore more "manly." In *Stand By Me*, a drama, the stakes are higher, as four twelve-year-old boys search the woods for the dead body of another boy, while in *White Water Summer*, a comedy, a group of slightly older boys must survive the perils of a summer rafting excursion. Despite genre differences, the message is the same: For boys coming of age is a personal trek over dangerous terrain in which triumph depends on the adult "male" ability to place mind over matter.

In a recent and highly acclaimed example, the young protagonist of *Good Will Hunting* (1997) reluctantly embarks on a figurative journey into the depths of his emotions, insecurities, and fears of success and love under the guidance of a therapist. As in the previous examples, the obstacles are encountered, eventually overcome, and the protagonist emerges mentally healthier, confident, and equipped to assume his place in the adult world. This pattern of male development is rarely duplicated in films involving female protagonists.

After examining two dozen popular films involving adolescent female characters in coming-of-age themes, I found that most of these films present the antithesis of the messages of self-discovery and self-validation that are generally present in similar films about males. Rather, in film after film, the same conventions of plot and character development appear, instructing the adolescent female viewer to find her adult identity not in personal discovery of her self-worth but through social recognition and validation by her involvement in various activities.

These activities include participation in sexual activity and romantic love, winning peer acceptance, use of drugs and alcohol, criminal behavior, and engaging in public performance. It is through these behaviors that girls are able to focus attention on themselves—despite the brief, insincere, or even negative quality of that attention—and to gain if not approval, at least recognition from external sources. As stated above, the object of desire for this recognition varies, but is usually focused on boys, parents, teachers, and peers.

A film moment that combines both the sense of societal pressure on girls to seek approval as well as their corresponding desperate desire to gain approval is the fantasy of twelve-year-old Dawn, the protagonist of *Welcome to the Dollhouse* (1995). Dawn dreams she heroically rescues her younger sister, who has been kidnapped, and subsequently all of the people in her life shower her with praise, recognition, and validation. In a series of cuts, first her parents, then her older brother, then her pseudo-boyfriend, then the seventeen-year-old object of her crush, then an elementary school tag-along, and finally all of her classmates assembled in the school lunchroom shout at her, "We love you, Dawn! We love you Dawn!" The dream has far less to do with the rescue, but everything to do with Dawn's being able to experience the love and acceptance of her whole world. In stark contrast with reality, she is no longer the ignored middle child, the inexperienced girl, the ugly duckling, or the unpopular nerd. Her ultimate fantasy is that she is universally recognized as being worthy of love.

Lyn Mikel Brown and Carol Gilligan observe that "for over a century the edge of adolescence has been identified as a time of heightened psychological risk for girls. Girls at this time have been observed to lose their vitality, their resilience. . . their sense of themselves and their character."[12] Moreover, they argue that adolescence for females "goes hand in hand with evidence of a loss of voice, a struggle to authorize or take seriously their own experience."[13] In the tendency of adolescent girls to discount their experiences of the world, it seems probable that they seek representation elsewhere, specifically in the media and on the big screen. If girls are accepting cinematic images and messages as valid depictions of their reality, it is imperative that those images and message be analyzed for their content. In this essay I argue that many of the most popular films targeted at adolescent female audiences convey the message that becoming an adult female means being approved of and validated by particular societal standards of behavior. Hence, the worth of a woman alone—without society—is nothing. Through my examination of a sample of films dealing with the coming of age of adolescent female characters—films that the female teen viewer is likely to encounter either in the theaters or at the video rental store—I was able to identify three themes that were repeated to the point of approaching conventionality. My primary aim is to describe these themes, which are "sex and romance"; "peer acceptance," which frequently involves drug use and/or participation in criminal activities; and "performances," which present a socially focused but more positive vision of coming of age. I will describe the mode of presentation of these themes in particular films and raise questions about possible effects on female adolescent viewers. I will conclude by examining some films that present "alternatives" to these general depictions of female coming-of-age films.

Sex and Romance

> "You're in need of a ravisher."
>
> —Jeremy Irons to Liv Tyler in *Stealing Beauty*

In coming-of-age films, the most prevalent and perhaps the most obvious theme is the discovery of sexuality. In some ways, this seems an appropriate topic for such films, merely because the transition from childhood to adulthood involves the physical maturation that opens doors to sexual capability. "All theories of adolescent development give sexuality a central place in negotiating the transition from child to adult."[14] However, the assumptions that are made about female sexuality are culturally constructed ideas that reinforce the demand for external validation that is placed on women. The loss of virginity and subsequent heterosexual activity does not merely signal biological entry into adulthood; it constitutes a male acceptance of the female into her place in patriarchal society—namely as sex object and eventually as child-bearer. However, the role of sex in guiding girls through adolescence to a meaningful identity formation and adulthood must be questioned. Sociologist D. P. Orr, et al.

found a link between early sexual initiation and poor self-esteem for girls . . . Sex can . . . become the inappropriate focus of identity formation, for example the person who feels they are defined by their level of sexual attractiveness. Selverstone suggests that sexual involvement is one of the ways we learn to feel lovable, but that inappropriate involvement and sexual risk-taking can be counter-productive in the quest toward self-definition and personal integration.[15]

Moreover, in regard to the role girls play in the male-dominated youth subculture, sociologists have observed that "insofar as [a girl] is a sex object, a commodity, she is actually diminished by sex, she is literally worthless, she has been romantically and materially partly consumed."[16]

Regardless of any notion of possible danger to the self-concept, Sharon Thompson reported that the girls in her case studies "indicated that first intercourse would be worth whatever it took because of the knowledge it would bring."[17] Indeed, "boys were . . . often less important in themselves than for the affirmation they could confer. Sex was the final test, the apotheosis of romance, its transubstantiation into the body, and a rite of passage."[18]

The goal of achieving sexual validation is repeatedly posed in films for girls. It is shown to be an end in itself, not just a step toward adulthood, and it often signals the full realization of adult status. Since Bradley S. Greenberg et al. "confirm that young adolescent girls actively use sexual media content as they learn more about the world of sex, love, romance, and relationships,"[19] an examination of cinematic messages about female adolescence and sex sheds light on ideas that girls may internalize about coming of age.

A clear-cut and blatant example of sexuality as validation and thus coming-of-age is Bernardo Bertolucci's 1996 *Stealing Beauty*. We know from the first few sequences that introduce the setting and characters that the primary conflict and theme of this film are of a sexual nature. With the opening credits we are given grainy, documentary-style footage of Lucy, the nineteen-year-old female protagonist (played by Liv Tyler). She is traveling by train to her literal destination of Tuscany and her figurative destination of adulthood. The camera pans over the sleeping traveler, her foot, her face, her arm, leading to her hand, which is conveniently placed on her thigh. Following is a prolonged extreme close-up of the crotch of her jeans; Bertolucci doesn't leave us wondering as to what Lucy will find in Italy. As the exposition continues, Lucy—who we will soon learn is still a virgin—arrives at the villa of an old friend of her mother. As she enters the house, she plucks a cherry out of a bowl, and eating it, proceeds to the back porch; her point of view shots reveal a bird's nest, bees hovering over flowers, and a framed plate from the Kama Sutra, making references to some of the best known symbols of increasing knowledge of sexuality. Throughout the film, the bohemian artist community of her mother's friends takes an overt interest in Lucy's virginity and seems intent on forcing her to "grow up." Indeed, after confessing her virgin status to a writer (played by Jeremy Irons), he tells her "You're in need of a ravisher." As the film progresses, Lucy has numerous encounters of a sexual nature with various men; however, to everyone's disappointment, she is emotionally unable or unwilling to have sex with any of them.

At long last, Lucy takes a different step on her road of enlightenment, and pieces together the secret of her mother's affair and thus the identity of her father, a now happily married artist. Subsequently, she confronts and is recognized and accepted by her biological father. It is this resolution of conflict regarding her father-daughter relationship that allows her to move into a sexualized male-female relationship. On her last day at the villa, after being stung by a bee—again, Bertolucci's lack of subtlety—she conveniently encounters the shy Italian boy who has been pining for her on the sidelines. After a few hours of walking through the countryside and talking, she finally loses her virginity to the "good guy" underneath a massive oak tree. Within approximately two minutes the movie is over. Lucy parts from the Italian boy and walks toward the villa, now an "adult woman," as the credits roll. Her goal has been accomplished, her questions have been answered, her body has realized its potential, and ultimately, its purpose. Beyond the sexual act, we see no further process of maturation, because the process is over, at least in the ideology of the filmmaker. Lucy's coming of age has been accomplished by an act of sexual validation, a rite of passage made seductively attractive by the highly romanticized depiction of tender, satisfying, consensual sex between two attractive young people. However, it is the cinematography, the appearance of the actors, the Italian countryside, and the simplistic ending of the film that are agreeable to the viewer's sense of aesthetics. Not so appealing is the idea that the evolving adult self-worth and identity of this character has just been defined by the sexual act.

Even when the actual physical act of sex does not appear in a film, the intensity with which teen characters are shown to focus on the topic expresses a similar attitude of endorsement of sex as a path toward adulthood. An example of this type of teen story is John Hughes's *Sixteen Candles* (1984). Hughes's skill as a writer and director in representing overtly stereotypical suburbs peopled with witty, minimally introspective, highly misunderstood teen heroes opposed by "square," gullible adult villains made him a leader of the 1980s youth market. Young people were—and still are—drawn to his images of teen maturation as manifested in films like *Sixteen Candles, The Breakfast Club* (1985) and *Weird Science*, and *Pretty in Pink* (1986) and *Ferris Bueller's Day Off* (1986). Indeed, *Sixteen Candles* was screened for a university audience as part of the campus film series during the semester I conducted the research for this chapter.

Sixteen Candles follows a day in the life of Sam, played by the 1980s teen idol Molly Ringwald. However, this is no ordinary day, but it is her sixteenth birthday, a landmark which has, most likely because of an association with the independence of a driver's license, gained cultural significance as marking a threshold of adulthood. With her first lines, Sam identifies immediately with the importance of the occasion and with the drastic changes that are expected to coincide with it. Looking at the profile of her body in the mirror, she remarks disappointedly to herself, "Chronologically you're sixteen today; physically, you're still fifteen. Hopeless." Obviously, to her the age of sixteen is supposed to imply a more adult body, which, as is soon demonstrated, implies her desirability to men and the potential for sex. Indeed, sociological research showed that "in 1979, half of the fifteen to nineteen-year-olds living in metropolitan areas reported having had intercourse. Sixteen was the average age for a girl's 'first time.'"[20]

Her birthday is completely forgotten by her predictably flighty, preoccupied parents (typical of Hughes); at school Sam and a classmate discuss the ideal sixteenth birthday:

> **Sam:** "Since I was about twelve, I've been looking forward to my sweet sixteen, you know, a big party with a band and tons of people."
>
> **Friend:** "And a pink Trans-Am in the driveway with a ribbon around it, and some really gorgeous guy you meet like in France. And you do it on a cloud without getting pregnant or herpes."
>
> **Sam:** "I don't need a cloud."

Although the girls mention the other significations of approaching adulthood—the party, which is indicative of an entry into a more formal social world, and the car, which signals freedom and independence—Sam's main response is in regard to the sexual aspect, indicating that even much less perfect sex than on a cloud would satisfy her expectations for her coming-of-age event. The audience is quickly introduced to the object of Sam's desire, Jake Ryan, the senior athletic star of the high school, who is flattered and intrigued by Sam's crush.

As the film progresses, Sam's dream birthday comes true in stages, even if parts of it are a little less than ideal, with sex always an underlying theme. The first aspect of the birthday fantasy comes true when Sam goes to the school dance, quite literally "a big party with a band and tons of people." Discouraged, however, by Jake's lack of attention, she ends up in the metal shop of the school, sitting in the seat of the front half of an old chopped convertible. The image is a visual joke on the earlier dream of receiving a Trans-Am for her birthday; moreover, the image is a metaphor for her stage of adolescence. Just as it is only half a car, and driving at sixteen allows for only half freedom, Sam is only a half-adult. Appropriate to the sexual preoccupation of the film, Sam experiences a pseudo-sexual encounter in the car with a freshman admirer. Although he "confesses" to her that he's never "bagged a babe," he at first awkwardly attempts to mount her in the driver's seat, and finally just asks, "Would it be totally off the wall if I asked you to have sex with me?" Sam declines, saying, "I'm saving myself for Jake Ryan." It seems that Sam is still hoping for the ultimate satisfaction of her birthday fantasy, which would more than compensate for the other unfulfilled wishes.

Eventually, Hughes's ending implies the realization of these dreams. Despite misunderstandings and a nearly missed opportunity, Jake—to whom Sam had heretofore never spoken—appears at the last moment to ask her out. In the last scene, the two face each other over a birthday cake glowing with sixteen candles, and Jake advises her to "make a wish." As the music rises, Sam replies, "It already came true." All of the hurt feelings at being forgotten by her parents, all of the insecurities about her body, and all of the frustrations and awkwardness of being a "half-adult" in high school are erased by the validation and approval of the older, mature "man" who realizes she has become a woman. Moreover, with her birthday wishes having "already come true," one does not much wonder whether or not Sam decides to do without the cloud and achieve the estimation of adulthood that she correlates with her sixteenth birthday.

Although the sexual method of coming of age is not explicitly shown in *Sixteen Candles*, the pervasive sexual content and the romantically charged ending fulfill the same end. Probably with maximum marketing potential in mind, Hughes's choice of keeping the explicit visual material out of the film earned it a rating of "PG," making it accessible at the theaters to all ages, as opposed to, for example, *Stealing Beauty*, which carried an "R" rating, making it available to only (theoretically) those viewers over seventeen. Therefore, the on-screen images and dialogue which implicitly condone sex as a viable way of conceiving of adult behavior are available to audiences of adolescents who are that much younger and more impressionable as they construct their attitudes about obtaining their adult identities. At even earlier ages, girls may be induced to consider age sixteen and the romantic and sexual acceptance of a man as a means to escape the problems of adolescence.

There are some films featuring female teen protagonists that are slightly more reflective about the influences that cause girls to view sexuality as an acceptable avenue of maturation; however, they do not seriously question the validity or implications of that message. A notable example is *Mermaids* (1990), starring Cher as a single mother in the 1960s and Winona Ryder—a female teen idol of the early 1990s—as her eldest daughter, Charlotte. Charlotte's mother has a fear of long-term commitments to a job, a home, or a man, and compensates by moving nearly every six months. Although a mother of two girls and ostensibly an adult, her transience, her blatant sexuality, and her frequent but short-lived romances make her a source of embarrassment to her daughter. Charlotte compensates for her mother's behavior with an extreme religious approach, having decided that she wants to be a Catholic nun, even though, as her mother points out, they are Jewish. In an early contrast in the film, Charlotte is shown watching *The Flying Nun* on television while her mother prepares to go out, with the song "Fever" blaring on the radio. Charlotte expresses her feelings about the division between her and her mother, telling her "Sometimes I feel like you're the child and I'm the adult."

Convenient to Charlotte's plans of becoming a nun, her family's newest home is next door to a convent where she observes the nuns living in blissful, asexual simplicity, playing games on the lawn and giggling like children. Although she idealizes this lifestyle, Charlotte is plagued by sexual and romantic thoughts about the attractive and older Joe, a groundskeeper at the convent. She attempts to ward off her feelings toward him and to maintain her purity in thought and deed, but still manages to contrive opportunities to spend time with him. However,

Charlotte is eventually forced to choose between her distaste for her mother's "impure" habits and her desire to assume her own identity as a woman. When she sees her slightly intoxicated mother kissing Joe when he drops her off from a New Year's Eve party, Charlotte "declares war" on her mother for Joe's affections.

A few evenings later, with her mother out for the evening, Charlotte sets into motion her plan for achieving the adult status, which will finally, in her mind, make her and her mother equals—and rivals. Singing the words to "Fever" and drinking several glasses of wine, Charlotte uses her mother's makeup, dresses in one of her mother's form-fitting dresses and sets out to the convent to seduce Joe. Ascending the rather phallic bell tower, she finds the object of her desire, this man who could be possibly ten years her senior, and makes an advance toward him. He responds to her as he would to an adult woman, not like the sixteen-year-old she is, and they have sex in the tower. Although Charlotte is now on an adult level with her mother sexually, her childlike irresponsibility caused her to neglect watching her younger sister, who had meanwhile fallen into a frigid stream. Charlotte's sexual maturation leads to an adult realization of a different kind, namely that actions have consequences.

Even though the little sister recovers, and although Charlotte has decided she will not see Joe again, the whole experience has brought her closer to her mother. She reveals her hurt feelings at her mother's "betrayal" with Joe and, although she takes responsibility for her neglect, essentially blames her sexual encounter and the ensuing accident on the "competition" her mother had created. The two forgive each other and are now able to exchange stories about love and sex. Charlotte abandons her dreams of the convent, her teen angst, and her drab clothes, and becomes a popular girl at her high school, wearing make-up and snug dresses. The film makes it clear that it was a confrontation with her mother's behavior and the emulation of it that led to Charlotte's sexual encounter, but the film also ends with the absence of conflict and a much happier, more confident young woman; obviously sexual behavior has its sources and its consequences, but ultimately, it makes a woman through its validation of an ability to attract the desire of a man and through an acceptance into the ranks of adult (i.e., sexually active) women.

As was shown in the discussion of *Sixteen Candles*, explicit sexual behavior need not be displayed on the screen in order for the film to convey a message advocating sexual validation. Films in which young female protagonists find adulthood through romantic love, which usually translates to marriage, make essentially the same statement. Notions of romantic love and marriage are intimately linked with ideas of sexuality. Romantic love is the result of at least some level of sexual attraction, and marriage is the social, legal, and/or religious sanction of a sexual union. Indeed, Thompson argues that

> girls receive encouragement to fuse sex and love from countless cues, experiences, responses, and stories that construct femininity—from talks of Beauty taming Beast and Cinderella's bringing her prince to his knees . . . . Through [romance] novels—and thousands of movies and songs modeled on the same lines—girls experience the fusion of sex and love that traditional female development through attachment requires.[21]

The notion of romantic love is possibly even more manipulative than sexual content because of its subtlety and the almost universal acceptance of its inclusion in stories for children of every age. Jane D. Brown asserts that "girls continue to be seduced by a romantic myth of heterosexual love that trivializes personal achievement and satisfaction by any other means than through a man."[22] Additionally, media theorist Tania Modleski proposes that the standard romance plot gives "the illusion that femininity will make men grovel with desire, [which] entices girls and women to give up any vision of equality for the chimera of female sexual power. Read this way, the plot of the basic teenage romance . . . leads straight to victimization."[23] In older films or films targeted at children, the realization of romantic love or marriage is frequently used to resolve plot conflicts and questions of coming of age for young girls in place of the sexual act itself.

One of the best-known and very popular stories in which romantic love and marriage result for a young female protagonist is *Cinderella*, a fairy tale long considered appropriate for telling children of the youngest ages. Since 1950 American children have been primarily exposed to this ultimate rags-to-riches love story through the Walt Disney animated version. Indeed, it is probably safe to say that this film figures more or less in the childhood experiences of almost all young girls at least in the United States. In *Cinderella's* opening song, we are informed that this is, indeed, "the sweetest story every told," a cheerful assurance—or perhaps an admonition—to girls that the acceptability and the validity of this fairy tale and its moral need not be questioned. The premise of the film is familiar: A beautiful young girl trapped in servitude to her lazy, selfish, and ugly stepmother and stepsisters is eventually rescued from her situation by a prince who marries her. However, a detail peculiar to the Disney version is the reason for the prince's introduction to Cinderella.

The first time we enter the royal palace, we meet not the prince but his father. The king has decided that it is time for his son to marry, so he plans a ball to contrive the prince's meeting of an appropriate girl. The question is, why is it so important for the prince to marry? It turns out that the motive is the king's personal desire for grandchildren. In delightfully animated sequences we are allowed to experience his dreams and fantasies about bouncing babies on his knee and giving toddlers rides on his back. Therefore, the ball is really an opportunity for the king, through his son, to acquire a brood mare who will provide him with children—and heirs. The individuality of any girl the prince would pick is entirely inconsequential; it is the female ability to reproduce that is the only true requirement.

However, this ulterior motive is quickly masked beneath the notion of romantic love for both the prince and Cinderella. Thus, the invitations for the ball are issued, Cinderella—whose age is never explicitly stated but who appears to be between sixteen and eighteen—makes her first appearance into society and into the pool of women of breeding age, and the prince "falls in love" with her because she is the most beautiful choice in the "pasture." The two are married in the final scene, and with the marriage Cinderella is transformed into a princess, but more importantly into a wife and soon-to-be mother. Under cover of the romanticized version of love and marriage, the more subtle message is that Cinderella's transformation from an unloved, mistreated child—whose value lies in her ability to work at chores—into a beloved adult bride and princess, lies not even in her individual sexuality and body, but in her universal female quality of being able to reproduce. Ostensibly, it is the bearing of children that makes women of value as adults. Ironically, this view of the role of women in society hearkens back to the distinctly nonromantic feudal conception of marriage, an institution necessary to ensure the availability of male heirs and the correct paths of inheritance.

In line with the ideology of Disney's version of *Cinderella* is another, more recent film fairy tale about the coming of age of a young girl: *The Little Mermaid* (1989). It was extremely popular and viewed as a comeback for Disney after a string of less successful films. In fact, *The Little Mermaid* was called by Roger Ebert "a movie so creative and so much fun it deserves comparison with the best Disney work of the past."[24] In addition, the movie was touted by many as breaking the stereotype of the weak, helpless Disney heroine. Ebert says that the female protagonist Ariel "is a fully realized female character who thinks and acts independently, even rebelliously, instead of hanging around passively while the fates decide her destiny. . . She's smart and thinks for herself."[25] Reviewer Hal Hinson of the *Washington Post* remarked that "it's refreshing . . . to see a heroine who has some sense of what she wants and the resources to go after it."[26] However, this popular opinion of the film's stronger message for young girls does not bear up under the weight of a closer look at the messages and imagery which lie beneath the bubbly musical numbers.

It is true that Ariel goes against the wishes of her father by venturing to the surface of the water to find out more about the outside world. However, what seals her decision to go to shore is her encounter with a human male, Eric. The sixteen-year-old mermaid is immediately attracted to the adult prince, exclaiming that "he's so beautiful," musing on "what [she] would give to stay beside [him]," and vowing that "someday I'll be part of your world." Thus, what causes Ariel to act "independently, even rebelliously" is her instantaneous teenage crush on a male and her decision to give up her entire nature as a mermaid to follow him. True, she is not passively letting "the fates decide her destiny"; instead, she is quite actively and willingly giving up her identity for a man.

To this end, Ariel enters into a pact with the evil sea-witch Ursula, who is a clear Satan type, overflowing with seductive encouragement and temptation. With Ariel's introduction to Ursula, there is no doubt that the romantic love she is pursuing as part of her quest to grow up and leave her childhood home in the sea has a sexual coming of age at its heart. As Ariel enters the female octopus's cave, a few moments of film display a brief but unmistakable view of the interior of the cave as an anatomically correct vagina. Throughout the scene, the pink and red folds of the cave serve as a fleshy background. Although this imagery may be almost subliminal, Ursula's demeanor is blatantly sexual. She is drawn as a caricature of an aging madam of a brothel, complete with wild hair, flame-red lipstick, and a black low-cut dress. She is also the only mother figure in the film, as Ariel's own mother is never mentioned. In exchange for her most outstanding feature, her voice, Ursula offers Ariel the opportunity to become human so that she may pursue Eric. As

Ursula points out in her bawdy song, this is not really a problem anyway because it is well known that "she who holds her tongue gets a man." This message is an undiluted statement describing the expected demeanor of women that is long familiar in the socialization of young girls. "As Mary Belenky, Blythe Clinchy, Nancy Goldberger, and Jill Tarule have described, continuing observations suggest that adolescent and adult women silence themselves or are silenced in relationships rather than risk open conflict and disagreement that might lead to isolation or to violence."[27] Ursula, although the villain, provides the most pointed commentary on the message of the film. When Ariel observes that "if I become human, I'll never be with my father or sisters again," Ursula remarks, "But you'll have your man. Life's full of tough choices, isn't it?"

Ultimately, Ariel makes her choice: She follows her man and marries him, giving up her family and her life as a mermaid. At sixteen Ariel becomes an "adult," by departing from the ownership of her father directly into that of her husband, a man she has known for three days. So, for this adolescent female character, being "smart, thinking for herself," and "knowing what she wants" entails following long-standing and socially accepted standards of female behavior. Her fate is not in her own hands, but in that of the traditions of patriarchal society, as is the fate of nearly every character I have discussed so far. The common thread that unites all of these characters is their dependence on some form of sexual or romantic validation in order to bring about their entrance into adulthood.

Peer Acceptance

> "If you want to be able to fuck with the eagles,
> you have to learn how to fly."
>
> —Heather #1 in *Heathers*

These words of wisdom are imparted from Heather #1, the beautiful, poised, immaculately groomed but ruthless high school socialite, to Veronica, a younger, more naive new addition to the most popular clique in the film *Heathers*, the 1989 black comedy directed by Michael Lehmann. This line and the movie as a whole express a recognition of the importance of peer acceptance in coming of age for adolescent girls. To Heather, who also proclaims that she "teaches people about real life," the "eagles" are the upper-crust power cliques of the society that waits outside what she considers the rather banal high school scene. It's "learning how to fly"—learning how best to fit into that society—that is the most important goal of her own teenage experience and that of her elite group of friends, namely two other Heathers and now Veronica. The girls use their own peer group as a training ground for their eventual entry into "real life" by pressuring each other to wear particular clothes, to shun unpopular people, to avoid dating "immature" high school guys, and to engage in "appropriate" activities, such as their afternoon croquet matches.

Indeed, the need to be accepted into a peer group is an element of coming of age for adolescent girls that is stressed in reality and on the big screen. In the teenage years, the peer group becomes more and more important as the teen attempts to distance herself from her childhood, as represented by her family, in order to enter adulthood, as represented by the generation of people who will eventually form her adult society. The desire of adolescents to become part of the emerging identity of their own generation manifests itself in the desire to fit in with one of the groups that will eventually comprise the foundation of their adult world. Susan Moore and Doreen Rosenthal describe the "shift [in adolescence] from a primary orientation to one's family to a reliance on peers for providing guidelines for attitudes and behavior . . . . So, the adolescent learns to locate himself or herself within a network of like-minded and similar others."[28] While still in the context of adolescence, at a time when identity is forming and constantly in transition, teens look to the peer group for structure. Although participation in groups is necessary for living in a society, it is the disproportionately high value placed on acceptance by peers that is problematic in the maturation of adolescents. A perceived necessity to gain the acceptance of a group leads to conformity to the preexisting ideals of that group—literally "fitting in"—thereby stifling development of individual values, attitudes, and beliefs. Sociologist Valerie Hey notes "the 'natural' tendency for girls to institute their friendships through the categories of 'sameness' as 'normality.'"[29] She further remarks that the practices of the girls in her studies "had as their major aim the making of feminine identity or reputation through the axis of conformity to classed sexual codes."[30] Likewise, Thompson concedes that in her studies of girls, "popularity require[d] conforming for the most part."[31] Even so, she emphasizes that "popularity rehearses sociality not intimacy."[32]

In an example from *Heathers*, Veronica asks Heather #3, "If everyone jumped off a bridge, would you?" Heather's honest response is

"probably." Films targeted at adolescent girls routinely portray the overwhelming desire of their characters to gain peer acceptance, a feeling that
is familiar to these viewers. However, what is portrayed as a "happy ending"—namely the protagonist finally finding her place to fit in—
emphasizes that seeking validation from external sources is the pro-
scribed way to achieve maturation. This is equivalent to telling girls that
becoming an adult is all about finding a group with which to jump off the
bridge, when they should be encouraged to find their own way into the
water. Notions of individuality, uniqueness, and the option of avoiding
conformity are ignored in this type of film.

It is in yet another John Hughes film about girls growing up that we
can see the message of peer acceptance played out. *Pretty in Pink* (1986),
like *Sixteen Candles*, stars Molly Ringwald as Andy, another teen girl
looking for love, acceptance, and adulthood. However, this time, as a
child of a working-class family attending an upper-class suburban high
school where peer groups are a strict function of socioeconomic status,
Andy is out of place. Although she has friends with similar backgrounds,
she is subjected to the ridicule of the girls who are from wealthy families
and are therefore popular and accepted. Peer groups collide when Blaine,
a rich boy, falls for her. Both the lower-class teens—represented by
Duckie, Andy's best friend and admirer since childhood—and the upper-
class teens—represented by Blaine's clique—oppose the match, and
Andy is torn. She has strong ties to the lower-class group she has always
known, but that group is "socially unacceptable" within the dominant
group of upper-class teens. Conversely, Andy is impressed with the
wealth of the upper-class teens but disgusted by their decadent partying
and drug use.

The crisis comes with the nearing of the high school prom, that teen
symbol of entry into the adult world beyond high school. When Blaine
bows to the pressure of his friends and breaks his prom date with Andy,
she believes that it is impossible for her ever to find acceptance in the
peer group of the upper-class world. So, in the final scenes, she makes
the bold decision of going alone to the prom, seemingly achieving a
measure of independence by refusing to rely on convention. However, on
her way she encounters Duckie, the symbol of not only her socioeconomic peer group but also of her childhood. Entering the prom with
Duckie, it appears that Andy has decided to "stick to her roots," to accept
the group which has already accepted her, despite its lower status within

her teenage world. However, Andy's evening takes another turn when she encounters Blaine, who has decided to go against the opinions of his own peer group and ask for a second chance with Andy. As she hesitates with her answer, Blaine exits to the parking lot, and she is momentarily caught between two worlds. Will she stay with her childhood friend, someone who has always accepted her, or will she choose to pursue the dominant ideal symbolized by Blaine? Duckie, seeing her decision in her eyes, lets Andy go, saying, "You'd better go get him." Andy's childhood world and her original peer group gracefully bow out, allowing Andy to pursue the possibilities of entering a new group within the "adult" world beyond high school. Andy and Blaine are reunited, and the film ends with a kiss, in typical John Hughes fashion.

The most disappointing aspect of *Pretty in Pink's* resolution is that Andy abandons the sense of self-actualization and independence that initially enabled her to attend the prom alone. Once she actually arrives at the event, she first relies on the safety of her childhood peer acceptance to get her in the door, and then is whisked out again in pursuit of acceptance into a different, seemingly more adult group—which includes the heterosexual romantic love interest. The character who actually risks nonacceptance and acts independently is not our female heroine, but Blaine, the male, whose decision to return to Andy is not based on his desire to be accepted, but on his personal preference for her. Thus, this particular adolescent girl does not so much cross into adulthood herself as she is pulled into it by way of her search for acceptance in the eyes of a male and of a more attractive, dominant social group.

In films in which the theme involves coming of age through being accepted by a peer group, two strains repeatedly appear as a means to achieving that acceptance: the social use of drugs and participation in criminal activities. Films frequently portray these scenarios as a way to show how groups initiate members they are considering for acceptance. Therefore, by an indirect relationship, it may appear that drug use and crime are modes of coming of age in and of themselves. However, the overriding importance of drug use and crime is that they provide a means of joining a certain peer group which incorporates such activities into its group identity. It is still acceptance that the characters crave, not alcohol, drugs, or delinquency.

Drug use as well as sex factor into the coming of age of *Stealing Beauty's* Lucy. In her first few days at the villa, Lucy forms a bond with

Jeremy Irons's character, who is a member of the adult community. As they exchange stories late one night, they also share a joint. Irons's character remarks to Lucy that "there's nothing more transporting [than sex], I seem to remember; except perhaps good grass." This marks the beginning of her evolving acceptance into a group of adults, who prior to this only remember her as the quiet fourteen-year-old daughter of a friend. Even so, it is Lucy's lack of experience with sex that keeps her as an outsider to this group. However, in a scene mid-way through the film, Lucy and a group of people her own age are depicted in friendly conversation, drinking wine and sharing marijuana. This bonding experience initiates Lucy's acceptance into the society of those in her own generation, and it is ultimately with one of the young men in this group with whom she has her first sexual experience. Thus, it is Lucy's use of drugs that introduces her to and connects her with a peer group that will eventually provide her with the opportunity of truly coming to adulthood through sex.

Not surprisingly, John Hughes uses a shared drug experience in one of his most popular teen films, 1985's *The Breakfast Club*, which he both directed and wrote. The film groups five teens from different high school clique stereotypes—the "athlete" (played by Emilio Estevez), the popular and rich "princess" (Molly Ringwald), the "brain" (Anthony Michael Hall), the "criminal" (Judd Nelson), and the "basket case" (Ally Sheedy)—in Saturday detention. Conflict initially arises among the students, who under any other circumstances would never associate with one another. Against their own inclinations, the five are forced to interact, and they eventually band together to retrieve a bag of marijuana from the criminal's locker. In the film's pivotal scene, the five discuss parents, sex, and popularity over several joints. It is the influence of the drug as well as their mutual conformity to a peer norm of drug use set by the criminal, the dominant teen in the group, which allows them to break down the barriers between their cliques to form a group of their own. When Sheedy raises the question, "will we still be friends on Monday?" it at first seems that the answer has to be "no." However, the teens grow closer throughout the day, and by the end of the film, the princess is romantically paired with the criminal, and the basket case ends up with the athlete.

The maturation experience for this group is achieved when they are able to recognize their commonalties as peers and to disregard the stereotypes that separate them. Additionally, it is interesting to note that in the teen world of John Hughes, the roles available for females are either the spoiled, rich princess or the basket case, both of whom confess themselves to be virgins. In the scenario of *The Breakfast Club*, the two unite only to pursue their romantic interests, with the princess giving the basket case a makeover, and the basket case providing the princess with the courage to approach the boy she desires. Again, it was clearly the peer bonding provided by the common drug experience that allowed the clique distinctions to be even temporarily removed to allow the "Breakfast Club" to take shape.

A film that combines both drug use and crime as modes of peer group formation is the 1996 release *Foxfire*. Like *The Breakfast Club*, this film centers on the development of a temporary peer group comprised of five girls who would be unlikely friends. Madeline, an artistically gifted student; Rita, a shy loner; Violet, the class tramp; Goldie, a drug-addicted rich kid; and "Legs," a mysterious and angry young drifter initially unite in a physical assault on a lecherous, predatory male teacher, an act that causes them to be suspended from school. The first emotional bond between the girls occurs when Madeline seeks Legs at her temporary home in an abandoned house in the woods. There she tells Legs of her suspension, and the two share a bottle of whiskey. The next time all five girls meet, they decide to commit another crime, breaking into the school at night to retrieve Madeline's art portfolio. Accidentally setting off a fire alarm, the girls are chased by the police but escape back to the abandoned house. High on the adrenaline of the incident, they tattoo themselves in a ritual that is facilitated through sharing marijuana and a bottle of whiskey.

The girls are now bound to one another by their complicity in two criminal offenses and in their almost ceremonial use of drugs and alcohol. The next few weeks are documented in a montage of the group hanging out together, drinking and using drugs, and stealing a car from a group of jocks, which ends in a police chase and a car accident. Despite the consequences, this string of drug use and crime only further cements the attachment of the girls to one another. Finally, in a misguided attempt to aid the heroine-addicted Goldie, the girls engineer an armed kidnapping of Goldie's father, but things spin out of control when Rita slips and accidentally shoots him in the shoulder. At this point there is a group crisis as Madeline and Legs struggle for control of the situation. Legs's anger at men in general mounts until she seems ready to kill Goldie's father, while Madeline becomes the voice of reason. Ultimately Madeline prevails, and the father is saved, but Legs leaves town quickly. Madeline's voice-over in the final scene explains that "the rest of us have drifted, but we still embrace when we meet—veterans of a sort." Indeed, the formation of a peer group through an initial act of cooperative delinquency allowed the girls to find unique acceptance in acting out "teenage wildness." Moreover, their experiences also caused them to mature to the point where they could realize that abandoning themselves completely to that wildness can have destructive consequences. The girls are "veterans" of a common coming of age in which they learned both the "freedom" of crime and the responsibility of its consequences in the context of a facilitating peer group.

The depiction of the peer acceptance that results from a common involvement in drug use and crime is a tempting idea for teens, as they are likely to be attracted to acts that serve as a rebellion against society and parents and as an identification with others their own age. Whether crime and the use of drugs are viewed as a means to peer group formation or as events in themselves, there is an obvious physical and social danger in portraying them as options for rites of passage into adulthood.

There are films that examine and reverse the message of the importance of peer acceptance in the maturation process. Surprisingly, the glam, deliberately faddish and highly successful film *Clueless* (1995), directed by Amy Heckerling, which popularized the sayings "as if" and "whatever," is one of these. The film's protagonist is Cher (played by Alicia Silverstone), who is the epitome of the affluent, popular, trendsetting fifteen-year-old and whose primary pastimes are shopping and obsessing over her appearance. As a friend remarks, "Cher's main thrill in life is a makeover." Following the story line of Jane Austen's *Emma*, from which *Clueless* was adapted, Cher takes on the new girl at school as her pet project, determining to overhaul "Ty's" behavior and appearance in order to gain admittance for her to the popular clique. However, this plan works too well, and Ty becomes even more popular than Cher. This combines with Cher's growing awareness of her own shallowness and lack of social consciousness, and culminates in the flunking of her driving test. When she fights with Ty, who terms her "a virgin who can't drive," Cher hits rock bottom and realizes that she is the one who is "clueless"—about her values, her beliefs, and her surroundings. She discovers that popularity and peer acceptance are fickle and transitory and have not led her to any kind of identity formation, uniqueness, or maturation; they have not even provided her with "adult" experience—in sex or in driving. With this revelation, and since she is no longer the center of her peer group, Cher begins to spend time at home and on community volunteer projects. Ultimately, she finds that through the cultivation of her unique interests, talents, and qualities, she is able to provide herself with the validation that her peers, sex, or even a driver's license could not. In the end, Cher is a more self-aware, socially aware, and mature teenager, with her coming of age resulting from her rejection of the importance of societal and peer validation.

Like *Clueless*, *Heathers* questions the need for peer acceptance and conformity in coming of age, but with a darker, satirical edge. The film constructs a world of extremes and a group of girls within which conformity is at first the only pathway to acceptance for Veronica, the young female protagonist. In the film's opening, we see the girls exhibiting their "refinement" by playing an afternoon croquet match, always sure to walk in step with one another. However, the illusion of this socially harmonious, polite world is immediately called into question with a shot of the girls walking through a flower bed, deliberately crushing the flowers under foot. Suddenly their timed steps look less like the walk of decorous girls and more like the march of trained soldiers. When we learn that three of the four girls are named "Heather," the feeling of sinister sameness increases.

There is a clear leader of the pack, Heather #1, who is consistent in her efforts to remind herself and her friends that they are far superior to their high-school classmates. She is also quick to inform people that they need "to grow up" and to remind her friends of the favor she is doing them. "You were playing with Barbie before I met you. You were a Bluebird, a Brownie, a girl scout cookie," she tells Veronica. Heather #1 also ensures that none of the girls associate with anyone from a lower popularity rung and is sure to make arrangements to party with the far more acceptable college crowd. However, at these "cooler parties," she inevitably ends up performing oral sex on a relative stranger, paying her dues, in a sense, for the superior status of the party scene and for the acceptance of the older crowd. The audience is not left to assume, though, that Heather is unaware of her complicity in her slavery to popularity, acceptance, and "growing up." We are shown Heather in a rare moment alone, gazing at her reflection in the mirror. Suddenly, a disgusted look comes over her face, and she angrily spits at her image. Even at the peak of the popularity game, her self-loathing can only cause her to question its rules.

Veronica's voice-over narration reveals directly to the audience her distaste for the society she has created with her popular friends. Writing in her diary, Veronica confesses that she thinks frequently about killing Heather #1 and prays to go to sleep and "dream of a world without Heather." By this point the film's symbolism is becoming clear: Heather represents the most rigid standards and hypocrisies of a society that raises its youths to believe in the dire need for conformity and peer acceptance as well as the urgency of passing out of adolescence as quickly as possible. Veronica is a youth herself, caught between her hatred of society and her fear of being expelled from it. This is the dilemma when Veronica meets the new boy at school, Jason Dean (played by Christian Slater), who dresses all in black and sticks closely to his cynical air about the superficiality he perceives all around him. "Seven different states, seven different high schools, and the only thing that changes is my locker combination," he comments. The significance of his name, with its similarity to "James Dean," and of his initials, which are common slang for "juvenile delinquent," are blatant and mark him as the symbol of rebellion and anti-establishment views. He is the "Other" to Veronica's socially structured world, and she falls in love with him as an outlet for her own contempt, symbolically joining herself to his ideology and directly controverting the mandate of the Heathers by having sex with him—in the middle of the croquet lawn.

However, things take an extreme turn when Jason decides to help Veronica realize her secret wish to escape societal conformity, i.e., to kill Heather and others like her. Then, when Jason engineers three deaths, Veronica is forced to question whether breaking from society's mold requires that mold to be literally exterminated. The final crisis comes when Veronica discovers Jason's plot to blow up the entire high school. Believing that "the school is society," he desires to take his anti-establishment beliefs to their ultimate end, envisioning a way to "clean the slate" by creating "a Woodstock for the 80s [where] burning bodies will be the ultimate protest."

Veronica finally realizes that, despite the imperfections of society, its annihilation is not the answer. In a last minute struggle with Jason, she gets him to remove the bomb from the school, and then she watches while he blows himself up. Ironically, this all occurs on the day of the prom, and still black from the explosion of Jason, she approaches an overweight, handicapped girl, one of the "untouchables" of the teen social scene. "My prom date kinda flaked out on me," she says. "You want to rent some new releases and pop some popcorn?"

Finally Veronica achieves a personal balance between the two extremes which confronted her: She rejects the notions of social conformity by rejecting the prom and the teen caste system of popularity, yet she also disavows the need to destroy society because of its flaws. Rather, she chooses an individual place in the middle, one in which she remains within a societal framework but behaves according to her personal preferences and value judgments. *Heathers* succeeds as a carefully constructed allegory that comments on the extreme models of society, ultimately advocating the path of the individual, who is, in this case, a female.

Performances

> "You want to ride your race, take your risks, and win?
> You want to win over them all, in sight of the world,
> Velvet Brown before the king and queen, is that it?"
>
> —Mickey Rooney to Elizabeth Taylor in *National Velvet*

Velvet's answer in the affirmative to this question determines the climax of *National Velvet* and can also serve as a model for a particular type of female coming-of-age film that occupies a unique place within the bounds of my argument. I have argued that films that depict external validation and social acceptance as the key to maturation are problematic to the development of female teens; however, films that focus on performances or public displays of individual talent deal with this message in a different way. There is a subgenre of films targeted toward preadolescent and adolescent girls that depicts the rise to recognition of their female protagonists through the use of some special talent or skill. Themes of coming of age are frequently tied into the story line, demonstrating the power of the process by which one conceives of a dream, strives toward it while facing obstacles, and eventually achieves it. Almost by definition, such a story must involve social recognition and validation, for a performance necessarily demands an audience; without consumers for a display of talent, performers go unnoticed. While this recognition is not strictly necessary—a talent may very well exist to enrich the experience of only its possessor—it is not obviously negative either. Moreover, filmic versions of talent stories emphasize the importance and positive nature of performance by creating a "follow your dreams" theme. Typically, the protagonists possess a burning desire to do something or to be recognized for a particular quality, and this drives them to overcome all obstacles to achieve that affirmation of their abilities. Thus, while they are seeking a public outlet and social validation for their talents, they are also in the process of achieving an individual goal which is important to their own sense of self-worth. This emphasis on actively striving toward a personal goal may be viewed as a positive message for girls to receive during adolescence, for it encourages them to take themselves seriously, to value their dreams, and to believe in their ability to pursue and realize them successfully.

As alluded to above, *National Velvet,* directed by Clarence Brown and released in 1944, portrays this search for simultaneous personal and social validation. The film tells the story of twelve-year-old Velvet Brown (played by Elizabeth Taylor), a British girl with an all-consuming love of horses and a great knack for handling them, who dreams "all day and all night about horses." She says of herself, "I want to be a famous rider; I should like to hunt, to ride to hounds; I should like to race." Velvet's goals are specific and passionate, and she seems confident of her ability in achieving them as soon as the right opportunity comes along. Upon acquiring her dream horse, she contrives to enter him in the prestigious and grueling Grand National Steeplechase. Despite the pessimism, discouragement, and skepticism of her family and friends, Velvet refuses to be denied and trains tirelessly. Eventually Velvet and her horse arrive in London, where Velvet decides to ride in the race herself, proclaiming that she wants to win along with her horse. Her trainer asks her, "So now it's the glory of winning you want for yourself, is that it?" and Taylor, as Velvet, gives an unhesitating nod, practically glowing with confidence and a sense of her own self-worth. To her, riding and winning are the ultimate proof of her belief in her horse and in herself.

After a lengthy but intense sequence of shots showing the dangers of the race and the skill of the jockeys—a visual metaphor for the "race of life" into which Velvet has entered herself by bringing her ambitions to a public forum—she wins the Grand National, thereby bringing her dreams to reality. Although officially disqualified as the winner because of her gender, Velvet is a heroine in the popular opinion, and more importantly, in her own opinion. Therefore, we are presented with a female character who finds validation in both the societal view and in her own sight by the public display of her dreams. Although it is not assumed that Velvet is now an adult as a result of this experience, her fierce devotion to attaining a high goal may be viewed as an important development in her adolescence. As Velvet's mother told her, "Win or lose, it's all the same; it's how you take it that counts, and knowing when to let go, knowing when it's over and time to move on to the next thing." Clearly Velvet's dream has come to a successful end, and she can now move on to the next stage—and dream—of her life.

With the 1991 film *Wild Hearts Can't Be Broken,* directed by Steve Miner, we see a more contemporary horse movie, a true story about Sonora Webster, another "girl who dared to live her dreams," to quote the opening titles. Set in the Depression era South, the film begins with the tomboyish Sonora running away from home. Intrigued by an ad that reads "Young Girls Needed for Diving Horses; Must Be Willing to Travel," she arrives at a local carnival to apply. Although Sonora has both the riding ability and the courage to dive the horses off a high platform into a pool of water, Dr. Carver, the owner of the show, tells her "You're too young and puny to be a diving girl." However, he reluctantly hires her as a stable hand, and Sonora, enticed by the applause of an audience, becomes determined that she will one day be a performer with the diving horses. Eventually Carver trains Sonora, and she goes on to become a popular diving girl, realizing her dream of performing.

At long last, she is offered a contract at Atlantic City's Steel Pier. Approaching the pier, Sonora has a point of view shot of the huge billboard that reads "Where Your Dreams Come True," a very apt sentiment in her case. Another form of coming of age also enters in at this point, as she accepts the marriage proposal of Carver's son, Al. However, tragedy strikes during her first dive, when she is startled and leaves her eyes open as she hits the water. Her retinas are damaged and she goes blind. After a brief period of despair, Sonora decides she must perform again, both for herself and the show. In scenes parallel to her original training, Sonora relearns mounting and riding with the additional challenge of her blindness. In the climax of the film, Sonora ascends the ladder to the platform, makes the dive, and emerges from the pool in dramatic slow motion to thunderous applause. In closing, she remarks in a voiceover that, "I found my destiny not in far away places, but within myself." As in *Na-*

tional Velvet, the validation that comes from the public's recognition of a special ability is intimately linked to the self-validation of the girl. The personal journey of striving toward a dream and overcoming obstacles is foregrounded, and social approval is included as merely secondary to that end.

An excellent model of how performance of a talent coincides with the coming of age of an adolescent female appears in *Little Women*, a Civil War era story popularized in its original telling in Louisa May Alcott's novel and in four film adaptations. I based my observations on the most recent version, released in 1994 and directed by Gillian Armstrong. *Little Women* details the lives of the daughters of the March family, centering on Jo, the spunky, tomboyish middle sister (played by Winona Ryder). Jo's primary passion in life is writing, and she frequently stays up late into the night penning action/adventure melodramas for her sisters to perform, while cherishing the idea of one day being published. Indeed, she loves the thrill of performance in general, proclaiming that "If I weren't going to be a writer, I'd go to New York to pursue the stage!" In contrast with her other sisters—Meg, who is preoccupied with dreams of marriage; Amy, who wants to be rich above all else; and Beth, whose happiness lies in caring for her family—Jo has a career goal and is fully confident in her ability to achieve it. Furthermore, Jo is so focused on her dream of a career that she is almost incapable of understanding the goals for adulthood her other sisters have set, goals that were more socially acceptable for women of the day. For example, upon learning of Meg's engagement, she laments, "Why do we have to get married? Why can't everything stay the same?" Critic Ruth Goldstein comments that "Jo's gloves, Jo's dress, Jo's hair, Jo's manners were unwomanly, but even in Miss Alcott's lifetime, Jo's mentality was acknowledged to be the most interesting in the novel."[33] It appears that even women of the nineteenth century were drawn to a female character who did not conform to typical paradigms for women.

When Jo decides to go to New York City to realize her dream of living as a writer, she remarks that she "stepped over the boundary from childhood into all that lay beyond." However, she and her writing only truly develop when Beth falls ill and dies. Jo's reaction to her profound grief is to write the stories of triumph and tragedy of her own family. Not only does the experience prove cathartic, but Jo is able to explore the substance of her childhood to discover who she is and how she became that person and to develop her true voice as a writer. It is this introspective experience that forms her actual coming of age, and when her family memoirs are published, she achieves the external validation she had been seeking. Therefore, Jo's process of striving toward her personal goal of being publicly recognized for her writing leads to an introspective maturation and adult identity formation that allow her to enter into traditional adult society as represented by her marriage. Ultimately, as Goldstein observes, "For all its quaintness, *Little Women* lays less stress on being ladylike than on being human."[34] As in the case of *Clueless*, *National Velvet*, and *Wild Hearts Can't Be Broken*, Jo's unique journey from childhood to adulthood serves as an alternative to portrayals of sexual validation and the all-consuming desire for peer acceptance.

Alternatives

> Despite its obvious dependence on the young, the American film industry has been spectacularly unsuccessful in depicting adolescence.[35]
>
> —David M. Considine, film theorist

Examination of films about female adolescents gives particular validity to Considine's remark. During my research I became overwhelmed by the dearth of positive or even original depictions of coming of age for girls. I tended to agree with Goldstein, who comments on the vast number of films that "tell twice-told tales about children and adolescence. They have been made to conform, in small ways or large, to the stereotypes. Their authors or directors or producers have not learned . . . that in life, 'There are no types, no plurals.'"[36] However, when I looked hard enough, I eventually discovered that since 1990 or so, films that present an alternative way of depicting stories about adolescent females seem to have been slowly pushing themselves to the surface amidst the flood of mainstream formula films. These are films "made not by manufacturers of products, but by artists . . . [who give] us sensitive, truthful, sometimes overwhelming pictures of childhood and adolescence."[37]

A strong example of such films is the 1991 release, *Gas Food Lodging*, directed by Allison Anders. The film intricately weaves together diverse influences from family dramas, romances, Westerns, feminism, Chicano culture, and coming of age themes to produce a quietly expressive film about the complexity of personal experience and the frequent incompatibility between expectations and reality. Set in a small desert town in New Mexico, *Gas Food Lodging* focuses on the lives of a single mother and her two teenage daughters, Trudi and Shade. The younger daughter, Shade, is the central character, a fifteen-year-old who spends her free afternoons immersed in melodramatic Spanish films starring Elvia Rivero, her favorite actress, who she says "could put into words everything I was thinking." However, the world on the movie screen is significantly different from Shade's own life, where she lives in a trailer park with her divorced waitress mother and Trudi, her hot-tempered, promiscuous older sister. Her only memories of her father are contained on a ribbon of film from a home movie. Rapidly maturing and inspired by the romantic images of Elvia Rivero, Shade wishes to experiment with male-female relationships herself, namely with regard to her best friend, Darius. Role models in that department, however, are conflicting and few. Although she idolizes the fiery and sensual Elvia, her example is not exactly practical for Shade's life. Moreover, her mother bears such a bitter grudge against Shade's father and her other failed relationships that she hasn't even dated in over two years and in Shade's view "just hates men." Trudi is reckless in her encounters with men, seemingly unfazed by her numerous one-night stands.

When Shade decides she is ready to approach Darius, she tries to follow Trudi's advice of becoming Darius's "dream woman"—Olivia Newton John—and to "throw him down and make him want you." Dressed in a blond wig, silver sequined shorts, and platform shoes, Shade attempts an awkward seduction. It apparently never occurred to her that he might be gay, despite some rather stereotypical signs. Darius gently rebuffs her advances, and she flees in humiliation to a nearby curb. There she has her first meaningful encounter with Javier, a Chicano youth. Attempting to make friends, he tells her, "I like the way you normally dress . . . . I liked your hair before just fine." When she removes her wig to show her natural hair, he responds enthusiastically with "*That's* the stuff."

So, in a matter of minutes, Shade goes from a rejection of her attempt to mimic popular standards of attractiveness to a sincere affirmation of her own unique qualities. This experience does not correspond with either her sister's advice or her mother's distrust of men. As a result, her interest in Javier grows, despite the fact that her female friend is plainly disdainful of him, stereotyping him based on his ethnicity as a "*cholo*, pure gangster. They deal dope; they kill each other for fun; they gang rape girls."

Meanwhile, various other upheavals and contradictions impact what Shade has long regarded as givens in her life. Trudi falls in love with a man who is genuinely interested in her, but soon finds herself pregnant and him mysteriously missing. Disillusioned once again, Trudi's love turns to hatred and mistrust of all men. At the same time, Shade's mother finds herself losing her cynicism toward men and falling for a young, kind satellite dish installer. Finally, Shade meets her father, who has moved back to town, and finds out that he is neither the monster her mother has always made him out to be nor the prince charming she herself fantasized that he could be. In this tumultuous world, Shade is at a loss to define herself in terms of her culture, her friends, or her family because of the wide divergence between them and her own experiences and beliefs. So, atypically, instead of following the example or advice of anyone close to her, she learns to follow her own intuitions and to determine the truth of things for herself.

This theme is beautifully dramatized in a scene in which Shade visits Javier at home. She meets his mother, who is deaf, but who can dance gracefully and rhythmically by feeling the vibrations in her feet. Javier and his mother pull Shade into their dancing, teaching her to dance to a rhythm that is not heard but felt, just as she is constructing her own identity by learning to rely on what she feels within herself, not on the "music" of the world around her. The afternoon ends with a tender encounter between Javier and Shade during which he speaks in flowing Spanish, which she cannot necessarily literally interpret, but from which she can understand his confessions of love. Again, she must rely on what she feels and understands from context, not on what is overtly said. Her relationship with Javier facilitates her discovery of herself, for as she said "it was like we'd finally met our twin . . . . In his arms I knew who I was: Shade, just Shade, and that was enough."

In the final scenes of the film, Shade again discovers that what often seems apparent is not always what is true. Stopping at a roadside rock stand, Shade learns that Trudi's lover had not abandoned her but that he was killed in an avalanche. The film ends as Shade walks into the desert, playing on the Western motif of the lone cowboy riding into the sunset. Although she is walking alone with a newfound maturity and understanding of her world, Shade's journey will take her home to a community in which she has both an identity of her own construction and people who love her. The adolescent female heroine has come of age, but by means of observing and experiencing life and various people's interpretations of life and then by thoughtfully determining what aspects she wishes to add to herself. The film does not just question but excludes the typical paradigms of female coming-of-age films, creating instead a complex tapestry of experiences and influences which is arguably more representative of the nature of individual realities.

Another recent film that attempts to change the way in which adolescents' stories are told is *Welcome to the Dollhouse*, which won the Grand Prize at the 1995 Sundance Film Festival, and which critic Barry Walters of the *San Francisco Examiner* described as "perhaps the only true-to-life film ever made about the seventh grade."[38] With similar praise, *New York Times* reviewer Janet Maslin reported that *Welcome to the Dollhouse* "displays wrenching emotional acuity."[39] Throughout the course of the film, twelve-year-old Dawn Wiener is subjected to perhaps more than her share of the tortures of middle school. Among her peers she is unpopular and a target for insults like "Wiener dog," "Dogface," and even "Lesbo." Asking one particularly menacing girl, "Why do you hate me?" she gets the response, "Because you're ugly." However, in keeping with social and media paradigms pushing peer acceptance, Dawn is "far from hating the bullying peers who pick on her; she simply wants to belong."[40]

Dawn's teachers ignore her or punish her when she asks for help, telling her she has "no dignity." With her parents, Dawn feels neglected and betrayed, considering that the majority of their attention is focused on her "adorable" six-year-old sister. In terms of boys, Dawn again follows the typical social and cinematic advice, and "she picks two impossible boys with whom to prove her self-worth."[41] She has the choice of either Steve Rogers, the seventeen-year-old object of her crush, who she is told, "will go all the way with anyone . . . as long as she's a girl and willing"; or Brandon, a boy her own age who forces her to go to an abandoned house with him under threat of rape, but then who really just wants to kiss her for the first time and to have someone to talk to.

Even Dawn's external appearance—all pastel shorts and kittycat shirts—is at odds with her inner self, which listens to heavy metal music when she does things like severing the heads of Barbie dolls and smashing a video tape of her sister. *Welcome to the Dollhouse* is more a montage of adolescence than a narrative of a path through it. Dawn merely strives to cope with her humiliations as they come, to endure her family and school, and to attempt to discover any significance.

Dawn finally asks her older brother if eighth grade is any better than seventh. "No," he replies matter-of-factly. "What about ninth?" she asks. "All of junior high school sucks," he says. However, he relents somewhat with the observation that high school is "better." "They'll call you names, but not as much to your face."

The film ends without a true climax, merely with Dawn on a bus trip to Disney World with the school chorus. The girls are singing as they travel, and as the camera closes in on Dawn in her bus seat, the voices of the other girls fade out, leaving only Dawn's immature but clear soprano as the screen fades to black. There is no packaged conclusion, no resolution of Dawn's adolescent issues, no real hope for the future beyond the weak promise of a more subtle torture in high school and a somewhat reassuring sense that Dawn is developing a lone but distinct "voice." The message is a realistic one, namely that there is no path through adolescence that culminates at a huge billboard proclaiming the entrance to adulthood. Adolescence is shown to be not a linear process beginning at age eleven and ending when a particular act is completed—such as sex or initiation into a group—or when a certain realization is made. Rather, life is presented quite accurately as a motley assortment of events, some progressive, some regressive. As Walters puts it, *Welcome to the Dollhouse* is "a horror film starring reality in the monster role."[42] Indeed, the cinematic reality created in this film comes closest to representing the experiences of actual adolescent girls by completely deconstructing the entire notion of "coming of age" as an event, replacing it with a far more complex and less definite process.

Conclusions

> The making of oneself as a girl is thus not an easy thing,
> but an activity fraught with all sorts of
> ambivalences and contradictions.[43]
>
> —Valerie Hey, sociologist

Hey's statement rings true enough in the context of her exploration of the real-life influences on girls as they struggle through adolescence. However, her words have special meaning when one begins to account for the millions of media influences ingested by young females during their transitional years between childhood and adulthood. Particular messages are continuously repeated and become conventional and therefore almost

invisible beneath relatively minor variations in actresses, plots, characterizations, and settings.

From film to film, the general ideology remains stable: As a female,
receiving acceptance and approval from those around you is the key to
happiness and is the only way to survive in the teen or the adult world.
The self is important only in its relation to social standards of acceptability. Films not only present this general directive, but simultaneously provide specific avenues by which to reach this state. Sex and romantic love
are shown as physical and social rites of passage that demonstrate the
girl's acceptance of her role in patriarchal society. Finding peer approval
is depicted as a means of providing the girl with a group in which to ori-
ent herself for the negotiation of adolescence and eventually adulthood,
with alcohol and drug use or criminal activity often being necessary for
initiation. Performing for an approving audience, though perhaps the realization of a personal goal, is glorified as the supreme validation for talent or hard work.

It is at the point of interaction between these glamorized, fictional
realities with the personal realities of the particular female adolescent
viewer that the ambivalences and contradictions arise. How do screen
scenarios compare to the real experiences of girls? How do cinematic
directives compare to girls' individual beliefs, values, morals, and preferences? Ultimately, who wins out, the individual or the media? Sociological research seems to indicate that, especially with girls, films often
have the upper hand. However, the familiar question also arises: Is the
relationship between girls and film a case of life imitating art or art imitating life? Perhaps this question is unanswerable, for as Considine
points out, "As we gaze into the mirror of youth [on screen] it is necessary to keep in mind that the images we see, the plots we encounter, the
recurring themes and motifs that unfold, reflect not simply the views and
values of the audience, not only the attitudes and ideas of the film creators, and not just the social conditions of the day, but an intricate and
interwoven association of all these factors."[44]

Thus, although it is easy merely to state that a change must be made
in the messages young girls receive from the media, and it is also relatively easy to describe what changes need to be made, the real problem
becomes determining where they need to be made. Will filmmakers per-
ceive the need to represent the uniqueness of female adolescent life? A
small minority has answered and will answer "yes," but the general an-

swer is likely to be "not as long as the stereotypes are what sell." An even more unsettling question is, can uniqueness, by its very definition, be represented in traditional forms of narrative and the media? Conversely, is society able—or willing—to teach girls to recognize the problematic discrepancies between mainstream film images and their own beliefs and experiences? Again, a small minority will answer "yes," while the majority will still feel compelled to turn their eyes to the neatly packaged happy endings flickering on the screen.

Changing deeply entrenched cultural stereotypes and conventional modes of cinematic representation can only occur through a slow process of action and reaction between film reality and human reality. Jane Brown proposes this relationship, noting that "since girls do use media as they learn more about available options and cultural expectations, the media could play an important role in creating alternative life scripts, especially if we also encourage girls to continue to listen and speak their own minds."[45] Fortunately, there have been some filmmakers and some young women on the margins of the dominant discourse who have taken and are taking the first steps in this process. The work of effecting a positive change on the interaction between girls and film takes on a sense of great urgency when we fully examine just how fragile and important are the emerging identities, the confidence, and the self-value of adolescent girls.

Girls on the screen and in reality can and do subvert the dominant paradigms that have been prepared for them by society. The frequency with which they do this and the probability of their arrival at positive, self-affirming identities is a movement that must be engineered and encouraged by parents, filmmakers, sociologists, politicians, and the girls themselves—and then must be relentlessly advanced into society at large.

Notes

1. Susan Moore and Doreen Rosenthal, *Sexuality in Adolescence* (London: Routledge, 1993), 30.

2. Sharon Thompson, *Going All the Way: Teenage Girls' Tales of Sex, Romance, and Pregnancy* (New York: Hill and Wang, 1995), 42. Cited from Carol Gilligan, *In a Different Voice: Psychological Theory and Women's Development* (Cambridge, MA: Harvard UP, 1982).

3. Moore and Rosenthal, 31.

4. Bradley S. Greenberg, Jane D. Brown, and Nancy L. Buerkel-Rothfuss, *Media, Sex, and the Adolescent* (Cresskill, NJ: Hampton Press, Inc., 1993), 45.

5. See Greenberg et al.

6. Greenberg et al., 56.

7. Richard Allen, *Projecting Illusion: Film Spectatorship and the Impression of Reality* (Cambridge: Cambridge UP, 1995), 2.

8. Greenberg et al., 245.

9. Jon Lewis, *The Road to Romance and Ruin* (New York: Routledge, 1992), 3.

10. David M. Considine, *The Cinema of Adolescence* (London: McFarland, 1985), 3.

11. Considine, 2–3.

12. Lyn Mikel Brown and Carol Gilligan, *Meeting at the Crossroads: Women's Psychology and Girls' Development* (Cambridge, MA: Harvard UP, 1992), 2.

13. Brown and Gilligan, 6.

14. Moore, x.

15. Moore, 38.

16. Mike Brake, *The Sociology of Youth Culture and Youth Subculture* (London: Routledge and Kegan Paul, 1980), 145.

17. Thompson, 20.

18. Thompson, 5.

19. Greenberg et al., 193.

20. Thompson, 19. Citing Sandra L. Hofferth, Joan R. Kahn, and Wendy Baldwin. "Premarital Sexual Activity Among U.S. Teenage Women over the Past Three Decades," *Family Planning Perspectives,* 19.2 (Mar./Apr. 1987): 47.

21. Thompson, 44–45.

22. Greenberg et al., 194.

23. Thompson, 45. Citing Tania Modleski. *Loving with a Vengeance: Mass Produced Fantasies for Women* (New York: Methuen, 1982).

24. Roger Ebert, *Chicago Sun-Times*, 17 November 1989. http://www.suntimes.com /ebert.

25. Ebert.

26. Hal Hinson, *The Washington Post,* 17 November 1989. http://www.washington post. com.

27. Brown, 3.

28. Moore, xi.

29. Valerie Hey, *The Company She Keeps: An Ethnography of Girls' Friendship* (Philadelphia: Open University Press, 1997), 130.

30. Hey.

31. Thompson, 55.

32. Thompson, 77.

33. Ruth M. Goldstein and Edith Zornow, *The Screen Image of Youth: Movies about Children and Adolescents* (Metuchen, NJ: Scarecrow, 1980), 312.

34. Goldstein and Zornow.

35. Considine, 9.

36. Goldstein and Zornow, xviii.

37. Goldstein and Zornow.

38. Barry Walters, *San Francisco Examiner*, 31 May 1996, http://www.sfgate.com.

39. Janet Maslin, *New York Times*, 22 March 1996, http://www.nytimes.com.

40. Peter Stack, *San Francisco Chronicle*, 31 May 1996, http://www.sfgate.com.

41. Stack.

42. Walters.

43. Hey, vii.

44. Considine, 11.

45. Greenberg, 194–95.

Bibliography

Allen, Richard. *Projecting Illusion: Film Spectatorship and the Impression of Reality*. Cambridge: UP, 1995.

Brake, Mike. *The Sociology of Youth Culture and Youth Subculture*. London: Routledge and Kegan Paul, 1980.

The Breakfast Club. Dir. John Hughes. Perf. Molly Ringwald, Ally Sheedy, Judd Nelson, Emilio Estevez. Paramount, 1985.

Brown, Lyn Mikel, and Carol Gilligan. *Meeting at the Crossroads: Women's Psychology and Girls' Development*. Cambridge, MA: Harvard UP, 1992.

Cinderella. Dir. Wilfred Jackson. Voices: Ilene Woods, William Phipps, Verna Felton, James MacDonald. Disney, 1950.

Clueless. Dir. Amy Heckerling. Perf. Alicia Silverstone, Stacey Dash, Brittany Murphy. Paramount, 1995.

Considine, David M. *The Cinema of Adolescence*. London: McFarland, 1985.

Ebert, Roger, *Chicago Sun-Times*, 17 November 1989, http://www.suntimes.com/ebert.

Ferris Bueller's Day Off. Dir. John Hughes. Perf. Matthew Broderick, Mia Sara, Alan Ruck, Jeffrey Jones, Jennifer Grey. Paramount, 1986.

Foxfire. Dir. Annette Haywood-Carter. Perf. Hedy Burress, Angelina Jolie. Samuel Goldwyn Co., USA, 1996.

Gas Food Lodging. Dir. Allison Anders. Perf. Brooke Adams, Ione Skye. IRS Media, 1991.

Goldstein, Ruth M., and Edith Zornow. *The Screen Image of Youth: Movies about Children and Adolescents*. Metuchen, NJ: Scarecrow, 1980.

Good Will Hunting. Dir. Gus Van Sant. Perf. Ben Affleck, Matt Damon, Robin Williams. Miramax, 1997.

Greenberg, Bradley S., Jane D. Brown, and Nancy L. Buerkel-Rothfuss. *Media, Sex and the Adolescent*. Cresskill, NJ: Hampton Press, Inc., 1993.

Heathers. Dir. Michael Lehmann. Perf. Winona Ryder, Christian Slater, Kim Walker, Shannen Doherty. New World Pictures, 1989.

Hey, Valerie. *The Company She Keeps: An Ethnography of Girls' Friendship*. Philadelphia: Open UP, 1997.

Hinson, Hal. *The Washington Post,* 17 November 1989, http://www.washingtonpost.com.

Lewis, Jon. *The Road to Romance and Ruin*. New York: Routledge, 1992.

The Little Mermaid. Dir. John Musker, Ron Clements. Voices: Jodi Benson, Christopher Daniel Barnes, Pat Carroll. Disney, 1989.

Little Women. Dir. Gillian Armstrong. Perf. Susan Sarandon, Winona Ryder, Gabriel Byrne, Kirstin Dunst, Claire Danes. Columbia Tristar, 1994.

Maslin, Janet. *The New York Times*, 22 March 1996, http://www.nytimes.com.

Mermaids. Dir. Richard Benjamin. Perf. Cher, Winona Ryder, Bob Hoskins, Christina Ricci. Orion Pictures Corp., 1990.

Moore, Susan, and Doreen Rosenthal. *Sexuality in Adolescence*. London: Routledge, 1993.

National Velvet. Dir. Clarence Brown. Perf. Elizabeth Taylor, Mickey Rooney. MGM, 1944.

Pretty in Pink. Dir. John Hughes. Perf. Molly Ringwald, Andrew McCarthy, John Cryer, Harry Dean Stanton. Paramount, 1986.

Romeo and Juliet. Dir. Baz Luhrman. Perf. Leonardo di Caprio, Claire Danes. Twentieth Century Fox, 1996.

Sixteen Candles. Dir. John Hughes. Perf. Molly Ringwald, Justin Henry, Michael Schoeffling. Universal Pictures, 1984.

Stack, Peter, *San Francisco Chronicle*, 31 May 1996, http://www.sfgate.com.

Stand by Me. Dir. Rob Reiner. Perf. River Phoenix, Wil Wheaton, Jerry O'Connell, Corey Feldman. Columbia Pictures, 1986.

Stealing Beauty. Dir. Bernardo Bertolucci. Perf. Jeremy Irons, Liv Tyler. Fox Searchlight Pictures, 1996.

Thompson, Sharon. *Going All the Way: Teenage Girls' Tales of Sex, Romance, and Pregnancy*. New York: Hill and Wang, 1995.

Walters, Barry. *San Francisco Examiner*, 31 May 1996, http://www.sfgate.com.

Welcome to the Dollhouse. Dir. Todd Solondz. Perf. Heather Matarazzo, Brendan Sexton III, Eric Mabius, Angela Pietropinto. Sony Pictures Classics, Columbia Tri-Star, 1995.

Wild Hearts Can't Be Broken. Dir. Steve Milner. Perf. Gabrielle Anwar, Cliff Robertson, Dylan Kussman. Buena Vista Pictures, 1991.

Chapter 10

Sound and Visual Misprecision in *Faces of Women*: Visual Difference Redefined in Thought

Binnie Brook Martin

The illusion of profundity is not the same as being profound. True, in a world where the will to say prevails (a "good" work is invariably believed to be a work "that has something to say"), the skill at excluding gaps and cracks which reveal language in its nakedness—its very void—can always be measured, and the criteria for good and bad will always exert its power.

—Trinh, *When The Moon Waxes Red*

Each language has its own music and its practice need not be reduced to the mere function of communicating meaning.

—Trinh, *Framer Framed*

Something different happens in what is called modern cinema . . . . What has happened is that the sensory-motor schema is no longer in operation, but at the same time it is not overtaken or overcome . . . . [At some point], perceptions and actions ceased to be linked together, and spaces are now neither co-ordinated nor filled.

—Deleuze, *Cinema 2: The Time-Image*

What connects these passages is a consciousness of the quest to create meaning in visual language by hiding the "gaps and cracks" in the visual field, a field in which the voids are beginning to show. In Hollywood film, editing usually disguises these voids, a technique that pushes back the unfastened, discontinuous elements between images and instead constructs a smooth, unified-looking cinematic text. The aural and visual elements, in particular, are coordinated to promote the cohesive sound/visual motion-of-picture. They are coordinated to form a precise relationship, in which sound supports the narrative direction of the moving visual image. This sound/image relationship closes off any currents of expression or elliptical threads that reside outside screen construction. Thus, it is in the composition of the attributes called "succession" and "correlation" in the motion-of-picture that gives screen narrativity the illusion of visual reality. Hollywood montage functions in this manner, and, accordingly, the spectator is conditioned to respond to the illusion of congruous flowing images in film space. Although western viewers hold fast to the construction of visual believability and continuity of motion, filmmaking practices in societies other than Hollywood may free up the filmic constructs of sound/visual images to permit the viewer to receive what lies outside of the formulated and the familiar in screen expression, where dialectical meaning is displaced and the awareness of gaps alights. The cinema of which Deleuze and Trinh speak embraces the same filmic crevices that Hollywood cinema avoids. Postcolonial African cinema makes known the gaps and cracks in the visual/aural field, and the distribution of such African films to western cultures summons a new relationship between the western viewer and the nonwestern screen image. The gaps in African cinematic images and the Cartesian mode of looking in western spectatorship open up the viewer's classical notions of image cohesiveness as the gaps enlist him or her to renegotiate the aural/visual terms in those images. This viewing relationship dismantles the spectator's normative perceptions of the African screen image as Other—all by virtue of apprehending the screen image's aural and visual unfastened elements—in a less fastened manner.

All of these observations therefore suggest that the redefining of the visual field calls for another kind of viewing, a thought induced viewing, from the western spectator. As the dismantling of normative perceptions ensues, the viewer's function of thought reappears; when the screen image's formerly assigned significations are upset, the spectator is summoned back to thinking and to exploring thoughts from outside themselves, thereby revealing an unthought in the thought. At this point, viewers reemerge as creators of new concepts vis-à-vis the screen subject and themselves. Each viewer's active involvement in developing new psychic connections suggests that the function of thinking on difference/otherness in the screen subject begins and then continues with the spectator.

Postcolonial film—well-known for its unconventional editing and filmic techniques—invites an active viewing that is nurtured by encountering disconnected, and hence defamiliarizing images.[1] These disconnected images and the gaps they expose are akin to Deleuze's filmic concept of the time image, wherein the time image consists of shots which present images that do not connect or corroborate the film's classical narrative function of linear, subject-centered storytelling. They present independent optical and aural elements and situations that slacken the spectator's sensory-motor connections, thus enabling him or her to see and hear what is "no longer subject to the rules of a response or an action."[2] In the breaking down of the sensory motor links, the correlation of situation and action in the viewer's mind can no longer be maintained.[3]

These spatializing conditions, predominant in normative film spectatorship, are subordinated to the privileging of temporal aspects that prevail in time images. Essentially then, with the emergence of time images, the filmic constituents of time and space reverse hierarchical positions within the power structure of the screen, thereby making the screen's space and movement, which normally propel image perceptions into actions, subordinate to the screen's temporality. It is by the forerunning of temporality that the image situations are released as independent functions. Subsequently, the autonomous shots of aural and visual expressions do not cohere from shot to shot, or shot to aural appendage. Time images are the lacunas outside of the screen construction of the "understood" narrative world, gaps that open to a specular world that is not iconoclast with meanings. Because these images do not produce the typical "sensory-motor situation" of linear, subject-centered narrativity, the spectator's standard role of classifying and reasoning out everything he or she sees and hears breaks down.[4] As time images loosen the sequential, continuous flow of the film's narrativity, they subsequently invoke the screen viewer to observe the image's gaps and hicccups as well as consider what the visual discontinuity might suggest. Emphasis on filmic gaps provides an effective method for disconnecting the viewer long enough from the screen image's story line to expand one's thinking of screen spatiality by occlusion of fixed memory cycles and the ensuing psychic effect this occlusion confers upon the viewer's shifting subjectivity.

Two of the ways in which time images expose the voids in filmic images are by multiplying and destabilizing the spectatorial positioning of the viewer and also by unhinging the sound elements from the visual components of the image on screen.

In Désiré Ecaré's Ivory Coast film, *Faces of Women (Visages de femmes,* 1985), time images come forth from the conscious disjunctive editing of sound image. The anachronous elements in this film deliver a disconnection of voice-to-lips movement (lip-sync) and a dislocation of sound-to-body proximity (i.e., a voice that sounds much closer, pervasive, or distanced than its body's actual location). When western spectators encounter the unsynchronized sound image formations, their spectatorial disposition is disrupted. As previously suggested, the new, and strange, sound image configurations defamiliarize the viewing experience, and, subsequently, the spectator's accustomed mode of filmic apprehension. At this point, a different spectatorial persuasion emerges from the deterritorializing meeting between the western screen viewer and the nonwesternized screen image. By turning to *Faces of Women* as illustration, I want to rethink western spectatorship of African films within the context of Deleuzeian time images. This spectatorial approach explores western viewers' experience in an alternative persuasion of filmic apprehension, thereby focusing on how spectators are situated to negotiate notions of difference/otherness in African screen images by discovering the existing otherness within themselves rather than in the screen subject.

The film *Faces of Women* is constructed in a rhythmical fashion by integrating the oral storytelling traditions of dance, music, and singing, with the more conventional, linear stylistics of action driven narration. The director, Ecaré, weaves these different styles of construction in and out of the three separate (yet complementary) segments of the film. Each of these segments narrates the life path of a particular African woman. The spectator follows each woman, two from a rural environment and the other from the city, as they struggle for their economic and sexual independence. Their stories illustrate how these women make choices (with mixed success) to empower themselves as subjects in pursuit of their own desires. While each articulates herself quite differently from the other, the young woman from the village, Affoue, most notably ex-

presses her subjectness in an aural/visual manner, a manner which is un-
hinged from the unified western perception of the "Third-World woman"
other.

The segment of *Faces* on which I focus is shot from multiple angles
and comes forth in the forms of voice-offs and voice-overs, and in the
synthesis of acoustic-visual misprecision. These filmic techniques create
some of the sensorial expressions and aberrant movements that produce
the time image spectatorial conditions in the film. In this particularly
long ten-minute scene, Ecaré presents the two characters, Affoue (the
young woman) and Kouassi (the young man), in a lengthy exchange of
sexual love play, in which the main subject in each frame is unques-
tionably Affoue. Affoue takes charge of the process that originates the
intimate sharings between them. Throughout the sexual exchange, she
initiates the turns of their often libidinous and sometimes tender intimacy. She shifts the predominant terms of the rendezvous from male to
female empowerment by guiding their bodily movements when and as
she desires. Unlike the depiction of the western love scene, Affoue vo-
calizes her sexual dislikes as well as her interests. Kouassi, at first, attempts to "make love" to Affoue in an ascribed triphasal manner (i.e.,
foreplay, intercourse, and postcoitus), and in so doing, he endeavors to
take the dominant male lead. Affoue, however, presses him to suspend
his tactics and heed to her voice and body's callings. Kouassi listens and
takes heed. In a responsive and more coequal sensibility, they engage in
explicitly vivid and varied manners of coupling, followed by a long af-
fectionate afterplay.

The rich sense of female empowerment in this scene is moreover
propelled by the filmic techniques that transport the scene's cinematic
release. Its extensive and diverse series of shots submit disunited visual
and aural situations, as well as a conventional specular position for the
western viewer to occupy. Ecaré frames the activity of sexual expression,
during their intercourse and afterplay, in extreme close-ups, long-
distance, high-angle, and partial-body shots; there are stationary and
moving-camera shots, as well as long stills. "When you focus on a subject," Trinh explains, "you don't see it from a single plane. Instead, you
move to different positions near and far and from side to side."[5] Shooting
near a character (as Trinh expresses) suggests spectatorial designs that
diverge from classical specular positioning. Hollywood cinema has per-
petually positioned the western spectator behind the main screen charac-

ter's point of view in order to enforce identification and sympathy with that character.[6] Perhaps it goes without saying that the mainstream typography of this character befits the white, heterosexual, and gender codings of the culture's phallocentric formula for mirroring the desired ego.[7] However, most screen representations of image otherness in western contexts (i.e., the marginalized Black, Hispanic, Asian screen subjects) are not designed to embody or reflect the viewer. The image other rarely represents the primary identificatory source or the point of view of the western viewer; in fact, this character is usually constructed to play the role of the secondary character foil, who serves to contrast and affirm the superiority of the preferred main character. Therefore, the screen image other, in its representation of lack, also reinforces the same imperialist desires as the main hero by positioning the other as the social binary of the main screen character. Hence, the image other also becomes the social binary of the screen viewer.[8]

In light of these pervasive western positionings, it seems that the spectator has been heavily sutured into a colonizing perspective and thereby conditioned to ascribe meanings to screen subjects and objects as that particular viewing position confers.[9] The encounter, then, of the western viewer vis-à-vis the nonwestern subject upends the viewer's habitual identification process of sustaining self-sameness (hence narcissism) through the screen subject.[10] In *Faces*, the main identificatory figure in each shot of the love scene segment is Affoue. Throughout this segment, the spectator is peripatetically located to either share her viewing perspective or to view her in a multivalent manner. We see in this instance how the viewer is not politically positioned to observe Affoue from any single viewpoint or position—neither that of the female African subject nor that of an omniscient third person. The viewer's framework and visual boundaries continue to shift, and by turns, resist a positional anchoring. In this instance, shooting *near* the subject instead of *about* suggests that Affoue's subjectness remains predominantly aimed at rather than represented. E. Anne Kaplan expands Trinh's term: "'Nearby is not knowing, but in the gap.'"[11] Kaplan gleans further the implicit intimacy conveyed in the word itself, showing how close-by positionings and perceptions suggest new connective possibilities between the viewer and screen image. In turn, she highlights further the spectatorial openings that looking *nearby* imputes.

Western viewers cannot necessarily categorize Affoue with an already assigned meaning from preconceived images. As Ecaré does not presuppose a vantage point for the spectator nor select a single viewing of the screen subject, the multiple framings and distances enable him or her to explore various ways of visualizing Affoue. Thus, we see how this segment's environmental compendium, with its different perspectival angles, distances, and durations, from a sometimes moving, sometimes stationary camera, shifts the eye to a degree of freedom in looking. The resulting questions now *en route*: Has the observer been liberated from assigned perceptions or has he or she been merely shifted from the traditional positioning of spectatorship that embodies screen representations to an alien spectatorship that invests the viewer with a looking that results in yet another set of perceived image paradigms? Conversely, is it possible that the peripatetic positioning causes the viewer to observe screen images that are not yet enlisted into representations? As implied from the description of the scene, the development of the spectator's viewpoint is simultaneously elided as well as made rhizomic. This viewing condition forms, in Deleuzeian terms, a "dehiscence" in the apprehension of the screen image. In reference to the love scene, the dehiscence pertains to the unexpected yawning, that is, the opening that emerges from the multiple disruptions and changes in spectatorial positioning. When viewers encounter the visual openings, there occurs, as mentioned above, a severance from their normal point-of-view reference, and, imminently, a severance from normative associations with the screen subject. The discharge of preconceived screen apprehensions and ideas (invoked from the multivalent perspectives and the screen image's gaps) is also accompanied by the spectator's new engagement with the "not yet" reality attributed to time images. This phrase portends that in a becoming but not-yet manner, ". . . the viewer brings into being that which does not yet exist."[12] The viewer first arrests the transferring of his or her percept to a perception. Received percepts come from the observer's very first visual, tactile, or aural encounter with an image. The viewer comprehends the image merely through sensations received by the mind through the senses.[13] When the spectator encounters a time image situation (in this case, induced by multivalent viewpoints of the screen subject), the spectator lacks the paradigm of past perceptions for the instant transference of the initial percept into a perception. The viewer's percept thus incurs an image percept, thereby suggesting the emergence of an image that engenders thought. The "not-yet" process conveys the existence of the indeterminate nature within apprehensions. Consequently, the not-yet process then calls upon the viewer's psychic capacities from unconscious memory cycles to merge new links to the image—without forgetting to carry along the problem of the indeterminate nature within apprehension—a nature that always remains present. In examination of the "not-yet but becoming" mindfulness, we see how the spectator is realigned to the process of thinking as he or she creates new perceptions with inconclusive terms. In essence, when the time image components enable the viewer to capture an expression of the screen image, arrested from its clichés, it in turn ascends the viewer into his or her spectatorial independence as a decolonized, active viewer, empowered to attribute "other" links to the screen subject while new representations begin to form.

We have observed in this instance how the emphasis exhibited in depicting Affoue in spatial multiplicity suggests the deemphasis of a spectatorial agenda. However, these observations furthermore propose a shift in the importance and persistence of preserving an all consuming narrative intent. The subordination of narrative intent derives partially from the scattering of a singular point-of-view; thereby, it originates a sexual encounter that is—although still fastened to the narrative—also separate from narrative anticipation. The ideological investment within certain cinematic images is strongly embedded in the western viewer's expectations. One of these images is the western love scene. The love scene images reinforce the cultural and psychic templates of seeing a certain way, of apprehending in a certain way. In this instance, the western love scene abides as a requisite model of identificatory cultural gender relationships. Particular to the subject under discussion, the love scene pervades as a predominant signification of women's agency. Gina Dent explains the western expectations of sexual love-on-screen in the following terms: "[T]he sexual relation, that is, our narration of the act of sex, hangs on a fantasy of oneness—phallocentrism, but also our longing to be 'as one with another'—that the idea of woman comes to support."[14] The indentured love scene exhibited in so many western films signifies both the woman's secondary position in heterosexual relationships as well as her role in supporting the hegemonic construction in spectatorship. These ideologically based anticipations are further glued by the idyllic, ethereal conditions within a love scene's imagery: The western audience expects the love scene to occur with a consummating sense of perfection and completion, ending "in a climactic, metaphysical ecstasy."[15] In a film of incommensurable shots like *Faces*, however, the occurrence of time images loosens the narrative intent in the images of sexual exchange, and thereby transforms the closed category of the "love scene" into a long open series of sexual expressions. Thus, the spectator's identificatory process no longer culminates in the transference of visual perceptions into an action in order to move the plot along its narrative track. In fact, the track no longer exists as a stable factor in the film, for the unity of situation and action have broken down. It is as though the series of love image shots subordinate the text's motion-of-picture to a filmic plan of its own terms, whereby the love scene becomes a "happening" rather than a totalizing consummation. The spectator experiences the love images as a happening because the autonomy of the images gains a material reality that imputes to them an importance in themselves. Furthermore, the creation of this happening becomes in great part a specular process in which the viewer returns to the spectatorial practice of conceptual construction. Thus, having liberated the spectator from the usual ends directed expectations, Affoue's bodily articulations are received with a less cohesive, and subsequently, less ideologically occupied agenda. As Trinh intimates, by getting away from the "desire not to simply mean,"[16] the viewer's renewed conceptual process suggests a reception outside of the reductive parameters of the already established cinematic meanings in imagery.

The concept of speaking *near* versus speaking *about* the screen other communicates both the postcolonial issue of women and voice and the western tendency to regard African women as the monolithic other.[17] In the homogenizing of the women's voice in film, the African director has struggled against western associations of African women as the erotic spectacle. The primary perceptions of the Third-World female other are based upon western humanist beliefs, francophone culture and language, as well as the colonizing ideology germane to Hollywood cinematography. Trinh's intimations on speaking *about* resonates this ideology in motion pictures, in that speaking about suggests a "possession or pretending knowledge *of*"[18] the other, based on already received categories and concepts. For example, African women in western films are usually portrayed as the "sensuous, bare breasted object, submissive to male demands and having a minute role or none in societal matters."[19] The per-

petuation of the African subject as the exotic erotic object for western
viewing and subjugation continues to determine the boundaries of Third-
World women's agency. Subsequently, African films that address the
subject of women's voice, as well as acquire international distribution,
encounter these normalized perceptions in western spectatorship.[20] Director Ecaré demonstrates a deterritorialization of Third-World female
representation by devoting his thematic workings to the subject of
women's resistance to the social and cultural oppressions of their agency.

Besides the shift to peripatetic viewing of screen image otherness,
Ecaré's singular filmic structuring in *Faces* manifests the subject of
women's voice in the cinematic forms of sound and visual expression.
Most notably, the message of female empowerment comes forth in the
film's creative expression of voice and body heautonomy (the independence of audio and visual components that form the filmic images). These
composing elements prevail as paradoxes in that they each act independently as distinct "incommensurable" units while they also remain "complementary" to one another.[21] Although the problematizing of female
agency is of course manifested by placing the African woman in primary
active roles of narrative action—all the principal characters in *Faces* are
women—it is further achieved, as we have discussed, by arresting the
western viewer's normative mode of apprehension, and furthermore,
from the viewer's raised consciousness of the screen subject's
heautonomous expression. We have already observed how the spectator's cultural gaze is decolonized. Conversely, how do viewers plumb
into their psychic stores of memory to apprehend the other? The answer
is: By linking with the other as self. This conceptualizing process reprob-
lematizes the notion of African female agency in western spectatorship
as the viewer encounters the film's visual/aural interstices, created by the
visual/aural counter "sync." A closer focus on the meaning of misprecision in the series of love scenes in *Faces* further illustrates this shift in
cinematic apprehension.

Mary Ann Doane writes in "The Voice in the Cinema: The Articulation of Body and Space" about the relationship between sound and visual
expression in western cinema, particularly on the cinematic protocol and
audience demand for appropriate voice and body articulation. It is understood that lip-sync precision sets the narrative standard in mainstream
cinema. Film sound, Doane declares, authenticates film movement and
validates the visual image. The simultaneity of sound and screen move-

ment assures a visual realism and verisimilitude in film. She further explains that there is an instilled fear on the part of the audience of being "cheated" if sound and movement do not resonate the precise degree of synchronization, especially with regard to voice and lips. To meet standards of sound/image "correctness" and audience expectations, the techniques of sound and image missynchronization are acquired gingerly.[22]

During the series of love images, the viewer is openly cheated from authenticated movement by sound. Narrativity by lip-sync and aural-to-visual exactness loosen considerably during the particular series of shots, when Affoue meets her lover, Kouassi, for their first-time tryst in a secluded cove. While the sexual encounter unfolds, the spectator observes several temporal dislocations of sound to its respective body or object. During the sighs, murmurs, and the swishing sound Affoue's body makes in the cove, the viewer hears unleveled, unbalanced auralities. Ecaré does not exact synchronicity with multiple timbrous elements. Instead the shots' various tonalities of sonorities incongruously compose the splashing sounds of the body, the water, her verbal commands, and other utterances. As Doane intimates, the spectator has been robbed of the corroborating oneness of body-to-voice synchronicity. At certain instances, the distance of Affoue's body from the camera would realistically position her voice at an almost imperceptible distance to the camera. However, the timbrous quality of Affoue's voice resonates the proximity of a close-up. Conversely, several of the lovemaking shots frame her from close and medium shots, even though her voice deliverance is obversely distanced. This spatial discrepancy creates an omniscient, voice-off existence for the subject, even though she is "in" the scene. The audio elements, independent from their correlating visual components, reveal visual interstices that travel apart from the aural/visual adhesions within normative diegetic expression. Indeed, these gaps of disjunction claim rights over the spatiality, or the diegetic zone, of signification. Because the optical and aural situation replaces the image's motor action, the spectator is then enabled to turn the image from its exteriority or extensiveness in space toward an origin in mental relations or time. In the scattering of the sounds-to-words-to-lips theory, the now prevailing gaps in the text evince more than scenes of incommensurable elements floating in time; they determine a sound/image relationship that does not rely upon the image's comprehensiveness in space.

The relationship between the sound/image components and the observer is in great part created by the spectator during an ongoing state of
dehiscence. In fact, the spectator reinvents what the film industry calls
the desired state of "presence" in the film text.[23] Doane articulates how
the condition of "presence" from sound and image correlation is the
sought-after effect in cinema. "The term presence offers a certain legiti-
macy to the wish for pure reproduction and becomes a selling point in
the construction of sound as a commodity."[24] That is, sound editing justifies the visual image in an effort to engender a truth and realness in the
screen representation as being whole in itself. According to the industry's terms of voice-to-body articulation, the image of Affoue is inade-
quately "present"; her voice and body do not compose a commodified
product since her aural articulations are not altogether localized to her
body. Contrary to the normative contingencies of sound in relationship to
screen spatiality, Affoue is altogether "present" by virtue of her visual
and sound nakedness. In fact, the image of Affoue is everywhere. As already foregrounded, Affoue's utterances are disembodied as well as em-
bodied. Sound, in this case, does not serve the purpose of attributing the
usually predominant visual image with the sense of total imagery. Subsequently, viewers can no longer extend themselves in the film subject's
space. Because the expressions of Affoue's voice and body each construct themselves as self-contained, autonomous elements of composition, the voice-to-body misprecision actuality results in a voice-and-body
parallelism; sound is no longer the legitimizing force of the visual and
therefore no longer its subordinate. As such, the sound along with the
image create, instead of a commodified presence, a pervasive and con-
currently "elliptical presence." Furthermore, as has already been established, the aberrant sound and optical situations replace the faltering sensory motor situations; thereby, the "showing" of the screen image tran-
scends the "telling" of the image.[25] By breaking up the image's aural and
visual expression in space, the elliptical presence of Affoue's image su-
persedes the screen's motor action and therefore erodes the believability
in film space as a secure or stabilized arena for expression. In fact, these
independent elements signify, it seems, the impossibility of a stable identity or a totalizing image in film. Perceiving the frailty of filmic space is
the spectator's beginning of seeing otherness.

Another concomitant aspect to the sound and visual misprecision of
Affoue's voice and body relates to the voice-off and voice-over situa-

tions. As with the concept of "presence," however, the series of love scene images also subvert and attenuate the standard definitions of the terms voice-off and voice-over. Traditionally the voice-off refers to moments in which the spectator hears "the voice that is not visible within the frame."[26] The voice-over, by convention, refers to the presence of "a disembodied voice," as is employed during an interior monologue or a flashback. "It is its radical otherness with respect to the diegesis which endows this voice with a certain authority."[27] Normally, the voice-over speaks to the viewer without mediation from the voice's body. Both kinds of voice-otherness, having a presence on and off screen, possess power simultaneously by what they reveal in screen space and also by what they conceal.[28] In the instances of voice-over and voice-off in *Faces*, the voice and body of Affoue are both manifested on screen; however, the voice's timbre and voice-to-body proximity range from slightly to greatly disconnected from the voice's body. In fact, at one moment during this series of shots, Affoue gives clear voice-utterance while her head is under water. Although the image of Affoue's body is "there," she is not entirely inside it because her voice presents itself in definite and indefinite terms. It is an inside/outside space that is absolutely other and partially indeterminate, yet altogether present. Clearly, the viewer does not apprehend much of the screen subject in a congruent sense, owing to the fact that the viewer's imaginative forces transport him or her to an inside/outside spectatorial site. The spectator may see Affoue's visual expression, but her image's empowered self is imperceptibly reflected throughout—in the frame, and also outside of the *framed*—as a partially unseen, unknown, open whole. Thus, along with the consciousness of "we are not thinking yet," follows "we are not seeing yet." In visual and audio situations such as these, the spectator is placed in touch with what is "not yet—but becoming" reachable, with the emergence of the outside. Seeing from the outside materializes a heightened sensibility to the current agendas and possibly to the denied desires within our own subjectivities. By time image turns, we may transpierce the normally inaudible and unseen differences in the self.

From the meeting of the African image with the western spectator emerges a viewer as an inventor of connections and syntheses at the level of image construction. This process ensures a viewer who questions the act of referencing a screen subject, for we have witnessed through these heautonomous situations that ". . . there arises an act of historical imagi-

nation,"[29] in that the destabilized spatiality in *Faces* holds the viewer in
the process of connecting unlinked links, and in Deleuze's Foucauldian
notion of the viewer's power in the "unthought thought."[30] Apprehending
difference takes place during this process of which Deleuze speaks, in
the process of stirring up the preconceived thought's unthought sedi-
ments. In *Faces* is a processual presence of filmic images that enables
spectators to stay in thought and to resist the already seen/named thing.

Examination of Ecaré's *Faces* through the philosophical lens of
thought engendered by time images conveys the formidable resistance to
the spectatorial categorization of Third-World otherness. It further illuminates the gravity of postcolonial film concerns on the representation of
the female subject and on the presumptive position of western audiences
to define that subject. The encounter of time images at once challenges
the stereotypes of African female characters as well as opens up the subjectivity behind the spectatorial process of apprehending those African
images. These observations show that a spectatorial emphasis accomplishes more than the bringing-to-consciousness of the viewer's tendency
to classify African women based on western humanist terms. It also illuminates the occasion for viewers to see themselves as other. The apprehension of otherness occurs because the monolithic roles of both viewer
and the viewed have broken down because of the disposition of time over
space in spectatorship. The viewer emerges as an individual other and
also acknowledges the screen subject as an individual other. The question is no longer what is knowable or unknowable about the subject, but
rather, what differences may resonate in the self, invoked by the exchange in the elliptical presence of subjectness? Trinh conjectures the
following idea on the locating of difference: "[D]ifferences do not only
exist between outsider and insider—two entities—, they are also at work
within the outsider or the insider—a single entity."[31]

As these observations suggest, the spectator is enlightened by the aberrant manner in which the aural and visual are linked. Although they do
not link in complete or understood synchronicity, they link together
nonetheless in the decolonizing of the western mode of spectatorship.
However, the visibly ascribed links are now absent. Time images sum-
mon the spectator to submit to these unlinking links. The sound/image
expression of time imagery invoke the psychic energies and the symbi-
otic capacities within each viewer's subjectivity. In essence, the viewer is
constructing a new visual framework that recognizes invisible links—

understanding that the broken spider web is the mark of the spider's success.

Notes

1. Teshome H. Gabriel provides a concise summary of postcolonial filmic characteristics in his essay "Towards a Critical Theory of Third World Films," in *Colonial Discourse and Post-Colonial Theory,* ed. Patrick Williams and Laura Chrisman (New York: Columbia UP, 1994), 352–55. His synopsis distinguishes postcolonial filmic constructs as being in many cases opposite from those of the West, in great part because of their different cultural values of time. Gabriel suggests that western culture does not value the natural, slower passing of time on the screen, whereas the representation of time's natural process and passing strike the cultural touchstones of African cultures. Western cinema, however, manipulates the spectactor's notion of time to a far greater extent than that of postcolonial cinema. Therefore, the imaginative compositions of sound, silence, and camera shots (i.e., high/low angles, long pans, long shots, and takes with sometimes repeated images) that characterize postcolonial film create new spectatorial possibilities and hence a new way of seeing for western viewers.

2. Gilles Deleuze, *Cinema 2,* trans. Hugh Tomlinson and Robert Galeta (Minneapolis: U of Minnesota P, 1989), 3.

3. Deleuze, *Cinema 2,* xv.

4. When an image is conceived, Deleuze calls it the action-image: When encountering a screen image in the typical sensory-motor situation, the viewer connects with that image by associating it with previous experiences and associations. The viewer then proceeds to correlate a mental reasoning and inference on to the image, which assigns the image meaning and classification. The action-image, therefore, is an image to which spectators assign finite significance immanent to their psyche's past social and cultural construction. See Deleuze, *Cinema 2*, 2–9.

5. Minh-Ha T. Trinh, *Framer Framed* (New York: Routledge, 1992), 114–15.

6. See Robert Stam and Louise Spence, Introduction to *Colonialism, Racism and Representation*, from *Screen* 3.1 (1971).

7. Kaja Silverman intimates the western viewer's "proprioceptive" apprehension (i.e., visual, cutaneous, and identificatory sensations) of the culturally coded screen subject. This screen apprehension ascribes to the viewer a sense of him- or herself as a body extended in film space. See Kaja Silverman, *Thresholds in the Invisible World* (New York: Routledge, 1997), 17.

8. Silverman, 23.

9. I refer to Griselda Pollock's explication of the colonizing cultural gaze, or the "male gaze," as the privileged and policing viewing position imposed upon the

viewer. See Griselda Pollock, *Vision and Difference: Feminism and Femininity in Art* (London: Routledge, 1995).

10. Kaja Silverman explicates Lacan's "mirror phase" and the western spectator's desire for the feelings of "wholeness" and "unity." The viewer attempts to sustain these feelings by "gratifyingly identifying with an ideal imago," 18. See also Silverman's explication of self-sameness, 18–26.

11. E. Ann Kaplan, *Looking for the Other: Feminism, Film, and the Imperial Gaze* (New York: Routledge, 1997), 201.

12. Gilles Deleuze, *Difference and Repetition* (New York: Columbia UP, 1994), 147.

13. Deleuze, *Cinema 2*, 22.

14. Gina Dent, "Black Pleasure, Black Joy," in *Black Popular Culture* (Seattle: Bay Press, 1992), 9.

15. Catherine Clémont's *Syncope: The Philosophy of Rapture,* trans. Sally O'Driscolle (Minneapolis: U of Minnesota P, 1985), 186.

16. Trinh, *Framed,* 113.

17. Minh-Ha T. Trinh, *When the Moon Waxes Red: Representation, Gender, and Cultural Politics* (New York: Routledge, 1991), 47–49.

18. Trinh, *Framer Framed,* 114.

19. Nwachukwu Frank Ukadike, *Black African Cinema* (Berkeley: U of California P, 1994), 221.

20. Ecaré's intent of distribution for *Faces*, it seems, was distinctly planned to move beyond the Ivory Coast. In the year the film was released, it was successfully distributed to the major cities in France, England, Germany, Holland, Canada, and to several major cities in the U.S. as well as on the U.S. Bravo cable channel. See Ukadike's *Black African Cinema*, 222–25.

21. See D. N. Rodowick's, *Gilles Deleuze's Time Machine* (Durham: Duke UP, 1997), 145.

22. Regardless of the many experiments performed on sound/image relationships, sound-to-image (especially voice) synchronization remains the dominant ideal for film procedure. In practice, the level of the voice generally determines the levels of sound effects and music. See Mary Ann Doane, *Femmes Fatales: Feminism, Film Theory, Psychoanalysis* (New York: Routledge, 1991), 35.

23. Doane states that "presence" justifies the screen image and meets the viewer's expectation of "pure production," 41–42.

24. Doane, 37.

25. Showing versus telling may also speak to the oral tradition of African texts. Ecaré is interpreted by Ukadike and others to regard this tradition in his own work. *Black African Cinema*, 213–15.

26. Doane, 37.

27. Doane, 42.

28. Doane, 40.

29. Rodowick, 143.

30. See Rodowick, 180–81, for further explication on the unthought in thought.

31. Trinh, *When the Moon Waxes Red: Representation, Gender, and Cultural Politics*, 76.

Bibliography

Clémont, Catherine. *Syncope: The Philosophy of Rapture,* translated by Sally O'Driscolle. Minneapolis: U of Minnesota P, 1985.

Deleuze, Gilles. *Cinema 2.* Trans. Hugh Tomlinson and Robert Galeta. Minneapolis: U of Minnesota P, 1989.

———. *Difference and Repetition.* New York: Columbia U, 1994.

Dent, Gina. "Black Pleasure, Black Joy." In *Black Popular Culture.* Seattle: Bay Press, 1992.

Doane, E. Ann. *Femmes Fatales: Feminism, Film Theory, Psychoanalysis.* New York: Routledge, 1991.

Faces of Women (Visages de femmes). Dir. Désiré Ecaré. Perf. Sidiki Bakaba and Eugenie Cissé Roland. Gerick Films, Ivory Coast, 1985.

Gabriel, Teshome H. "Towards a Critical Theory of Third World Films." In *Colonial Discourse and Post-Colonial Theory,* edited by Patrick Williams and Laura Chrisman. New York: Columbia UP, 1994.

Kaplan, E. Ann. *Looking for the Other: Feminism, Film, and the Imperial Gaze.* New York: Routledge, 1997.

Pollock Griselda. *Vision and Difference: Femininity and Feminism in Art.* London: Routledge, 1995.

Rodowick, D. N. *Gilles Deleuze's Time Machine.* Durham: Duke UP, 1997.

Silverman, Kaja. *Thresholds in the Invisible World.* New York: Routledge, 1997.

Stam, Robert, and Louise Spence. Introduction to *Colonialism, Racism, and Representation. Screen* 24(2):2–20.

Trinh, T. Minh-Ha. *Framer Framed.* New York: Routledge, 1992.

———. *When the Moon Waxes Red: Representation, Gender, and Cultural Politics.* New York: Routledge, 1991.

Ukadike, Nwachukwu Frank. *Black African Cinema.* Berkeley: U of California P, 1994.

List of Contributors

Margaret Allison is Honorary Senior Lecturer in French Studies at the University of Bradford, UK. Her research is in media analysis with particular emphasis on the representation of women in the political arena in Britain and in France, including the elections of May and June 1997. She has published articles on abortion in France and on French media representations of sexual harassment. With Richard Cleminson she co-edited *In/visibility: Gender and Representation in a European Context.* She also co-edited a volume with Owen Heathcote, *Forty Years of the Fifth French Republic: Actions, Dialogues and Discoursed,* (1999). In *Women in Contemporary France*, eds, Abigail Gregory and Ursula Tidd, (2000), she contributed a chapter on the portrayal of women, and also their professional role, in contemporary French media.

Karen Boyle is a Lecturer in Women's Studies at the University of Wolverhampton, UK. She has published her research on pornography and screen violence in a number of journals and is currently working on *Feminist Perspectives on Media Violence* (for Pearson) and (with Paul Sutton) on *Contemporary Hollywood Film: Politics and Pleasure* (for Arnold).

Ann Hardy lectures in Screen and Media Studies at the University of Waikato in Hamilton, New Zealand. She has previously been a television news journalist and video producer, as well as producing a body of critical work on New Zealand women filmmakers for Australasian journals, such as *Illusions* and *S.P.A.N.* Her most recent publication is a chapter on Jane Campion's film *The Piano* in the Cambridge Film Handbooks series. She is currently completing a doctoral thesis about the construction and reception of themes of religion and spirituality in New Zealand film and television.

Alexandra Heidi Karriker is Associate Professor of Modern Languages, Women's Studies, and Film at the University of Oklahoma. Her articles, translations, and reviews have appeared in *Iskusstvo kino, World Literature Today, Canadian-American Slavic Studies, Russian Review, West Virginia University Philological Papers, Kinovedcheskie zapiski, The European Legacy,* and in collections. Her monograph, *Turmoil on the Screen: Shifting Perspectives in Soviet and Post-Communist Cinema,* was published in 1993. She is completing a book on Andrei Tarkovsky's writings and films.

Jane Knox-Voina is Professor of Russian Language, Film, Culture and Women's Studies at Bowdoin College and a Research Associate at the Davis Center of Russian Studies at Harvard University. Her research is widely published and she has received numerous grants from the International Research and Exchanges Board for studies of Russian and Soviet film.

Binnie Brook Martin is a Ph.D. candidate in the Comparative Literature Program at Purdue University. Her thesis topic is "The Effects of Nonwestern Image Flows on Western Spectatorship," and her areas of research interest include visual culture in West African literature and film, western, and nonwestern visual theories on spectatorship, and narrativity in literature and film.

Amanda Maxfield is a 2000 *summa cum laude* graduate of the University of Oklahoma, holding bachelor's degrees in English Literature and in Letters. She is pursuing a career in law while maintaining an interest in film scholarship and media theories.

Susan Smith Nash has taught literature and film classes since 1993 at St. Gregory's University, the University of Oklahoma, the Universidad Católica, and the Paraguayan-American Cultural Center in Asunción, Paraguay. Her research on Paraguayan filmmakers and writers has been ongoing since 1996, and her book, *First Light: An Anthology of Paraguayan Women Writers,* a critical edition of poetry and prose was published in 1999 by Texture Press and the Centro Cultural Paraguayo Americano.

Katherine J. Patterson received a B.A. and two M.A. degrees from the University of Alabama. She is completing her dissertation, "The New Money Shot: Male Frontal Nudity, Spectatorship, and the Masochistic Mainstream Film Text of the 1990s–2000." She has taught at the University of Alabama, University of Oklahoma, University of Alabama in Birmingham, and Miles College. She represented the United States at the "Women's Political Empowerment Conference" in New Delhi, India, in 1999. Her areas of interest include feminist film theory, women's studies, gender theory, women's literature, minority/world literature, and feminist art theory.

Paul Sutton lectures in Film Studies at the Bolton Institute in the UK. Currently completing a doctoral thesis on deferred action and spectatorship, he has published articles on film and critical theory in journals such as *French Studies*, *Parallax* and *Angelaki*. His articles have appeared in *French Cinema in the 1990s* (Oxford University Press), *Jean Baudrillard* (Sage), and the forthcoming *Sensual Reading* (Bucknell). He has also published an extensively annotated translation of Félix Guattari's *The Three Ecologies* (Athlone).

Davinia Thornley is a media/cultural studies doctoral candidate at the University of North Carolina at Chapel Hill. She is originally from New Zealand and writes on New Zealand nationality and cinema.

The History & Art of Cinema

Frank Beaver, *General Editor*

Framing Film is committed to serious, high-quality film studies on topics of national and international interest. The series is open to a full range of scholarly methodologies and analytical approaches in the examination of cinema art and history, including topics on film theory, film and society, gender and race, politics. Cutting-edge studies and diverse points of view are particularly encouraged.

For additional information about the series or for the submission of manuscripts, please contact:

Peter Lang Publishing, Inc.
Acquisitions Department
275 Seventh Avenue, 28th floor
New York, NY 10001

To order other books in this series, please contact our Customer Service Department at:

(800) 770-LANG (within the U.S.)
(212) 647-7706 (outside the U.S.)
(212) 647-7707 FAX

Or browse online by series at:

www.peterlangusa.com

DATE DUE

MAY 05 03